Development and Supervision of Teaching Assistants in Foreign Languages

Joel C. Walz
Editor

D1521476

American Association of University Supervisors, Coordinators, and Directors of Foreign Language Programs (AAUSC)

Issues in Language Program Direction
A Series of Annual Volumes

Series Editor
Sally Sieloff Magnan, University of Wisconsin–Madison

Managing Editor
Charles J. James, University of Wisconsin–Madison

Editorial Board
David P. Benseler, Case Western Reserve University
Jean-Pierre Berwald, University of Massachusetts
Kenneth Chastain, University of Virginia
Claire Gaudiani, Connecticut College
Alice Omaggio Hadley, University of Illinois
Theodore V. Higgs, San Diego State University
Dieter Jedan, Murray State University
Claire Kramsch, University of California, Berkeley
Dorothy Rissel, State University of New York–Buffalo
Carlos Solé, University of Texas at Austin
Wilga Rivers, Harvard University
Albert Valdman, Indiana University

Development and Supervision of Teaching Assistants in Foreign Languages

Joel C. Walz
Editor

Heinle & Heinle Publishers
Boston, Massachusetts 02116, U.S.A.

© Copyright 1992 by Heinle & Heinle. No parts of this publication may be reproduced or transmitted in any form or by any means electronic, or mechanical, including photocopy, recording, or any information storage and retrieval system, without permission in writing from the publisher.

Manufactured in the United States of America.

Heinle & Heinle Publishers is a division of Wadsworth, Inc.

ISBN 08384-5124-1

10 9 8 7 6 5 4 3 2 1

Contents

III. Specific Aspects of TA Development and Supervision

Acknowledgments

As volume editor, I must express my most profound gratitude to Sally Sieloff Magnan, Series Editor, and Charles J. James, Managing Editor, for their constant help in guiding me through the editing process and for all the improvements they made in my work. The Editorial Board, whose members are listed elsewhere in this volume, were extremely considerate in both the speed of their evaluations and the helpfulness of their comments. I must also thank all of the authors with whom I worked by letter, phone, fax, and electronic mail for cooperating with me, often on short notice, in order to produce the final version of their work, which you have before you.

This volume and series would not be possible without the firm commitment of Stan Galek and his staff at Heinle & Heinle. I would like to thank Elizabeth Holthaus for supervising production, Philip Holthaus, who served as copy editor, and Frank Weaver, who was responsible for composition. Without the continuing dedication of these people, the members of the AAUSC would not be able to make such contributions to the profession.

I would like to recognize the Department of Romance Languages at the University of Georgia for bearing some of the expense of producing this volume, primarily through telephone, faxing, and e-mail services. Matthew Crew, an M.A. candidate in the department, helped by checking references.

In conclusion, I would like to call on all AAUSC members and other readers of this volume to join in my thanks in a very positive way: by undertaking to contribute articles to the future volumes listed on the back cover. The laudable actions of others must inspire us to create and continue traditions.

Joel C. Walz
Volume Editor

Introduction

In the ebb and flow of concerns expressed by professionals involved in higher education, teaching seems to have moved to the forefront. While few universities and surprisingly few colleges have abandoned their commitment to research, it does appear that interest in providing high-quality instruction for undergraduates is reaching a new peak. We can see this changed attitude in the numerous seminars and programs at many colleges and universities, where faculty and administrators are exploring new avenues for improving undergraduate instruction without reducing research. We can see it in articles and editorials in professional publications such as the *Chronicle of Higher Education* and, in foreign languages, in dramatically increasing attendance at professional meetings, such as those of the American Council on the Teaching of Foreign Languages, of regional conferences on language teaching, and of state associations.

The American Association of University Supervisors, Coordinators, and Directors of Foreign Language Programs (AAUSC), which produces this volume every year, is ultimately concerned with quality in teaching. Statistics continue to show that the vast majority of students learning foreign languages in America's universities are at the first- or second-year level. We know from experience that these courses are the domain of graduate student teaching assistants (TAs) in virtually all universities. When we add in classes taught by temporary and part-time faculty (lecturers, instructors, adjunct faculty), we must recognize that a substantial portion, perhaps even most, of America's efforts at educating its population in foreign languages at the postsecondary level is in the hands of teachers under the direct supervision of members of the AAUSC and their colleagues.

While the AAUSC has as one of its primary goals the encouragement and publication of research in the fields most related to our work (this volume being an example), we also spend considerable energy in the development and supervision of competent teachers. On the one hand, we have distinct advantages over our colleagues in schools of education, who must train schoolteachers via one or two methods courses and an eight- to ten-week teaching practicum. We supervise many of our teachers for a number of years. We have developed a variety of training aids, including preservice orientation sessions, many types of methods courses (several of which are described in this volume), in-service training seminars, and direct observation of novice teachers by veteran colleagues for a long period of time. Our TAs have many advantages over undergraduates who go directly into full-time teaching because of their extended coursework, increased opportunities for study in the target culture, contact with professors who serve as mentors, and supervision by a professional TA program director.

Yet no one has ever established that teaching at the university level is better, or produces better results, than teaching of any other type. Clearly, much remains to be done. The AAUSC is in a unique position to capitalize on the renewed interest in teaching in general and foreign language teaching in particular. The current volume, *Development and Supervision of Teaching Assistants in Foreign Languages,* the third in the series *AAUSC Issues in Language Program Direction,* produced by the AAUSC and published by Heinle & Heinle Publishers, presents a broad spectrum of articles that demonstrate how complex the development of successful teachers can be. The volume title reflects that complexity.

"Development" is a term that has replaced "training" in that the latter implies mechanical procedures and rote learning. Authors of this volume have interpreted development in a very broad sense, with many components and approaches. "Supervision" (literally, "to see over") is both an aspect of development and the format in which all development takes place.

We begin the volume with three articles that describe entire programs, thereby showing not only the diversity of approaches that long-range supervision entails, but also how such programs evolve given changing needs and the creation of new ideas. The second group of two articles describes radically different ways of defining the methods course. No longer a collection of "how-to" suggestions (in fact, it has not been for a long time), the new-generation methods course is based on research and immediate concerns of higher education. The last group of six articles discusses specific approaches to take in the supervision of TAs in their role as teachers and as professionals.

In the first article, "Undergraduate Teaching Assistants: One Model," Katherine Kulick suggests preparing undergraduates to assume the duties of TAs in colleges where the faculty teach all beginning courses. She emphasizes changes that have occurred in teaching theory since Rassias pioneered the model with an audiolingual approach. Benefits accrue to faculty, who have no increased teaching loads, to students, who have more contact time with the language, and to TAs, who develop responsibility and teaching skills.

Julia Herschensohn stresses change in her chapter, "Teaching Assistant Development: A Case Study," which she traces to an increased emphasis on excellence in teaching at her institution. She describes each aspect of the development program in French and how different offices involved with teaching at the university can be integrated into a coherent whole.

The less commonly taught languages have not participated equally in the methodological changes of recent years. Because TAs in Arabic, Chinese, Japanese, and Russian in particular do not receive the same education in language teaching as do their counterparts in French, German, and Spanish, we are not developing new TA program directors who can educate future TAs. Benjamin Rifkin, in "Breaking Out of the Vicious Circle: TA Training, Education, and Supervision for the Less Commonly Taught Languages," pleas for a break in this cycle and describes detailed steps that faculty members in these languages can take to improve TA training and to develop better materials for these languages.

Narrowing their focus to the methods course, Marva Barnett and Robert Francis Cook, in "The Seamless Web: Developing Teaching Assistants as Professionals," see no dichotomy between research and teaching. In their chapter they describe the methods course that they teach as a team, in which they integrate such seemingly diverse topics as teaching theory, research methods, bibliographical style, and ethics. All aspects contribute to the professional competence of future faculty members.

Another long-range approach to TA development is that of Keith Mason, described in "Beyond the Methods Course: Designing a Graduate Seminar in Foreign Language Program Direction." Taking his cue from evidence that many TA supervisors have their work thrust upon them with little preparation of their own, he describes a seminar he has given that will prepare future TA supervisors. He combines readings in language learning theory with a hands-on approach of observations and role-plays to prepare TAs for frequently offered positions in this field.

In the group of articles on specific aspects of TA development, Charles James introduces a set of five "tools" that he has found useful in supervising TAs in "What TAs Need to Know to Teach According to the New Paradigm." Among them is the Triangle showing the relationship between the learner and the language course, the keystone being the topic discussed and not the language itself. He applies Knop's Overview-Prime-Drill-Check method to communicative teaching and emphasizes small-group work as an effective way to achieve the goals of current theories of foreign language learning.

In "'Poof! You're a Teacher!': Using Introspective Data in the Professional Development of Beginning TAs," Mary Wildner-Bassett recommends the use of dialogue journals written by TAs to enhance their awareness in four areas: professional development as an ongoing process, teacher and learner roles in the classroom, anxiety and ways to reduce it, and learner styles. She quotes many insightful remarks made by TAs to show that they can assume much of the responsibility for their own development.

In the first of two linguistic approaches to TA supervision, Nadine O'Connor Di Vito, in "Sensitizing Teaching Assistants to Native-Speaker Norms in the Communicative Classroom," identifies a lack of knowledge about how native speakers use linguistic forms to communicate in true contexts. Using examples from French, she shows how traditional classroom and textbook descriptions do not accurately reflect native speech. She recommends a greater use of authentic oral documents and sensitizing TAs to such differences.

In "Toward a Revised Model of TA Training," Cynthia Fox shows how TAs need to have a knowledge about their target language that only linguistics can provide. Realizing that additional required coursework is unlikely in most departments, she argues for the integration of techniques such as language awareness activities into existing methods courses so that TAs will be prepared to discuss features of the target language in an accurate way.

Another important aspect of TA training is sensitivity to cultural differences, as explained by Madeleine Cottenet-Hage, John Joseph, and Pierre Verdaguer in "Thinking Culturally: Self-Awareness and Respect for Diversity in the Foreign Language Classroom." They describe how to "think culturally" and how to train TAs to use the classroom as a laboratory for the discovery of "small-c" culture.

We conclude this volume with a discussion of testing foreign language proficiency. Robert Terry describes two ways of scoring students' written and oral production in "Improving Inter-rater Reliability in Scoring Tests in Multisection Courses." He describes both global and analytic systems, offering a number of detailed scales created by himself and other scholars. He also recommends specific training procedures designed to help TAs become more consistent in scoring their students' tests in multisection courses.

The grouping of these chapters and the definitions given above do not imply that development and supervision are distinct entities nor that one is philosophical and the other mechanical. One cannot exist without the other. Development is a long-range goal; we attempt to achieve it through complex, multifaceted programs comprising many different procedures, techniques, and guiding principles and by supervising the entire process. The membership of the AAUSC hopes that the depth and breadth of the 11 articles presented in this volume will contribute to an understanding of the scope of the problems we face and provide solutions.

Joel C. Walz
Volume Editor
University of Georgia

Undergraduate Teaching Assistants: One Model

Katherine M. Kulick
The College of William and Mary

Faculty at four-year colleges and smaller universities regularly teach the entire spectrum of the foreign language curriculum from first-year language courses to advanced seminars in literature and civilization. Lacking the aid of the graduate students who frequently teach introductory courses at doctoral-granting institutions, these faculty members must themselves staff each section of every course. As a result, teaching loads are often heavy, with faculty members scheduled for six to nine classes per year. In order to balance student demand for courses with a fixed supply of faculty members, class size tends to increase, raising additional concerns for foreign language teachers. At a time when the foreign language professional community has demonstrated renewed interest in the teaching and evaluation of functional language skills (Omaggio, 1986; Byrnes & Canale, 1987; Rivers, 1992), faculty concerned with increased class size might do well to consider using undergraduate students as teaching assistants in the first-year foreign language program.

The decision to implement a cooperative approach to the first-year program involving faculty and undergraduate teaching assistants (UTAs) deals with issues fundamentally different from those raised in a discussion of graduate teaching assistants (TAs). Although appropriate pedagogical training and supervision of TAs represent shared concerns for coordinators of graduate as well as undergraduate teaching assistants, the use of undergraduate teaching assistants signals a shift in the basic design of first-year courses. UTAs do not replace faculty, nor do they reduce faculty time in the first-year classroom. Rather, they expand instructional time and opportunities for functional language practice for first-year students.

UTAs contribute to many successful programs in courses ranging from speech communications (Crawford, 1983, 1984; Baisinger, 1984; Gray, 1989; Ross, 1990) to persuasion (Larson, 1990) to journalism (Tait, 1989). For more than two decades Rassias (1983) has successfully integrated UTAs, known as "Apprentice Teachers," into an intensive first-year foreign language program, known as the Dartmouth Model. All subsequent efforts to use undergraduates as TAs in foreign languages are ultimately based, to some extent, on the earlier work of Rassias (Hirsch, 1982; Winston & Boots, 1987; Cormier, 1988). The following model is an adaptation and reorientation of the Apprentice Teacher program first introduced by Rassias. More recent attention to the humanistic and affective factors involved in foreign language acquisition (Young, 1990; Phillips, 1991) has resulted in a new perspective on the UTA's role in the first-year classroom. Our desire to reduce anxiety levels in the classroom (Oxford, 1990), and to provide real-world, contextualized language practice (Omaggio, 1986) in introductory language courses, has profoundly influenced the choice of instructional strategies and techniques in which the UTAs receive training. The training has fundamentally altered the interaction between UTAs and their students.

Brief Background and Description of One UTA Model

A model that has been implemented in eight languages at the College of William and Mary in Virginia carefully coordinates the efforts of faculty and UTAs in a collaborative approach to the first-year foreign language experience. In the mid-1970s the Department of Modern Languages and Literatures faculty elected to convert the foreign language program at William and Mary to an intensive format — with eight class meetings per week — patterned after the Dartmouth Model. Faculty members recruited undergraduate students to serve as Apprentice Teachers or "Drill Instructors" and were pleased with their classroom performance. As the name implies, the responsibilities of these "Drill Instructors" were limited to highly structured pattern drilling. Twelve years later, in 1986, a university-wide curricular review took place, resulting in the standardization of course scheduling times and the elimination of intensive-format courses during the regular academic year. At the same time, the Department of Modern Languages faculty began to reexamine first-year language teaching strategies in light of recent developments within the field of foreign language methodology (Omaggio, 1986). Under the revised plan, first-year classes were redesigned to meet five times per week and the role of the UTAs was greatly expanded.

For any institution, the decision to incorporate UTAs into the first-year program provides an opportunity to offer more contact hours for first-year language students than would ordinarily be possible if instructional time were limited solely to faculty members. Students increase their exposure to and practice with the target language by enrolling in courses that meet daily, rather than the more traditional offering of three times per week.

First-year foreign language students register for one section of a beginning language course that meets with a faculty member on Mondays, Wednesdays, and Fridays. At the same time, they also enroll in one section with a UTA that meets on Tuesdays and Thursdays (e.g., GER 101 and GER 101A). Rather than receiving two hours and 30 minutes of language instruction (3 days × 50 minutes) each week, students receive four hours and 10 minutes of language instruction (5 days × 50 minutes). The additional sessions represent an increase of 66% in contact hours. In some of the less commonly taught languages, the same format is repeated in the second-year sequence of courses.

Undergraduate Teaching Assistant Responsibilities

Within the context of the model being presented, several significant differences between the use of UTAs and TAs become quickly evident. First, UTAs do not carry complete responsibility for one particular section of a course. Unlike TAs, who introduce and explain new functions, structures, and vocabulary, UTAs do not make the initial presentation of new material. UTAs do not collect or correct homework assignments. They do not assign grades to students' oral or written work, nor do they write or administer examinations. All of the aforementioned tasks are performed by the faculty instructor responsible for the three weekly meetings with the class.

If we consider the presentation of new material as a three-step process that involves (1) introduction and explanation, (2) controlled practice, and

(3) open-ended, communicative activities, then UTA classes primarily focus on the second stage, what Rivers (1983) calls the "skill-getting" phase, and secondarily on the third stage or "skill-using" phase of instruction. In her description of what constitutes the skill-getting phase of instruction, Rivers (1983, p. 43) states that "whether we use the terms 'exercises,' 'drills,' 'intensive practice,' or 'activities' is immaterial; some kind of practice in putting together smoothly and confidently what they [the students] are learning is essential." In the sessions taught by UTAs, controlled exercises reinforce the forms and use of structures and vocabulary first presented in the faculty instructors' class. Capitalizing on their small class size, UTAs concentrate on the development of oral skills. Students do no written work in class, nor do they refer to textbooks.

At times the UTA class may include pronunciation practice, video viewing, or preparation and review for major examinations. The selection of activities in the UTA class depends upon the preceding class period with the faculty instructor. If on Monday the faculty member introduces a new grammatical concept in the latter part of the class period, then the UTA class on Tuesday is likely to include intensive drilling and practice of forms followed by more meaningful questioning to allow for some personalization of the new structure. On Wednesday the faculty instructor may elect to begin class with personalized, but controlled, questioning and then proceed to a more open-ended discussion, followed perhaps by the introduction of another new concept or structure. On Thursday the UTA class may follow up on the discussion with role-plays and also begin the very controlled practice and drilling of the newly introduced material.

UTAs do not limit their classes to simple mechanical drilling. With supervised preparation, they are thoroughly capable of implementing personalized questions, overseeing class discussions, and directing role-plays.

Recruitment of UTAs

Early in the spring semester the language coordinators for the first-year programs fix the date, time, and place of an informational meeting for prospective UTAs. In order to identify possible candidates for UTA positions, language coordinators place advertisements in the student newspaper, post notices at popular student spots on campus, and ask all foreign language faculty members to encourage their students in upper-division courses to consider applying. These brief announcements indicate that the department actively seeks students with ability and interest in Chinese, French, German, Italian, Japanese, Portuguese, Russian, or Spanish to assist in first-year programs. It is important not to overlook those students who are not currently enrolled in departmental courses or undergraduate native speakers of the foreign language who are majoring in other fields. An advertisement in the student newspaper and flyers in the campus center or student union building may turn up individuals unknown to the department faculty and staff, but who have an interest and the language ability to contribute significantly to the program. Many native speakers are eager to share their cultural knowledge and promote their language on campus through the UTA experience. Native speakers offer personal insights and valuable background information for the video segments that may be viewed in the UTA class. In the true sense of collaboration, native-speaker UTAs instruct fellow students on cultural issues while non-native-speaking UTAs can offer insight into particular difficulties for American speakers of the foreign language.

At the spring informational meeting the first-year foreign language program and UTA responsibilities are described and applications distributed (see Appendix A). The brief application elicits only basic, factual information. The students' summer addresses are requested for correspondence and updates regarding times and rooms for the orientation workshop. The number of applications for each language will help in determining handouts to be photocopied and the room size for break-out groups. Additional information is requested regarding coursework already completed in the target language and study, travel, or residency abroad. Although required as part of the application process, such information is not the main criterion for the selection of UTAs. The actual selection is proficiency-oriented, much like the road test for receiving a driver's license. Rather than competing on the basis of grade point averages, students must teach sample lessons and demonstrate their ability to apply what they are learning.

Selection Process

The selection of UTAs typically occurs in August, within the context of a workshop that takes place the week preceding the beginning of classes. Although a spring selection of UTAs for the fall semester would allow a longer period for initial training, it would also preclude the selection of students who participate in a Junior Year Abroad program. Upon their return to campus for their senior year, these students are often among the most eager to share their enthusiasm for the language and culture in which they have so recently been immersed.

The selection process takes place over a three-day period prior to the beginning of classes. The departmental methodologist, who serves as workshop director and coordinator for the UTA program, opens the workshop with a plenary session for all eight language groups. The director presents an overview of the content and schedule for the workshop and describes the first-year language program and the role that UTAs play within it. The director also discusses general employment guidelines and departmental policies concerning salary, earned credit, absences, weekly planning sessions, and specific UTA classroom responsibilities. Returning UTAs offer their perspectives on the selection process, the ongoing training sessions, and the classroom experience itself. A question-and-answer period follows and leads into a discussion of the selection criteria. The session wraps up with demonstrations in several different languages so that candidates may better envision the range of activities in which they will be involved. The demonstrations may be live, using faculty and experienced UTAs, or they may consist of videotaped UTA classes from previous years.

On the afternoon of the first day of the workshop and for the remaining sessions scheduled over the next two days, students meet in language-specific groups to view additional demonstrations, discuss techniques, and practice leading their group through a variety of activities from highly structured substitution drills to open-ended personalized questions and role-plays. Through a series of microteaching experiences, students receive encouragement and feedback on how they might improve their performance.

In the final selection process the first and most frequently raised question in the faculty discussion is whether or not the applicants possess sufficiently developed target language skills to serve as a model when teaching. Murphy (1991) recommends that standards for entering TAs be set at the ACTFL Advanced Level for the productive skills and at the Advanced High Level for the receptive skills. Yet Murphy goes on to note that many fourth-year undergraduate foreign language majors do not reach that level in the course of their undergraduate studies — even with study abroad options. Magnan (1986) confirms this fact, reporting that while 60% of the seniors did reach the Advanced Level in speaking, the remaining 40% did not. Within the context of the UTA model at the College of William and

Mary, we do not conduct Oral Proficiency Interviews as part of our selection process. With anywhere from one hundred to two hundred students applying for positions as UTAs, it would be unrealistic to place such a burden on the faculty. While Magnan's (1986) figures suggest that UTAs probably exhibit a range of oral proficiency levels from Intermediate to Advanced, it would appear that this range is sufficient to meet the responsibilities of a UTA. The restricted use of UTAs for skill-getting and skill-using activities, rather than for presentation, explanation, testing, and evaluation, represents a much more controlled environment — and one more closely supervised — than that of an entering TA with similar skills for whom the responsibilities are much greater.

The selection criteria for the UTAs include, admittedly, a combination of factors — some mechanical, others more impressionistic. In addition to a numerically scored evaluation sheet, an evaluator's narrative comments carry considerable significance. "Good teaching" by most definitions would be difficult — if not impossible — to reduce to a numerical formula. So called "good" teachers exhibit decidedly different profiles, with individual strengths compensating for occasional weaknesses. For this reason, the evaluation forms for the microteaching lessons attempt to address the candidates' abilities to adapt their teaching techniques to the type of activity in progress and in response to feedback from the students. In the course of the orientation workshop UTAs are advised to keep mechanical drills quickly paced and to offer immediate and direct error correction for student mistakes. In more communicative activities, on the other hand, UTAs practice responding first to content and then to form, reinforcing the natural exchange of information that takes place. UTAs use indirect error-correction strategies, often modeling the appropriate response. The affective atmosphere in the classroom, created and reinforced by the UTA, is considered, as are the language skills demonstrated throughout the duration of the lesson. As a basic threshold language ability, we look for UTAs who demonstrate a low frequency of error in the functions, structures, and vocabulary to be taught in the first-year program. Given their lack of experience, we look for only the most basic teaching techniques.

In the final stage of the selection process, each student presents a microteaching lesson that includes at least one mechanical drill and one communication activity. Each candidate is evaluated using the criteria previously discussed (see Appendix B). In some languages the first-year coordinator makes the final selection of students for the UTA positions, while in other languages the decision is made by a committee of all faculty scheduled to teach in the first-year program that semester. Those who are chosen to fill UTA positions begin almost immediately — in consultation with the coordinator — to prepare for their first day in class. Although the number of students applying for UTA positions varies from language to language, student interest in the program is high. Last year, one in seven students vying for a post in French was selected.

Training and Supervision

The training and supervision of the UTAs may be handled by one faculty member, the course coordinator for first-year language instruction, the departmental methodologist, or the responsibility may be shared with all faculty members involved in teaching in the first-year program. In some cases, one person may assume responsibility for the selection workshop, while the weekly planning sessions and classroom visits are rotated among several faculty members.

Weekly Planning Sessions

The orientation workshop at the beginning of the semester marks only the first step in what will become an ongoing process of UTA training. The forum for the additional training takes place primarily in the weekly planning sessions required of all UTAs.

The weekly planning session consists of three unequal segments. Each session begins with a discussion of specific concerns or problems that arose the previous week in class — a "trouble-shooting" period in which UTAs receive advice on how to handle students with particular difficulties, how to deal with pacing, and how to address discipline issues should they arise. The second portion of the session, representing the main focus, is a step-by-step discussion and demonstration of the lessons for the upcoming week. The faculty supervisor takes this opportunity to verify that the UTAs feel comfortable with the new material and that any questions they have concerning the lesson are answered. In addition, potential problem areas for first-year students are identified so that the UTAs can begin to anticipate student questions and concerns. If time remains, the final portion of the planning session is devoted to the continuing development of instructional strategies for the UTAs. Each week another technique is presented, demonstrated, and discussed, so that the UTAs are continually improving their understanding of the teaching process and their role in it. The topics for these discussions may arise from particular exercises and activities; they may be suggested by the faculty supervisor as a result of in-class observations; or they may result from a direct request from UTAs for additional instruction in certain types of techniques. If no time remains in the weekly planning sessions for discussion of new instructional strategies, the methodologist or language program coordinator may elect to offer an occasional seminar for interested UTAs.

Lesson Planning

For the first few weeks the supervising faculty member prepares the lesson plans, which serve as prototypes for future UTA lesson plans. Initially, the UTAs need time to adjust to being in front of a class, and they focus their efforts on issues of pacing, on encouraging class participation, and on providing appropriate feedback to their students. In an article on improving the performance of TAs, Rogers (1987, p. 403) notes that "teaching assistants with no prior pedagogical preparation nor instructional experience would use supervisor-prepared lesson plans to incorporate communicative materials and activities into their classroom."

It is important, however, to allow and even encourage the UTAs to personalize their lessons in some way so that their own identities can shine through. In the first few weeks of the semester, the "warm-up" and "wind-down" segments represent a good opportunity for individualization. In time, the UTAs contribute more and more toward the design of the lesson plans. The preparation of exercises to practice specific functions, grammatical structures, or vocabulary may be assigned to individual UTAs. Each one then brings an activity to the weekly planning session, where it is discussed and the lesson plan assembled. By second semester, pairs of UTAs may alternate class preparation by bringing an entire lesson plan to the planning session for feedback and revision.

Classroom Observations

UTAs are observed a minimum of three times each semester. The observations may be conducted by the first-year language course coordinator or rotated among several faculty members. The faculty supervisor maintains a file of observation notes for each UTA. These written evaluations provide the faculty supervisor with insights into techniques and issues that may need to be addressed in a future weekly planning session.

Because a number of faculty members are involved in classroom observations, those concerned expressed a desire to have a common form for note-taking during these visits (see Appendices B and C). The basis for the form is the same sheet used during the selection process and described earlier in this chapter. After some discussion, faculty members agreed upon two additions. The first is a brief questionnaire addressing overall classroom management skills; included are questions relating to UTA promptness in starting class, familiarity with the various activities of the day, appropriate use of the target language in class, attention paid to every student, appropriate respect shown to all students, and so forth. The questionnaire ends with an invitation to comment more extensively on the strengths of the UTA as well as to offer constructive suggestions for improvement. The second change to the form added several questions specifically designed to address the less structured classroom situations, such as group work and role-plays.

Just as learning styles vary from one individual to another, so too do teaching styles (Oxford, 1990). UTAs tend to develop a distinctive style and respond differently to suggestions from different faculty members. The rotation of responsibility for classroom observations among several faculty members offers UTAs a wide range of strategies and techniques from experienced faculty, all with their own teaching styles.

UTA Student Evaluations

Students enrolled in first-year classes evaluate their UTA twice each semester, at midterm and at the end of the semester. Students complete the evaluation forms during a 15-minute segment of each faculty member's class. In this way, the UTAs do not actually distribute the evaluations nor do they see the results of their evaluations until the semester has ended. By conducting evaluations at midsemester, the supervisor can identify problems with specific UTAs and provide additional training in pertinent areas. The student evaluations become an important part of the file on each UTA and play a role in determining whether to renew a UTA for the following semester.

The evaluation instrument currently in use combines numerical ratings and student narrative comments. UTA evaluations are consistently high, indicating that UTAs are well received by their students. One of the final questions asks students to rate the overall effectiveness of their UTA on a scale of 1 to 5 (1 being low and 5 being high). In the most recent semester, for

UTAs in French, 66% of the students completing the evaluation form gave a rating of 5 to their UTA, 28% rated the UTA at 4, and 6% entered a rating of 3. Slightly over 95% of the students enrolled in the course completed the evaluation form.

Regarding the written comments from that same semester, several common threads run through the narratives in response to the question "What do you feel are the greatest strengths of this UTA?" Thirty-six percent of the students completing the evaluation form specifically mentioned the positive manner in which the UTA corrected errors. Thirty-four percent of respondents noted the high level of enthusiasm as the greatest strength of their UTA. Twenty-three percent of the students spoke of a "positive attitude" that the UTA exhibited in the classroom, and 14% cited "patience" as the UTA's greatest strength. (The figures total more than 100% because some of the students noted two strengths.)

When asked "In which areas would you recommend improvement?," students showed less consensus, but mentioned three areas more frequently than others. Ten percent of the students felt that the UTA spoke too quickly and needed to slow down. Eleven percent expressed a need to have an exercise or activity explained more clearly since they were not always sure what was expected of them until the activity had begun. Finally, 10% of the students specifically requested that the UTA include more creative activities in the lesson plan and fewer structure drills.

UTA Remuneration: Salary or Course Credit

When implementing a model for UTAs, it is important to consider what form of compensation will be offered to the students participating as UTAs. Two clear choices are paying the students an hourly salary or offering them credit. If students are to be paid an hourly wage, the time used for class preparation — the weekly planning sessions and any additional time that the UTAs are expected to devote to the preparation of their classes — needs to be included on the timesheets. One suggestion is to pay them for their actual time in the classroom (two 50-minute class periods), plus the planning session, plus one to two hours of preparation for each hour in the classroom, for a total of approximately five hours per week. An alternative would be to award one credit for each semester of the UTA appointment. Students are often interested in receiving credit and official recognition on their transcripts for their teaching experience.

Legal restrictions may prohibit the awarding of academic credit for services for which payment is rendered. In the model being discussed, the initial form of compensation was an hourly wage for class preparation and teaching time. The issue of academic credit for the experience was raised by the UTAs themselves, many of whom indicated that they preferred to receive credit and a formal record of the teaching experience on their transcripts. A one-credit course has since been introduced that may be repeated each semester in which the student serves as a UTA. The credit is earned through a series of assignments ranging from participation in a series of pedagogical workshops, to observations of other UTA classes in the same or different languages, to reflective journal writing and videotaped classes followed by self-critiques. Each semester the language coordinator prepares a new list of workshops and assignments. From a list of eight options, UTAs select five that they must complete satisfactorily in order to receive the one credit.

Instructional and Motivational Benefits

First-Year Foreign Language Students

For students enrolled in the first-year foreign language course sequence (101–102), twice-a-week sessions with UTAs may offer several advantages. While class size for faculty members may vary between 25 and 30 students per class, the UTA class is restricted to 12 students. The smaller classes provide more opportunities for individual students to respond to questions, to receive feedback, and to participate actively in class discussions. Moreover, because they are scheduled separately from faculty classes, the UTA sessions represent a mix of students from all of the other classes. The alternating groupings from faculty and UTA classes provide a fresh start each day for students, offering them the opportunity to shed any embarrassment associated with errors committed the previous day. In addition, the new combinations of students ensure that communication activities that recycle the vocabulary, structures, and functions from the faculty class to the UTA class retain an element of spontaneity. Although similar questions may be asked in both classes, the answers to these questions continue to represent an exchange of new information within the context of two different sets of partners. Horwitz, Horwitz, and Cope (1991, pp. 32, 34) state that,

> Students who test high on anxiety report that they are afraid to speak
> in the foreign language. They endorse statements indicative of speech

anxiety such as "I get nervous and confused when I am speaking in my language class" (33%); and "I feel very self-conscious about speaking the foreign language in front of other students" (28%).

The faculty believe that the introduction of UTAs into the first-year foreign language program may lead to a less stressful learning environment. As noted earlier, student evaluations often cite a positive attitude, patience, and nonintimidating error correction techniques. Possible explanations for these comments include the following:

1) The limit of 12 students in each class provides for a smaller, more intimate setting within which students interact.

2) UTAs do not assign grades to their students. Without the pressure of grades and in the context of the smaller class size, a sense of camaraderie and cooperative spirit may develop, contributing to the feeling of a "positive atmosphere."

3) Students recognize that the UTAs are also undergraduates like themselves and not as removed from their experience as a faculty member or even a graduate student might be. In the course evaluations of UTA classes gathered over 10 semesters, first-year students frequently comment that the UTAs are approachable, nonintimidating, and understanding.

Another benefit that first-year students derive from participation in such a model is additional time to practice, internalize, and apply concepts before new material is introduced. The model provides a structured alternation between the faculty and UTA classes. For example, on Monday the faculty member may introduce the concept of the subjunctive and focus on the formation of subjunctive forms. On Tuesday the UTA would reinforce the formation of the subjunctive through a series of structured exercises and ask personalized questions requiring the subjunctive in the answer (not yet asking students to choose whether or not to use the subjunctive). On Wednesday the faculty member might introduce several different uses of the subjunctive and discuss what functions may be accomplished through their use. On Thursday the UTA class would focus on more open-ended activities requiring that students use the subjunctive or the indicative — whichever is called for to accomplish the task at hand. On Friday the faculty member might expand still further on oral work with the subjunctive or might focus class attention on a writing assignment in which students give their opinions on topics pertinent to their lives. Students recognize how useful the Tuesday/Thursday sessions are as a follow-up to one faculty class and as preparation for the succeeding one. The UTA classes offer students the opportunity to work intensively with the material first introduced by the faculty instructor before they are presented with new structures or functions. Attendance at the UTA sessions is mandatory; an absence from a UTA session is considered by faculty members to be the equivalent of missing a Monday, Wednesday, or Friday class. Although no formal studies have been conducted, student attendance is reported by the UTA to the faculty and there have been no surprises in this regard. Student attendance in the UTA classes appears to be problematic only for those students whose attendance is sporadic in the faculty member's class.

Undergraduate Teaching Assistants

Beginning foreign language students are not the only ones to benefit from this program. UTAs report a variety of motivations for choosing to participate:

1) To share their enthusiasm for the target language and culture with others

2) To find out what teaching is like and to decide whether or not they would like to pursue a career in teaching

3) For the unique responsibility and experience that teaching offers them while still undergraduates.

As a result of their advanced coursework or through residency abroad, these students are comfortable speaking the language and actively seek opportunities to use their skills outside the context of formal coursework. UTAs approach their classes with an energy level and an enthusiasm that are contagious. UTAs and their students have the opportunity to develop a unique and very special rapport with one another. In light of the fact that UTAs are undergraduate students, they serve as excellent models for first-year students of a level of language proficiency the latter might strive to attain. Students' identification with their UTAs and recognition that they too were once beginners offers first-year students a seemingly more reachable goal than that of attaining the proficiency level of a faculty instructor with years of foreign language experience. UTAs frequently report that at the beginning of each semester they are besieged with student questions regarding how long they have been studying the foreign language, their experience abroad, and how long it took for them to feel comfortable with the language.

For students who have already decided to seek secondary school certification, the UTA posts represent a valuable path to developing self-confidence and gaining useful experience prior to student teaching and entering the job market. Finally, students planning to continue their foreign language studies in graduate school often hope that the UTA experience will increase their chances of receiving a graduate teaching assistantship. Not only do they bring actual, although limited, teaching experience, they also have had some pedagogical training and can provide student evaluations and reference letters from a supervisor who has seen them teach. While two hours per week for a year is not a substantial amount of teaching experience, 60 hours of standing in front of a group of students, answering questions, encouraging participation, planning activities, managing time, and providing feedback does represent a substantial investment in the development of self-confidence and in alleviating the stage fright that is so often characteristic of first-time teachers. For a graduate program reviewing teaching assistantship applications, the additional information is bound to be welcome, providing more on which to base a decision than simply future potential.

While we may recognize the value of the undergraduate teaching experience for those considering teaching at the secondary or postsecondary level, it is important to underscore the fact that most students involved in the UTA program at William and Mary are not planning careers in teaching. Some of these students plan to do graduate work in other areas — business, law, or medicine — while others will enter the job market immediately upon completion of their undergraduate degree program. Such a unique position of responsibility and authority while an undergraduate offers students the opportunity to develop organizational skills, interpersonal skills, and leadership qualities that are valuable in many fields other than teaching. Each year brings requests from UTAs for letters of recommendation that specifically address their responsibilities as UTAs. Last year these letters were sent on behalf of applicants to law schools, medical schools, the federal government, and international business firms.

Faculty Teaching in the First-Year Foreign Language Program

Although the faculty of the Department of Modern Languages at the College of William and Mary has long endorsed the use of UTAs in the classroom, instructors from other institutions have more recently welcomed the contributions of UTAs (Laroche, 1985; Winston & Boots, 1987). Initial cautiousness and skepticism have given way to a strong belief that the first-year foreign language program has been greatly enhanced by the use of UTAs. For those programs shifting from a three-day to a five-day per week program, the pace of the first-year course has been relaxed. The guided practice offered in the Tuesday/Thursday classes alleviates the hectic pace of the Monday, Wednesday, and Friday class sessions. Knowing that a structure introduced on Monday has been reinforced and practiced on Tuesday enables the faculty instructor in Wednesday's class to focus more class time on personalized, open-ended activities. Language skill activities planned for a given week can be spread out over five class meetings rather than three.

In addition, the smaller Tuesday/Thursday classes permit the UTAs to work more closely with the students and to observe at greater length individual performance. As a result, student differences and learning difficulties become more quickly apparent in the UTA classes than in the larger classes of 25 to 30 students. Often the first indication that a student is having difficulty comes to light in the UTA class, and the faculty instructor is alerted to possible problems before they have developed very far.

Finally, a few years ago the French section decided that if the goals of the program were to be the development of all four skills plus culture, then it would be essential to incorporate some sort of oral testing into the first-year program. Concerns regarding class size, limited contact hours, and fairness to students were allayed by the twice-weekly sessions in small groups where the focus is specifically on the development of oral skills. Although no empirical data have yet been tabulated, the faculty is extremely happy with student performance on the oral examinations. We believe that students enjoy increased self-confidence in their speaking as a result of the small class size and positive atmosphere of the UTA classes.

Conclusion

The model described in this chapter has been in use for four years in eight languages (Chinese, French, German, Italian, Japanese, Portuguese, Russian, and Spanish). The decision was recently made to introduce an Arabic language program into the Department of Modern Languages and Literatures, and a new faculty member has been hired. Although the newly hired faculty member was not due to arrive on campus until this fall, news of the hiring has spread and half a dozen undergraduates have come forth to offer their services as UTAs in Arabic! The enthusiasm and interest that such a program engenders permeates the entire curriculum, from the students embarking upon their first year of study to senior-level students who hope to earn positions as UTAs.

Such a model is likely to be of interest to four-year institutions wishing to maximize language practice for students in their first year of study. With limited funding (Laroche, 1985; Winston & Boots, 1987), it is possible to enrich the first-year foreign language experience, expanding not only upon the contact hours, but also on the class setting in which students use their emerging foreign language skills.

Works Cited

Baisinger, Wilbur H. "Undergraduates as Colleagues: Using Undergraduates as Teaching Assistants in the Basic Course." *ACA Bulletin* 47 (1984): 80–83.

Byrnes, Heidi & Michael Canale (Ed.). *Defining and Developing Proficiency: Guidelines, Implementations and Concepts.* Lincolnwood, IL: National Textbook Company, 1987.

Cormier, Raymond. "Language and Cultural Immersion: A Winning Enterprise." Paper presented at the Northeast Conference on the Teaching of Foreign Languages, New York, 1988.

Crawford, John E. "Using Undergraduate TAs in the Basic Course." Paper presented at the Western Speech Communication Association, Albuquerque, NM, 1983.

———. "Maximizing Quality, Minimizing Costs: The Use of Undergraduate TAs in the Basic Course." Paper presented at the Western Speech Communication Association, Seattle, WA, 1984.

Gray, Pamela L. "An Alternative to PSI in the Basic Course in Speech Communication: The Structured Model of Competency-Based Instruction." Paper presented at the Speech Communication Association, San Francisco, 1989.

Hirsch, Bette C. "Beyond Rassias: Intensive Language Programs at Large and Small Institutions." *ADFL Bulletin* 13, 4 (1982): 1–2.

Horwitz, Elaine K., Michael B. Horwitz & Jo Ann Cope. "Foreign Language Classroom Anxiety." *Language Anxiety: From Theory and Research to Classroom Implications*. Ed. Elaine K. Horwitz & Dolly J. Young. Englewood Cliffs, NJ: Prentice-Hall, 1991: 27–36.

Laroche, Jacques M. "Undergraduate Internship in Conversation." *Foreign Language Annals* 18 (1985): 209–12.

Larson, Charles U. "Innovative Approaches to Teaching the Large Persuasion Class." Paper presented at the Annual Meeting of the Speech Communication Association, Chicago, 1990.

Magnan, Sally Sieloff. "Assessing Speaking Proficiency in the Undergraduate Curriculum: Data from French." *Foreign Language Annals* 19 (1986): 429–38.

Murphy, Joseph A. "The Graduate Teaching Assistant in an Age of Standards." *Challenges in the 1990s for College Foreign Language Programs*. Ed. Sally Sieloff Magnan. AAUSC Issues in Language Program Direction 1990. Boston: Heinle & Heinle Publishers, 1991: 129–50.

Omaggio, Alice C. *Teaching Language in Context: Proficiency-Oriented Instruction*. Boston: Heinle & Heinle Publishers, 1986.

Oxford, Rebecca L. *Language Learning Strategies*. New York: Newbury House Publishers, 1990.

Phillips, Elaine M. "Anxiety and Oral Competence: Classroom Dilemma." *French Review* 65 (1991): 1–14.

Rassias, John A. "New Dimensions in Language Training: The Dartmouth College Experiment." *Methods That Work: A Smorgasbord of Ideas for Language Teachers*. Ed. John W. Oller & Patricia A. Richard-Amato. Rowley, MA: Newbury House Publishers, 1983: 363–74.

Rivers, Wilga M. "Talking Off the Tops of Their Heads." *Communicating Naturally in a Second Language: Theory and Practice in Language Teaching*. New York: Cambridge University Press, 1983: 41–54.

——— (Ed.). *Teaching Languages in College: Curriculum and Content*. Lincolnwood, IL: National Textbook Company, 1992.

Rogers, Carmen Villegas. "Improving the Performance of Teaching Assistants in the Multi-Section Classroom." *Foreign Language Annals* 20 (1987): 403–07.

Ross, Roseanna C. "Utilizing Undergraduates as Teaching Assistants in the Basic Communication Course: A Model." *ACA Bulletin* 73 (1990): 45–52.

Tait, Alice A. "A Pre-Student-Teaching Experience for Secondary School Journalism and Publication Advisors." Paper presented at the Association for Education in Journalism and Mass Communication, Washington, DC, 1989.

Winston, Anne & Justine Boots. "A Modification of the Dartmouth Intensive Language Model." *ADFL Bulletin* 19, 1 (1987): 18–21.

Young, Dolly Jesusita. "An Investigation of Students' Perspectives on Anxiety and Speaking." *Foreign Language Annals* 23 (1990): 539–54.

Appendix A

Application for Teaching Assistant

Department of Modern Languages and Literatures

Name: _____

Summer Address: _____

_____

Telephone: _____

Native language(s): _____

Language you wish to teach: _____

Year of studies (fall semester): ____ Soph. ____ Junior ____ Senior

Previous experience as a teaching assistant?   ☐ Yes   ☐ No

If yes, please describe: _____

_____

Courses taken in the language you wish to teach:

_____

_____

_____

Study, travel, or residence abroad:

_____

_____

_____

Other pertinent information:

_____

_____

_____

Appendix B

Evaluation for UTA Microteaching Demonstrations
[Also used in conjunction with Appendix C for class observations]

Name: _____

Rating Scale
1 = Poor   2 = Fair   3 = Good   4 = Very Good   5 = Excellent

Highly structured mechanical drills

1. Instructions are clear. Models are provided
   (students know what is expected of them):   _____

2. Pacing is rapid and even: _____

3. All students are called on, in no discernible order: _____

4. Error correction is direct and immediate: _____

5. UTA's manner is pleasant, friendly, and
   enthusiastic. There is good eye contact: _____

6. UTA's language skills: grammatical accuracy _____
                                    pronunciation _____

Meaningful interactive activities (communicative in nature)

1. Questions are related by topic/theme and
   seem logical/natural for conversation: _____

2. Questions offer a range between "yes/no"
   and information-type questions: _____

3. Efforts are made to involve students other
   than the one directly asked the question: _____

4. Error correction is indirect or delayed: _____

5. UTA's manner is pleasant, friendly, and
   enthusiastic. There is good eye contact: _____

6. UTA's language skills: grammatical accuracy _____
                                    pronunciation _____

Additional comments:

_____
_____
_____

Appendix C

Supplemental Observation Forms for Classroom Visits

Name: _____

Date of observation: _____   Time of class: _____

Faculty member conducting observation: _____

Basic classroom techniques:

1. Did the UTA start class on time?   ☐ Yes ☐ No

2. Did the UTA take attendance?   ☐ Yes ☐ No

3. Did the UTA get bogged down
   in giving instructions?   ☐ Yes ☐ No

4. Did the UTA use English unnecessarily?   ☐ Yes ☐ No

5. Did the UTA seem prepared and comfortable
   with the material?   ☐ Yes ☐ No

6. Did the UTA listen attentively to student responses? ☐ Yes ☐ No

7. Did the UTA use appropriate
   error-correction strategies?   ☐ Yes ☐ No

8. Has the UTA established a good
   rapport with the students?   ☐ Yes ☐ No

9. Did the UTA use appropriate
   pacing throughout the lesson?   ☐ Yes ☐ No

10. Were all students called upon during the lesson?   ☐ Yes ☐ No

    —More or less equally?   ☐ Yes ☐ No

11. Was there a distinct warm-up and
    wind-down included in the lesson?   ☐ Yes ☐ No

General comments: Please write your narrative comments below. Please include UTA strengths as well as areas for improvement.

_____

_____

_____

Supplemental Observation Forms for Classroom Visits — *cont'd.*

Open-ended communicative activities (role-plays, groupwork, etc.)

1. Were the instructions clear? ☐ Yes ☐ No

2. Were all students at work on the task? ☐ Yes ☐ No

3. Did the UTA use appropriate
error correction strategies? ☐ Yes ☐ No

4. Were time limits established and followed? ☐ Yes ☐ No

5. Was time used efficiently? ☐ Yes ☐ No

Follow-up meeting with UTA to discuss classroom observation:

Date of follow-up meeting: _____

Summary comments (strengths and weaknesses):

_____

_____

_____

Specific recommendations for improvement:

_____

_____

_____

Teaching Assistant Development: A Case Study

Julia Herschensohn
University of Washington

The apprenticeship of teaching assistants (TAs) of foreign languages can be likened to language learning by a true beginner: both novices are required to gain mastery of several areas of expertise at once. The language learner must be able to pronounce the foreign tongue before using its salutations and syntax, yet must have some knowledge of the words before being able to pronounce them. Language students must learn rudimentary cultural characteristics in order to use forms as basic as the personal pronouns. Likewise, TAs are expected to have an understanding of administration, methodology, and content, that is, subjects ranging from placement tests to cultural subtlety. Language TAs are often given broader administrative duties than TAs in other disciplines (such as complete responsibility for their own class) and must excel in a methodology that is quite discipline-specific. The multifaceted role of language TAs requires that a training program address nearly simultaneously a wide range of issues that are of relevance to them. In addition, the home department must provide an administrative system that supports and enhances their teaching. The morale of language instructors is crucial to the excellence of the language program.

The first-year French program of the University of Washington teaches approximately one thousand students per year; over 80% of the classes are taught by TAs. Numbers such as these are typical of research universities with large language programs and graduate TAs. Our TA development program aims to provide TAs with necessary information regarding administration, methodology, and content to enable them to serve the undergraduate language population. This chapter describes the development program for graduate TAs in French at the University of Washington and the implementation of a one-quarter methodology seminar initiated in the fall of 1991. The first section presents an overview of the background and issues involved in foreign language teacher preparation in this country; the second section describes the rationale and planning of the TA program in French at the University of Washington; and the third recounts the implementation and evaluation of the TA seminar.

Foreign Language Teacher Preparation

In describing "What Constitutes a Well Trained Foreign Language Teacher" in the twenty-fifth anniversary issue of *Modern Language Journal,* Freeman (1941, p. 304) portrays an individual who "must possess a rich store of mature knowledge, untiring energy and vigor, contagious enthusiasm for his subject and his profession as a teacher, limitless patience, human understanding and sympathy." In the decades following his article, many others have built teacher preparation programs that aim to develop foreign language teachers according to Freeman's description (see, for example, Paquette, 1966; Brickell & Paul, 1982; Alatis, Stern & Strevens, 1983; Lange, 1983; Mellgren, Walker & Lange, 1988; Phillips, 1989; Morain, 1990; Richards & Nunan, 1990; Wallace, 1991; Woodward, 1991). Appropriately, one of the most thorough documents to articulate issues in foreign language teacher training, and a prototype for later work, was the fiftieth anniversary issue of *Modern Language Journal* (Paquette, 1966). In it Paquette incorporates relevant articles and documents dealing with foreign language pedagogy that ranged from content preparation and methodology to certification. An article by MacAllister (1966) deals with the role of TAs in college language teaching.

The "development" (a term Lange [1983] prefers to "training" or "preparation") of preuniversity teachers is similar, but not equivalent to that of TAs. Foreign language instructors in elementary and secondary schools are career teachers whose background and professional roles are broader and more complex than those of TAs. High school teachers, whose undergraduate specialization may not have been a foreign language, are perhaps better prepared in areas other than knowledge of the foreign civilization and proficiency in its language. This "content" knowledge is considered one of the most important prerequisites of the language teacher by most authors dealing with teacher education. Freeman (1941), whose ideal language teacher is both virtuously patient and maturely knowledgeable, underscores the necessity of thorough grounding in the target language and culture. The specific content that should be attained by foreign language teachers is spelled out in the MLA "Guidelines for Teacher Education Programs in Modern Foreign Languages" (Paquette, 1966, pp. 342–44). The seven areas of competence in which the teacher should achieve a level of "good" are as relevant today as they were 25 years ago: (1) oral comprehension; (2) speaking ability; (3) reading comprehension; (4) writing ability; (5) understanding of the structure of the foreign language and its systematic differences from the native one; (6) knowledge of the cultural context; and (7) "knowledge of the present-day objectives of modern foreign language teaching as communication." Phillips (1989, p. 12) points out the importance of content knowledge and makes recommendations to assure this competence in the certification of teachers.

Once certified, high school teachers represent their profession in interactions with colleagues in school and with members of the community. They are expected to be professionally active and to keep up with current ideas in the field. Extracurricular demands and multiple preparations for classes in varied fields are not uncommon for high school teachers. Finally, the necessity of teaching five to seven classes daily, with over a hundred students, and of handling disciplinary problems, requires that high school foreign language teachers deal with much more than simply the content of foreign language teaching.

TAs, on the other hand, are usually graduate students working on an M.A. or Ph.D. in the literature or linguistics of a foreign language while teaching one or two classes a term. TA training is designed more to expedite the teaching of beginning language classes than to prepare a teacher for a lifetime profession, as Benseler and Schulz (p. 94) deplored as long ago as 1980. Recent work in TA preparation (e.g., Henderson, 1985; Nyquist, Abbott, Wulff & Sprague, 1991; Rava, 1991) has emphasized the long-term importance of preparation in pedagogy, since teaching is the profession that many TAs will seek to enter. Such preparation is not, however, the first short-term priority in TA training, since some new TAs enter the program with no training whatsoever. Unlike high school teachers whose academic preparation may be in an area other than a foreign language, TAs in foreign languages must meet minimum requirements of language proficiency and academic preparation in the field of literature or linguistics to be admitted to a graduate program. Finally, TAs as teachers have far fewer extracurricular demands and disciplinary issues to deal with than high school teachers.

Studies that have looked at the training of foreign language TAs (Nerenz, Herron & Knop, 1979; Schulz, 1980; Gibaldi & Mirollo, 1980; Ervin & Muyskens, 1982; Azevedo, 1990; Murphy, 1991; Waldinger, 1990) bear out MacAllister's (1966, p. 402) comment: "As to the training given these assistants before or during their first experience, the situation with respect to methods courses proved to be more complex and varied than could be reliably ascertained by a questionnaire." Di Donato (1983, p. 34) echoes MacAllister in lamenting the inadequacy of much of TA training. "These observations and studies on TA training and supervision make it clear that improvements are still needed." He furnishes a checklist that makes recommendations similar to those of the articles he cites and others dealing with training (see also Gilbert & McArthur, 1975; Henderson, 1985; Lalande, 1991; Strozer, 1991). The main areas he delineates are TA orientation, in-service training, and TA evaluation, areas described in typical programs of TA preparation. Within each category he makes suggestions for procedures.

To summarize his checklist for TA orientation, he recommends: (1) a "shock" foreign language lesson; (2) role-play of Day One; (3) administrative information; (4) language lab tour; (5) presentation by experienced instructors; (6) panel of experienced instructors; (7) observation of teaching video; (8) office sharing with experienced TAs; (9) videotaping of new TAs; (10) idea sharing; (11) incorporation of target culture; (12) classroom problems; and (13) classroom procedure. For in-service training he recommends: (1) methods course; (2) observation of experienced TAs; (3) videotaping of new TAs; (4) observation by experienced TAs; (5) materials file; (6) introduction to professional organizations; (7) program articulation; (8) upper division literature; and (9) counseling. For TA evaluation he recommends: (1) predistribution of an evaluation checklist; (2) visitation by more than one supervisor; (3) peer observation; (4) preobservation conference; and (5) consideration of student reaction. Judging from the literature, methodology courses for TAs are closely tied to other aspects of the training program, that is, orientation, supervision, observation, and evaluation (see Gilbert & McArthur, 1975; Henderson, 1985; Strozer, 1991). The methods course is usually offered the first term the new TA is teaching, although it may extend for the whole year (as in Henderson's case). As do many other universities, the University of Washington French program closely ties together all aspects of TA preparation, integrating many of Di Donato's suggestions.

University of Washington TA Preparation

TA Training Before 1991

The seminar for French TAs at the University of Washington was a logical addition to an apprenticeship program that was already in place. The training sequence before fall 1991 provided information on the mechanics of the course itself and on campus resources, while attempting to acquaint TAs with issues in language pedagogy and a repertoire of classroom techniques. First-year French courses at the University of Washington are taught through a methodology that entails extensive use of the target language in the classroom and emphasizes communication skills, interactive presentation of grammar, and daily practice outside of class. Language learning requires skill acquisition as well as the cognitive integration of syntax, vocabulary, and culture. The goals of the first-year program are to develop the skills of listening, speaking, reading, and writing to a level equivalent to intermediate–low proficiency on the ACTFL scale (ACTFL, 1986), so that the student can communicate basic ideas in the target language and understand the cultural context of the language. Our methodology requires the use of a variety of materials — videotapes, recorded conversation and music, slides, overhead transparencies, maps, photographs and other visuals and cultural artifacts — to foster participatory learning on the part of the students. The role of the individual teacher cannot be underestimated in a language classroom requiring such intensive preparation and teaching.

In order to train TAs in our approach, we set up a program with the following components: an intensive, week-long orientation in the fall before classes begin; a weekly practicum to discuss ongoing issues in pedagogy; intervisitations by TAs; supervisor visitation; videotaping of TA classes; and meetings throughout the year to discuss issues and problems as they come up. In addition, with the assistance of the Center for Instructional Development and Research (CIDR) and the Language Learning Center (LLC), we have developed a computer-assisted language learning (CALL) program that students use to complete and self-correct their daily homework. The TAs also receive ongoing in-service enrichment to sharpen teaching ability and extend evaluatory and conceptual skills. Enrichment includes workshops given by professionals in language pedagogy such as Pierre Capretz and Claire Kramsch.

In principle, the first-year training program included necessary information and practice, but in reality it did not provide sufficient time to develop the requisite knowledge and skills. All Romance language TAs participated in a one-week orientation prior to the first day of classes in fall. Theoretical and practical information was conveyed in sessions covering a "shock" foreign language lesson, general methodology, program requirements, lesson planning, first-week activities, evaluation procedures, administration, CALL, potential problem areas, idea sharing, and the functions of the LLC. During the orientation experienced TAs gave model presentations and worked with new TAs in pairs and groups doing hands-on preparation of materials.

During fall and winter quarters the new TAs met weekly with the TA supervisor in a one-hour practicum to discuss lesson planning, supplementary materials, evaluation procedures, test writing, grading policies, campus resources, and idea sharing. The teaching issues were always dealt with experientially so that TAs learned through doing. For example, test correction and grading were presented through the experience of correcting a sample exam and subsequently comparing grades. Written guidelines were provided for the evaluation of oral interviews and compositions. Each new TA made a presentation of an original teaching technique and submitted sample lesson plans and materials. TAs received one credit for each quarter of the practicum.

The supervisor visited TAs once a year. She evaluated the class and spent an hour discussing it with the TA. TAs received a copy of the written report, which became part of their file. New and experienced TAs were expected to visit each others' classes and to turn in an evaluation indicating what they found useful in the visit. TAs were asked to have their class videotaped at least once by CIDR. They discussed the resultant videotape with a CIDR specialist and informed the supervisor of their response to the videotaping experience. CIDR performs this service on a strictly confidential basis.

Through our training program in the three areas of administration, methodology, and content, we tried to instruct TAs not only in the specifics of our language program, but also in general issues of pedagogy. We found, however, that one hour a week was insufficient to provide even the minimum necessary for the administration of the program, let alone instill an interest in the educational process that might shape their professional lives beyond French 101.

Entry Level Initiative

In the beginning of the 1989–91 biennium the University of Washington designated nearly $4 million to be used exclusively for the improvement of undergraduate education. This project, which affected courses with large enrollments of first- and second-year students, became known as the Entry Level Initiative. A task force on foreign languages worked intensively in the fall of 1989 to draft a proposal that would improve first-year language teaching. The major thrust of the Romance Languages' proposal was the development of a TA training program that would include both a generic methodology section and a language-specific practicum. The relevant excerpt of the proposal reads as follows (University of Washington Romance Languages Memo, December 1989):

> We take as [our] premise that teaching excellence is central to the language learning process, and that it should be the focal point of undergraduate education. We believe that TA training, supervision, and support are the most important issues for entry-level language courses, for it is only through adequate preparation that language instructors can realize their own potential and improve the quality of the language program. The availability and development of techno-logical support systems, while useful adjuncts, cannot replace the teacher–student interaction at the core of the language learning process. Our top priority recommendation is a TA training program that would include an interdisciplinary graduate methodology course coupled with language-specific support and supervision. We view the TA training and support program as a necessity from two perspectives. First, adequate preparation of language TAs is essential for teaching excellence, a characteristic central to the improvement of the entry-level language program. Second, a top-notch training program accom-panied by adequate support and professional preparation are requisite to attracting outstanding graduate students to our language programs.

The Romance Languages' proposal was accepted in spring 1990; the recommended positions were funded; and, in addition, the College of Arts and Sciences decided to hire a language pedagogy specialist who would work with CIDR and the LLC as well as teach a generic methodology course. In the fall of 1991 the French section implemented the five-credit graduate seminar on language methodology. The Spanish section of the department has had a five-credit seminar in place since 1987 (Strozer, 1991).

TA Development Seminar

In expanding the TA apprenticeship from a one-hour practicum to a five-hour seminar, we retained many aspects of the program already in place. We covered most of the points in Di Donato's checklist, but a large amount of the training information was dealt with very intensely during the orientation. We wanted to reduce the information overload of the preservice orientation while providing adequate preparation for the first week of class. We saw all aspects of TA development as linked: the orientation, the seminar, coordinator evaluation, intervisitations, and videotaping. The seminar was then designed to integrate all these components.

We wanted to provide both "received" and "experiential knowledge" (Wallace, 1991, pp. 14–17). In the first, "the trainee becomes acquainted with the vocabulary of the subject and the matching concepts, research findings, theories and skills which are widely accepted as being part of the necessary intellectual content of the profession" (p. 14); in the second, "the trainee will have developed knowledge-in-action by practice of the profession, and will have had, moreover, the opportunity to reflect on that knowledge-in-action" (p. 15). We were interested in teaching process as much as content (Woodward, 1991, p. 4), in providing a holistic approach that would not only prepare instructors for the University of Washington French program, but also furnish the tools for language teaching and the development of cognitive skills beyond those needed for teaching first-year French. Richards and Nunan (1990, p. 9) describe a holistic approach as "the examination of the total context of classroom teaching and learning in an attempt to understand how the interactions between and among teacher, learners, and classroom tasks affect learning." They advocate a preparation that develops teaching strategies and problem-solving skills rather than simply the memorization of classroom routines.

The one-week preservice training program before the first week of classes in the fall was expanded to eight days in order to foster mentoring relationships among new and experienced TAs, promote acclimation to the University of Washington, and provide information necessary for the first week of classes (administration policies and pedagogical goals). The new preservice orientation focused more on the essentials for teaching the first chapter than on general issues of language pedagogy. We included a day of microteaching by the new TAs, who were videotaped by CIDR. As a group, the new TAs evaluated each others' video microlessons with a CIDR staff member. Another innovation was the use of experienced TAs not simply as presenters, but also as leaders of the practica in which the new TAs prepared lesson plans and materials.

At orientation TAs received a "TA Packet" that includes the following information sections: I. GENERAL INFORMATION FOR INSTRUCTORS; II. MATERIALS FOR DAY ONE; III. PEDAGOGICAL MATERIALS; IV. AUDIO-VISUAL MATERIALS; V. EVALUATING STUDENT PERFORMANCE. Section I includes a list of "TA Responsibilities" (see Appendix A) and a sample TA evaluation form (see Appendix B). TAs thus had from the outset clear, written guidelines concerning their responsibilities and the criteria on which their work was judged. Knop (1977, p. 634) points out that such guidelines are an integral part of TA development: "TAs react very positively to having such a checklist. They feel secure in knowing ahead of time the specific items that supervisors are going to look at and comment on after a visit. They use it for self-evaluation and for obtaining their students' evaluations."

The five-credit graduate-level course required of all new French instructors was offered during the fall quarter (two hours on Mondays and Wednesdays, one hour on Fridays). It was designed to include three components: on Mondays the two-hour lecture/workshops dealt with general issues of language pedagogy; on Wednesdays the two hours were devoted to particular aspects of the French language program (how to grade an exam, how to conduct an oral interview); and on Fridays the hour meeting was targeted to dealing with the grammar, vocabulary, culture, and idiosyncrasies of the chapter being taught. Both the general methodology and the language-specific sessions emphasized participatory learning on the part of the TAs.

Issues dealt with in the general theory of methodology sessions included (see sample syllabus, Appendix C): first and second language acquisition; history of language methodology; survey of current language methodologies; ACTFL Proficiency Guidelines; phonological, syntactic, and semantic variation among languages; interface of culture and language; emerging technologies in language pedagogy; curriculum planning; evaluation procedures; and teaching styles. The new TAs did weekly readings and completed a one- to two-page written assignment related to the week's topic or to an aspect of their teaching. For example, one assignment entailed short identifications of current methodologies, while another was a lesson plan that the TA had found worked well. Groups of new TAs worked together to develop classroom approaches drawing on authentic materials and audiovisual supplements.

The "French program" sessions dealt with language specific issues (e.g., lesson planning, inductive grammar presentation, using realia and audiovisual materials, exam writing and grading, oral interviews, calculating course grades, classroom techniques), class observation, and videotaping of the new TAs. Techniques included group work, panel discussions, role-playing, and use of video training tapes. TA intervisitation was modified to include a mentoring system by which new TAs were paired with experienced ones. We felt that for the new TA, senior TAs are an invaluable resource and are able to advise the new TA on their dual roles of teacher and graduate student. Senior TAs can also foster the socialization and integration of new TAs. In turn, the senior TA gains experience in interpersonal relationships and supervision. The methodology course also encouraged intervisitation among instructors (within French and in other languages) to foster cooperation and cross-linguistic sharing.

In order to develop a more interactive approach to class visitation (Acheson & Gall, 1987, p. 10), the coordinators established several feedback mechanisms. The TA responsibilities and evaluation form provided in the TA Packet were discussed in the seminar before class visitations, and TAs were given a preobservation form asking which particular areas they would like the supervisor to observe closely. Before receiving the supervisor's visit in the fall quarter, the new TAs were videotaped for a class period by CIDR. They reviewed their video with the assistant coordinator, who discussed the class in terms of the criteria on the TA evaluation form. After the visitation the supervisor and TA discussed the class using the evaluation form as a point of departure.

Evaluation of the new methodology programs was done by surveys distributed to TAs at the end of the preservice orientation and the methodology seminar. As the surveys conducted by Ervin and Muyskens (1982) and Nerenz, Herron, and Knop (1979) indicate, it is somewhat difficult to quantify responses that are in part attitudinal. In order to establish a baseline of comparison, we decided to compare responses of this year's TAs with those of earlier years. An examination of the responses of the new TAs and those prepared under the previous system shows a clear improvement in their perception of professional preparedness. We like to think that this apparent self-confidence contributed to greater self-assurance in teaching. The TAs were asked to "indicate how knowledgeable you feel about the following issues after your first quarter as a TA, on a scale of 1 to 3 (1 lowest to 3 highest)."

Figure 1
TA Response to Evaluation Survey (12/91)

Issue	New TAs	Experienced TAs
TA role in general	2.9	2.3
TA responsibilities	3.0	2.3
Departmental responsibilities	2.4	2.2
Language methodology (Theory)	2.4	2.1
Classroom technique (Practice)	2.6	2.3
Exam construction	2.4	1.9
Oral interview	2.7	2.1

The average of new TAs' opinion was 2.62, whereas that of experienced TAs was 2.17, an increase suggesting that the seminar attained its objectives of better preparing the TAs for their first quarter of teaching.

Conclusion

The development program for French TAs at the University of Washington seems to have been positively influenced by the addition of a methodology seminar. The seminar complemented other aspects of the program already in place and assured adequate preparation and feedback for the first quarter of teaching, and also provided a forum for discussion of issues. Continuing in-service workshops and projects for TAs after the first quarter gives them the opportunity of teaching at various levels and of gaining advanced training in language administration. Discussion of pedagogy and materials preparation in areas such as interactive reading or writing enables TAs to prepare for professions that will include those activities on a more advanced cognitive level.

Works Cited

Acheson, Keith A. & Meredith Damien Gall. *Techniques in the Clinical Supervision of Teachers: Preservice and Inservice Applications.* New York: Longman, 1987.

Alatis, James, H.H. Stern & Peter Strevens (Ed.). *Applied Linguistics and the Preparation of Second Language Teachers.* Georgetown University Roundtable on Languages and Linguistics. Washington, DC: Georgetown University Press, 1983.

American Council on the Teaching of Foreign Languages [ACTFL]. *ACTFL Proficiency Guidelines.* Hastings-on-Hudson, NY: ACTFL, 1986.

Azevedo, Milton M. "Professional Development of Teaching Assistants: Training *vs.* Education." *ADFL Bulletin* 22, 1 (1990): 24–28.

Bailey, Leona G. "Observing Foreign Language Teaching: A New Method for Teachers, Researchers and Supervisors." *Foreign Language Annals* 10 (1977): 641–48.

Benseler, David & Christine Cronjaeger. "The Preparation and Support of Graduate Teaching Assistants in Foreign Languages: A Bibliography." In Magnan, 1991: 207–32.

––––– & Renate Schulz. "Methodological Trends in College Foreign Language Instruction." *Modern Language Journal* 64 (1980): 88–96.

Brickell, Henry M. & Regina H. Paul. "Ready for the '80s? A Look at Foreign Language Teachers and Teaching at the Start of the Decade." *Foreign Language Annals* 15 (1982): 169–86.

Buerkel-Rothfuss, Nancy L. & Pamela L. Gray. "TA Training: The View from the Top." *Preparing the Professoriate of Tomorrow to Teach.* Ed. Jody Nyquist, Robert D. Abbott, Donald H. Wulff & Jo Sprague. Dubuque, IA: Kendall-Hunt, 1991: 29–52.

Di Donato, Robert. "TA Training and Supervision: A Checklist for an Effective Program." *ADFL Bulletin* 15, 1 (1983): 34–36.

Ervin, Gerard & Judith A. Muyskens. "On Training TAs: Do We Know What They Want and Need?" *Foreign Language Annals* 15 (1982): 335–44.

Freeman, Stephen A. "What Constitutes a Well Trained Foreign Language Teacher?" *Modern Language Journal* 25 (1941): 293–305.

Gibaldi, Joseph & James V. Mirollo (Ed.). *The Teaching Apprentice Program in Languages and Literatures.* New York: Modern Language Association, 1980.

Gilbert, Claire P. & James F. McArthur. "In-service Teacher Preparation of French Graduate Assistants: Design and Evaluation." *French Review* 48 (1975): 508–21.

Henderson, Ingeborg. "Training Teaching Assistants in the Yearlong Methods Course." *ADFL Bulletin* 16, 2 (1985): 49–52.

Knop, Constance K. "Developing a Model for Student–Teacher Supervision." *Foreign Language Annals* 10 (1977): 623–38.

Lalande, John F., II. "Advancing the Case for an Advanced Methods Course." In Magnan, 1991: 151–66.

Lange, Dale L. "Teacher Development and Certification in Foreign Languages: Where Is the Future?" *Modern Language Journal* 67 (1983): 374–81.

MacAllister, Archibald. "The Preparation of College Teachers of Modern Foreign Languages." *Modern Language Journal* 50 (1966): 400–15.

Magnan, Sally Sieloff (Ed.). *Challenges in the 1990s for College Foreign Language Programs.* AAUSC Issues in Language Program Direction 1990. Boston: Heinle & Heinle Publishers, 1991.

Mellgren, Millie Park, Constance L. Walker & Dale L. Lange. "The Preparation of Secondary Language Teachers through Postbaccalaureate Education." *Foreign Language Annals* 21 (1988): 121–29.

Morain, Genelle. "Preparing Foreign Language Teachers: Problems and Possibilities." *ADFL Bulletin* 21, 2 (1990): 20–24.

Murphy, Joseph A. "The Graduate Teaching Assistant in an Age of Standards." In Magnan, 1991: 129–49.

Nerenz, Anne G., Carol A. Herron & Constance K. Knop. "The Training of Graduate Teaching Assistants in Foreign Languages: A Review of Literature and a Description of Contemporary Programs." *French Review* 52 (1979): 873–88.

Nyquist, Jody D., Robert D. Abbott, Donald H. Wulff & Jo Sprague (Ed.). *Preparing the Professoriate of Tomorrow to Teach.* Dubuque, IA: Kendall-Hunt, 1991.

Paquette, F. André. "Guidelines for Teacher Education Programs in Modern Foreign Languages — An Exposition." *Modern Language Journal* 50 (1966): 323–425.

Phillips, June K. "Teacher Education: Target of Reform." *Shaping the Future: Challenges and Opportunities.* Ed. Helen S. Lepke. Middlebury, VT: Northeast Conference on the Teaching of Foreign Languages, 1989: 11–40.

Rava, Susan. "Minding Our Business." *ADFL Bulletin* 22, 3 (1991): 51–53.

Richards, Jack C. & David Nunan. *Second Language Teacher Education.* Cambridge: Cambridge University Press, 1990.

Schulz, Renate A. "TA Training, Supervision and Evaluation: Reports of a Survey." *ADFL Bulletin* 12, 1 (1980): 1–8.

Strozer, Judith. "The TA Training Program in Spanish at the University of Washington." *Preparing the Professoriate of Tomorrow to Teach.* Ed. Jody D. Nyquist, Robert D. Abbott, Donald H. Wulff & Jo Sprague. Dubuque, IA: Kendall-Hunt, 1991: 205–09.

Waldinger, Renée. "Training Ph.D. Students to Teach in College." *ADFL Bulletin* 22, 1 (1990): 20–23.

Wallace, Michael. *Training Foreign Language Teachers: A Reflective Approach.* Cambridge: Cambridge University Press, 1991.

Woodward, Tessa. *Models and Metaphors in Language Teacher Training: Loop Input and Other Strategies.* Cambridge: Cambridge University Press, 1991.

Appendix A

TA Responsibilities

I. PARTICIPATION IN TA ORIENTATION IN SEPTEMBER

II. CLASSROOM

1. Class list: monitor class enrollment, keep records of students, maintain grade book; post enrollment figures during first week.

2. Write lesson plans for each lesson; teach daily classes. If you are unable to meet your class because of illness or a conflict, arrange a substitute. Do not go through the supervisor or the secretaries. Each instructor is responsible for teaching or covering his or her class. New TAs submit to the supervisor two lesson plans and two examples of supplementary materials (e.g., quizzes, dialogues) in the fall quarter.

3. Enrichment: provide supplementary materials (e.g., cultural documents and realia) and quizzes, *dictées,* etc. Use slides, tapes, etc., as indicated to teach culture component of course.

4. Work in language lab; do oral comprehension testing; use available videotapes and slide programs as indicated on the syllabus.

5. Do correction of daily work, quizzes, midterms, and final exam. Collect workbooks during exams, and check that students have completed work. The teacher should randomly correct the workbooks for error, and should give pop quizzes taken from the workbook assignment for the day. Students are expected to do one or two short writing activities in each lesson.

6. Do oral grading; this includes one oral interview per quarter, and one class evaluation per quarter. The class evaluation may be a composite score (based on several observations) or a single-event evaluation.

7. Administer and grade quizzes, midterms, and final; keep track of student attendance.

8. Submit final grades to supervisor, indicating clearly the components (e.g., quiz average, oral interview).

9. Meet with supervisor to discuss her visitation to the class (fall quarter); arrange with CIDR to have class videotaped (winter quarter).

III. OUTSIDE THE CLASSROOM

1. Give one 7- to 10-minute oral interview with each student during the quarter; this may be accomplished by doing a pair interview, but each student should be allotted 7–10 minutes.

2. Be available for office hours at least two hours per week.

3. Attend meetings in fall and winter quarters; instructors will contribute ideas, comments, quizzes, material, etc., at each meeting.

4. Write sections of exams requested; participate in the composition meetings in which the exam committee critiques and puts together the parts of the midterms and final.

5. Make class visitations of other instructors: all TAs make two visitations in the fall; it is recommended that new TAs make additional visitations. New TAs should visit experienced ones, and vice versa.

6. Run off all personal dittos. Each exam committee is responsible for running off quizzes and midterm–final during its tenure.

7. Turn in all requested materials, including exam grading data, and especially final class grades (a copy of the grades should be kept on the tenth day enrollment list) for each individual file. TAs should keep the individual grade sheets used for calculating each student's grade for the academic year.

8. Have students complete the student evaluation form. The envelope with forms will be put in your box the week before the end of the quarter. Be sure that a copy is sent to the chair of the department.

9. Tell students *not* to call the department to leave messages for you. The secretaries in the main office cannot handle the potential volume of calls from two thousand students.

Appendix B

Teaching Assistant Evaluation

Instructor: _____   Course: _____

Date: _____   No. students: present _____
enrolled _____

I. ORGANIZATION OF COURSE

   A. Plan of class hour

   _____

   _____

   _____

	Needs attention		Exceptional
B. Organization			
• warm-up, review of previous lessons	–	0	+
• well organized, planned ahead	–	0	+
• practice of written/oral language	–	0	+
• skill-getting/skill-using activities	–	0	+
C. Tempo			
• set immediately, without waste of time	–	0	+
• sustained throughout the hour	–	0	+
• appropriateness of time management	–	0	+
• ten-minute rule	–	0	+
• effective use of book, board	–	0	+

II. CLASS ACTIVITIES

A. Teacher techniques			
• general student–teacher rapport	–	0	+
• include original materials	–	0	+
• target language used throughout period	–	0	+
• meaning reinforced via visuals, intonation, etc.	–	0	+
• inductive grammar presentation	–	0	+
• ability to deal with student difficulties	–	0	+

Teaching Assistant Evaluation — *cont'd.*

	Needs attention		Exceptional
B. Student participation			
• amount of teacher talk to student talk	–	0	+
• all small talk in target language	–	0	+
• personalization of materials	–	0	+
• mixture of choral/group/individual work	–	0	+
• all students called on	–	0	+
• cues for student self-correction	–	0	+

COMMENTS:

_____

_____

_____

Overall Rank: –   0   +

Evaluator: _____

Appendix C

French 590B   Fall 1991
Herschensohn

Date	Subject	Assignment	Reading
09/30	Language	IPA transcription	Ch. 1, #1
10/02	Exam construction		#8, #11
10/07	Language acquisition	Lesson plan 1	Ch. 2, #4
10/09	Teaching technique		
10/14	Methodology	Observation report	Ch. 3, #3
10/16	Observation discussion		Ch. 4, #6
10/21	CALL (K. Brandl)	Methodology ID	Ch. 13
10/23	CALL and homework		#10, #12
10/28	ACTFL guidelines	Lesson plan 2	Ch. 5, 6
10/30	Oral interview		#5
11/01	Moreau workshop, *"La presse quotidienne,"* 2 P.M.		
11/04	Curriculum, text	Text report	Ch. 12
11/06	No class		
11/11	Holiday		Ch. 7
11/13	Text discussion		(Ch. 8–11)
11/18	Cultural authenticity	Materials 1	#13 (1)
11/20	A-V, realia		
11/25	Styles (K. Brandl)	Materials 2	#13 (2)
11/27	Productive skills		
11/29	Holiday		
12/02	Comprehension	Materials 2	Project
12/04	Receptive skills		
12/09	Student presentation	Project report	
12/11	Final grading		

The weekly assignments, which are due on Friday of the week indicated, should be one to two pages.

Chapters 1–13 and readings #1–8 refer to Richard-Amato; #10–13 are indicated below [see Appendix D].

The final project will be a 7- to 10-page report including either: (1) a review of a book selected from the following list [see Appendix E]; the review will evaluate the book critically and relate it to pedagogical issues treated in FR 590; *or* (2) a short research paper dealing with a topic in language pedagogy (e.g., the writing curriculum, teaching literature in the language classroom).

Each student will give a 10- to 15-minute oral presentation of the report during the last week of class.

Appendix D

Required Readings for FR 590

Richard-Amato, Patricia. *Making It Happen: Interaction in the Second Language Classroom.* London: Longman, 1988.

#10. Ariew, Robert & Judith C. Frommer. "Interaction in the Computer Age." *Interactive Language Teaching.* Ed. Wilga M. Rivers. Cambridge: Cambridge University Press, 1987: 177–93.

#11. Herschensohn, Julia. "Toward a Theoretical Basis for Current Language Pedagogy." *Modern Language Journal* 74 (1990): 451–58.

#12. LaReau, Paul & Edward Vockell. *The Computer in the Foreign Language Curriculum.* Santa Cruz, CA: Mitchell, 1989: Chap. 2.

#13. Swaffar, Janet K., Katherine M. Arens & Heidi Byrnes. *Reading for Meaning: An Integrated Approach to Language Learning.* Englewood Cliffs, NJ: Prentice-Hall, 1991: Chaps. 1 and 2.

Appendix E

Bibliography for Report in FR 590

Berns, Margie. *Contexts of Competence*. New York: Plenum, 1990.

Brinton, Donna M., Marguerite Ann Snow & Marjorie Bingham Wesche. *Content-Based Second Language Instruction*. New York: Newbury House Publishers, 1989.

Carrell, Patricia, Joanne Devine & David E. Eskey (Ed.). *Interactive Approaches to Second Language Reading*. Cambridge: Cambridge University Press, 1989.

Goodluck, Helen. *Language Acquisition: A Linguistic Introduction*. Oxford: Blackwell, 1991.

Horwitz, Elaine & Dolly J. Young (Ed.). *Language Anxiety: From Theory and Research to Classroom Implications*. Englewood Cliffs, NJ: Prentice-Hall, 1991.

Johnson, Robert Keith (Ed.). *The Second Language Curriculum*. Cambridge: Cambridge University Press, 1989.

Krashen, Stephen. *The Input Hypothesis: Issues and Implications*. London: Longman, 1985.

Omaggio, Alice. *Teaching Language in Context: Proficiency-Oriented Instruction*. Boston: Heinle & Heinle Publishers, 1986.

O'Malley, J. Michael & Anna Uhl Chamot. *Learning Strategies in Second Language Acquisition*. Cambridge: Cambridge University Press, 1990.

Richards, Jack C. *The Language Teaching Matrix*. Cambridge: Cambridge University Press, 1990.

Rivers, Wilga (Ed.). *Interactive Language Teaching*. Cambridge: Cambridge University Press, 1987.

Wenden, Anita & Joan Rubin (Ed.). *Learner Strategies in Language Learning*. Englewood Cliffs, NJ: Prentice-Hall, 1987.

White, Lydia. *Universal Grammar and Second Language Acquisition*. Amsterdam: John Benjamins, 1989.

Breaking Out of the Vicious Circle: TA Training, Education, and Supervision for the Less Commonly Taught Languages

Benjamin Rifkin
University of Wisconsin–Madison

Recent political events transpiring across the globe, from Tiananmen Square to Red Square, from Berlin to Baghdad, and from Tokyo to Johannesburg, have drastically changed Americans' view of the world and their own place in it.[1] According to enrollment records reported in the *Modern Language Journal* ("Foreign," 1991), American university students are expressing greater interest than before in some of the less commonly taught languages (LCTs), including Chinese, Japanese, and Russian. Enrollments in Arabic may likely increase in the aftermath of the Persian Gulf War. Other sources also report increases in enrollments in some of these languages (National Foreign Language Center, 1991; Walker, 1991). As of 1990, there were approximately 45,000 college and university students of Japanese, 44,000 students of Russian, 19,000 students of Chinese, 3,000 students of Arabic, and 24,000 students of other LCTs (including other Asian languages, African languages, languages of native peoples of North America, Modern Hebrew, and other LCTs of Europe), for a total of 135,000 students engaged in the study of a less commonly taught language. Assuming a hypothetical student–teacher ratio of 30:1, one might safely conclude that there are more than four thousand teachers (professors, lecturers, and teaching assistants) at colleges and universities across the country.

Many of the introductory- and intermediate-level courses in these languages are taught by graduate teaching assistants (TAs) or native-speaker lecturers. These instructors often have little or no formal preparation in the foreign language pedagogy of their target language and also have little or no supervision in their work. Many of them ultimately earn doctorates, with dissertations in literature or linguistics, and take positions as junior faculty at institutions where they continue to teach language courses. Despite their own lack of any formal preparation in second language acquisition or in the methods of teaching their target language, they often find themselves responsible for supervising TAs.

Problems in the development of instructional materials and the implementation of teacher training, education, and supervision in the LCTs feed into a vicious circle: enrollments are not large enough to support the hiring of specialists in second language acquisition to provide programs of professional development for each of the LCTs, and thus there are few or no opportunities for teacher training (short-term workshops and orientations that are program-specific), education (long-term, not program-specific), and supervision. As a result, teachers are less likely to be able to help their programs retain students through higher levels of instruction to achieve better learner outcomes or to build their enrollments in the more advanced courses. In the remainder of this chapter, I will examine some of the factors contributing to the vicious circle and suggest steps that we can take to break out of it.

The Vicious Circle

Numerous articles describe foreign language teacher preparation programs in general (such as Rivers, 1983; Chism & Warner, 1987) and teacher preparation programs in the more commonly taught languages (for example, Bernhardt & Hammadou, 1987; Donahue, 1980; Gilbert & McArthur, 1975; Knop & Herron, 1982; Parrett, 1987; Pons, 1987; Rava, 1987; and Zimpher & Yessayan, 1987). Much has been written about teacher preparation for the international TA and especially for the native-speaker foreign language TA (Gutiérrez, 1987; Lalande & Strasser, 1987; Stern, 1983). However, very little has been written about professional development programs specifically for TAs in the LCTs. Since 1980 only two articles about TA or teacher training and education were published for Russian (Chaput, 1991; Ervin, 1981) and one for Arabic (Rammuny, 1989). None were published for Chinese or Japanese. Although a number of published works for all these languages have presented "prescriptions" or "recipes" for successful instruction, most are based only on personal experience (e.g., for Arabic — Younes, 1990; for Chinese — Packard, 1989, and Wang, 1989; and for Japanese — Jorden, 1987).

The lack of published works on programs of professional development in the LCTs may indicate that few such programs exist. In one survey of foreign language graduate programs, only 15% of programs in the LCTs reported that they required a graduate course in methods of teaching for their TAs (Devens & Bennett, 1985, p. 25), despite the fact that as long ago as 1980 there were close to 150 TAs in these languages (Schulz, 1980, p. 2). Given the tremendous increase in Japanese enrollments and significant increases in Russian and Chinese enrollments since that time, the number of TAs in these languages is likely to have increased.

Specialists in Arabic, Chinese, Japanese, and Russian interviewed for this study[2] agree that introductory-level and intermediate-level courses in these languages are quite commonly taught by TAs and native speaker lecturers at colleges and universities that often have made no provision for teacher preparation. One specialist — who asked for anonymity — described teacher training and education in his field as "haphazard at best," while another described her field's offerings as "sporadic." A third specialist said that TAs who demonstrated interest in pedagogy and had teacher training on their curricula vitae were often considered "tainted" in the job market.

Ronald Walton (1989, p. 18), writing of the situation in Chinese, complains, "There is no teacher training, but rather teacher adaptation to idiosyncratic institutional settings." Speaking of the less commonly taught languages in general, he notes that some programs, desperate for LCT teachers, hire instructors without going through the normal certification procedures or checks on professional competence. This leads to a perverse situation in which languages typically considered more "challenging" for Americans, such as Arabic, Chinese, Japanese, and Russian, which require a high degree of professional pedagogical training, are taught by instructors who are less qualified in some respects than instructors of the "less challenging," more commonly taught languages (Walton, 1991). Walker (1989b,

p. 119) concurs, noting the institutional lack of opportunities for teacher training, at both the secondary and postsecondary levels.

The consequences of the lack of teacher training are quite real in terms of learner outcomes. One study (Duff & Polio, 1990), for example, links teacher training to use of the target language in the foreign or second language (L2) classroom for both commonly taught and LCT languages. Although many untrained instructors may receive positive student evaluations, one must bear in mind that the "consumers" are often unsophisticated and may not know what they are missing. Sophisticated learners are frequently dissatisfied in LCT classrooms. One such learner of a less commonly taught language wrote of her disappointment in the instruction she was offered by noting the instructor's utter neglect to provide authentic input and opportunities for students to use the language in the classroom (Neu, 1991, p. 440). Complaints about poor teaching can be found in work by scholars of Arabic (Belnap, 1987, p. 37; Younes, 1990, p. 107); of Chinese (Walker, 1989a, p. 44; Walton, 1989, p. 8); of Japanese (Jorden, 1987, pp. 11–12); and of Russian (Baker, 1980; Chaput, 1991, p. 392, if only implicitly; Rifkin, in press, a).

One might view attrition rates in the LCTs as evidence of problematic instruction, despite student evaluations to the contrary. Belnap (1987, p. 31) reports a 50% per year attrition rate in Arabic. Dien (1985, p. 103) reports a 36–38% attrition *within* each of the first- and second-year Chinese courses he surveyed and what appears to be a 61% attrition rate *between* the first and second years. Kataoka (1986, p. 192) reports "considerable" attrition in Japanese language classes. The *National Foreign Language Center Survey of Russian Instruction* (in press) reports similar trends for Russian. Clearly, our students are voting with their feet.

Much has been written about the development of speaking skills or the development of instructional materials and assessment instruments for the LCTs, but, as one specialist (Allen, 1990, p. 2) points out, our profession may be neglecting items that should be at the top of our agenda:

> Any number of conference titles can be invoked to confirm the impression that, in planning programs of language teaching and/or learning, the most logical sequence is represented by something along the following lines: Goals, Curriculum, Teaching and Learning, Testing and Evaluation. Now, when we consult the proficiency "scenario" in its historical context, it becomes clear that the lion's share

of attention, debate, and controversy thus far has focused on the later (or, at least, the latter) end of this sequence. We are, in a very real sense, working from Z to A.

The vast majority of articles and surveys of instruction published since 1980 in the various professional journals for teachers of LCTs on problems in pedagogy, applied linguistics, and instruction avoid the broader question of professional development for TAs and teachers (for instance, for Arabic — McCarus, 1987; Parkinson, 1985; Younes, 1990; for Chinese — Chi, 1989; Dien, 1985; Packard, 1989; for Japanese — Jorden, 1987; Kataoka, 1986; Samuel, 1987; and for Russian — Launer, 1977; Thompson, 1977). In each of these fields, however, some do call for a commitment to teacher preparation: Ryding (1989) for the LCTs in general; Allen (1990) in Arabic; Walton (1989) in Chinese; Samuel (1987) and Jorden (personal communication) in Japanese; Rifkin (in press, a) and Thompson (1991) in Russian. These specialists believe that we must reassess our professional needs and establish as one of our top priorities the professional development of teachers, without which we will never be able to share in the progress made in understanding the processes of foreign language acquisition.

For most of the LCTs some programs for teacher training on the secondary level do exist; they are conducted during the summer and funded by organizations such as the National Endowment for the Humanities and the Ford Foundation. However, it is inefficient to provide special programs for secondary-level teachers while ignoring the professional development of the postsecondary-level teachers and TAs. If we establish regular programs for the professional development of postsecondary-level teachers, some of them will ultimately become teacher trainers for secondary-level teachers. Thus, programs for TAs and other postsecondary teachers would be an efficient means to promote the spread of instruction in the LCTs to the secondary level by providing for a larger range of options for secondary-level teacher education in these languages at institutions across the country.

As efficient as teacher preparation on the secondary level may be, few institutions provide for LCT TA professional development in a systematic way, according to surveys for Japanese and Russian conducted by the National Foreign Language Center and according to my interviews with specialists in Arabic and Chinese (see note 2). In the era of ever-tightening budgets, some institutions may reject requests to fund LCT teacher preparation because there are so few new teachers in any one of these languages in any given year or because many or all of the LCT TAs are native speakers and therefore may appear to administrators to have no need for such programs.

But those who hold that target-native speakers (i.e., native speakers of the foreign language that is the "target" of instruction) need no professional development programs to increase their understanding of learning and instructional processes are seriously mistaken: native proficiency in a language is not in itself sufficient preparation for teaching that language. In some instances graduate students in engineering and chemistry, originally from Taiwan or Egypt, are funded as TAs in Chinese or Arabic language classes, but this practice devalues the entire language learning enterprise by suggesting that the acquisition process is essentially a mechanical transfer of knowledge. Target-native speakers preparing to become language teachers, but who have no pedagogical training, often model their teaching on their own learning experiences in their native lands (Duff & Polio, 1990; Goodlad, 1983; Herold, 1977; Liskin-Gasparro, 1984; Walker, 1989a). The resulting instruction is often not in keeping with American students' learning styles and needs. As Jorden (1987) points out, target-natives are unlikely to understand or be able to predict areas where base-natives (i.e., native speakers of English in the American context) will experience intercultural misunderstandings, nor will they be able to provide adequate explanations of linguistic and cultural phenomena without special preparation to do so. Thus, LCT TAs, the next generation of assistant professors, deprived of opportunities for professional development, are trapped within the LCT vicious circle.

The view that foreign language instruction is a mechanical process that requires no professional preparation other than target-language competency is the legacy of instruction in Latin as a mental exercise. Swaffar (1989, pp. 123–24) discusses some of the assumptions about foreign language instruction that are a product of this view:

1) The goal of a language program is to teach its literature and its historical-linguistic development.

2) Teaching elementary language is not a university-level activity.

3) Elementary language learning is mechanistic, a matter of acquiring rote skills.

4) Instruction in beginning languages lacks the intellectual rigor of literary and linguistic theory.

Each of these assumptions is unfounded, both with respect to the more commonly taught languages and to the LCTs, regardless of the widespread perception of some of these languages as so difficult for Americans as to justify instructional methods unacceptable in the contemporary French, German, or Spanish classroom. Since the advent of the audiolingual movement, foreign language instructors in most languages have begun to respond to students' expressed interest in learning to speak a foreign language and have begun to focus their instruction on the development of more functional skills and communication or fluency activities, rather than devoting most of their attention to the analysis of language structures. In the face of changes that have swept the foreign language profession in the last 50 years, we have learned that the processes of language acquisition and language instruction are far from mechanical at any level of instruction, but rather are very complex processes requiring sophisticated instructional strategies in order to achieve successful learner outcomes. Academe has begun, slowly, to recognize the scholarly value of research in instructional methods and foreign language acquisition. The Committee on Institutional Cooperation, an organization consisting of representatives of the "Big Ten" universities, together with the University of Chicago and the University of Illinois at Chicago, urges that language program directors' research in pedagogy and related fields be counted toward tenure (Lee & VanPatten, 1990, p. 114). The Modern Language Association also recognizes the legitimacy of research in these fields (MLA Commission on Foreign Languages, Literatures, and Linguistics, 1986, p. 3).

The lack of teacher training, education, and supervision is but one of the more significant factors that binds the vicious circle for the LCTs. Another of these factors is the issue of instructional materials. When criteria for the evaluation of instructional materials established by Bragger (1985), Schulz (1991a), Swaffar, Arens, and Byrnes (1991), and Walz (1986) for the more commonly taught languages are applied to the materials available for the LCTs, the results are clear: instructional materials for our languages are, for the most part, catastrophic. As noted by Walker (1989b, p. 131), these materials are infrequently renewed, making improvements even less likely. Parkinson (1985, p. 18) and Walton (1989, p. 9) lament the quality of materials available for Arabic and Chinese, while Thompson (1991) and Rifkin (in press, b) voice similar concerns about materials for Russian. There seem to be fewer complaints *in print* about materials in Japanese, but in discussions with specialists in this field (see note 2), this writer heard of much dissatisfaction in terms of the lack of instructional materials that would provide for truly communicative activities in the Japanese classroom. Since LCT TAs often have little or no pedagogical training, they may rely excessively on the instructional materials they are given. Many foreign language teacher educators note time and again that they expect teachers to develop materials, exercises, and activities for their classes that the textbooks fail to provide (Andrews, 1983, p. 130; Ariew, 1982, p. 31), but in the LCTs, where instructional materials are generally deficient and teacher preparation generally lacking, TAs are simply not prepared to make up for these deficiencies.

Publishers are reluctant to become involved in textbook ventures for small markets that produce even smaller profits. In fact, the market for state-of-the-art instructional materials in the LCTs is even smaller than our enrollments might suggest; because so few instructors of LCTs ever have the opportunity to study methods of teaching foreign languages, they are often resistant to innovations in instructional methods and materials. Liskin-Gasparro (1984, p. 31) has observed that "the grammatically oriented text…has conditioned language teachers to make the *structure* of the language, rather than proficiency in the *use* of the language, the focus of a course of study" (her italics). Thus, many instructors prefer to use older instructional materials despite the availability of materials with newer approaches to foreign language study, such as a greater focus on communication activities and authentic input — for instance, *Let's Learn Arabic* (Allen & Allouche, 1988), *Ahsalan wa-Sahlan* (Alosh, 1989), *Japanese: The Spoken Language* (Jorden & Noda, 1990), *Learn Japanese* (Young & Nakajima, 1990), *Reading Real Russian* (Thompson & Urevich, 1991), and materials in Chinese, Japanese, and Russian available from the American Council on the Teaching of Foreign Languages (*Instructional Materials for the Teaching of Less Commonly Taught Languages,* n.d.). Resistance to and suspicion of innovation in instructional strategies is a significant factor in the LCTs, according to all those interviewed for this study, despite the fact that all the evidence to date suggests that authentic input and opportunities to practice language use (fluency activities) are the most efficient route to the development of communicative performance in commonly and less commonly taught languages alike (Brumfit, 1983; Dvorak, 1977; Rivers, 1986; Savignon, 1983; VanPatten, 1988, 1992a, 1992b).

Traditional instructional materials, in which so much attention is devoted to structure, may remain popular for a variety of reasons. They are the most familiar. They present an overview of the entire grammatical structure of the target language. They also devote considerable attention to instruction in the writing system, especially of languages with a nonalphabetic script. The prevalence of traditional materials is self-generating: textbook writers are often inspired by the books they themselves used when they were students. Leaver (1991), in a review of a new textbook for Ukrainian, noted that it lacked authentic reading and listening texts and that the authors made little attempt to develop communicative competence. The review (p. 282) concludes: "The teacher concerned with communicative competence can supplement these materials with authentic reading and listening materials and with more communicative classroom activities." Realistically speaking, however, many instructors of this language may not seek out such supplementary materials and activities, since few may know that they promote the process of language acquisition. Furthermore, those instructors who are sufficiently well informed to want authentic reading and listening texts are unlikely to have the resources to find them themselves.

LCT instructors across the country continue to produce their own materials in relative isolation, often reinventing what others have already done. Again and again one hears the refrain, "We have been so frustrated for so long that we have developed our own materials." While some of these materials might be very good (in which case one would hope that they would be published and shared with the entire teaching community), often locally produced materials are likely to be problematic, since they may be designed by people with no methodological training. Jorden and Walton (1987, p. 122) observe, "Parallel to the mistaken assumption that anyone who knows a language is automatically qualified to teach it is the equally mistaken assumption that the same individuals are equally qualified to produce text materials." Those who create "home-grown" instructional materials without careful collaboration with other specialists tend to produce materials that emphasize linguistic theory at the expense of authentic input or communicative activities, or materials that provide authentic texts or activities lacking a rigorous linguistic foundation (Jorden & Walton, 1987, p. 114). Furthermore, the current lack of communicative textbooks in Chinese and Russian is more than regrettable. The pervasive use of older materials feeds into the vicious circle in that TAs and junior faculty who use these materials, but who never had opportunities for professional development, are likely to resist the introduction of new instructional materials as well as the methods they represent.

Breaking Out of the Vicious Circle: Professional Development for LCT TAs

Some authors are currently writing communicative instructional materials for some of the LCTs, including Arabic, Chinese, Japanese, and Russian, but these materials, no matter how high their quality, will disappear if our departments are not prepared to adopt them for instruction. Furthermore, unless we undertake reform and work to change attitudes within academe, we will not be prepared to accept the next pedagogical innovation when it appears in the years to come. The most important changes that we need to make lie in the area of providing for our TAs' professional development. We must recognize the fact that most teachers with Ph.D.'s in languages and literatures, whether more or less commonly taught, spend a good deal of their time in language instruction.

We need to establish programs for teachers' professional development and provide all graduate students (whether they become TAs in our programs or not) with opportunities to participate in them. Even those graduate students who are not employed as TAs in our own programs are likely, some day, to be teaching language at some other institution. The Ph.D. is not only a recognition of scholarly research, but also a license to teach, and we have an obligation to ensure that all those to whom we grant the Ph.D. are competent to teach their target language. Some of us have collaborated with colleagues in the more commonly taught languages, bringing our TAs together for joint workshops and methods courses (Garner, Geitz, Knop, Magnan & Di Donato, 1987), which is certainly one way of overcoming the financial barriers to programs for the professional development of TAs for small departments. In some circumstances, however, the needs of LCT teachers may be neglected in the context of a teacher preparation program in which 95% of the participants are teachers of French, Spanish, and German. A solution to this problem would be to bring together into one group the teachers of all the LCTs for a separate professional development program at each institution. Participants in a program dedicated to serving the needs of LCT TAs would be able to share with one another their unique perspectives and needs, making explicit some of their notions of language learning and instruction relevant to their target languages as they grow toward a better understanding of the language acquisition process. The professional development program for LCT TAs should include three distinct components, each with its own goals and corresponding design: teacher training, teacher education, and teacher supervision.

LCT TA Training: The Preservice Workshop and In-Service Practicum

Once LCT TAs have been selected, they should be enrolled in a training program consisting of a preservice workshop and an in-service practicum. The preservice workshop should familiarize new TAs with the language programs in which they are about to participate, the instructional materials they will use, and the kinds of tasks they will face in working with the learners in their classrooms. Chism & Warner (1987) offer a number of descriptions of preservice workshops.

The preservice workshop should be dedicated to the TAs' most immediate classroom needs in order to be most effective (Ervin & Muyskens, 1982; Larsen-Freeman, 1983): planning an introductory lesson, presenting a pattern drill, introducing a dialogue, and taking care of pressing administrative details. The preservice workshop should provide TAs with opportunities to observe sample lessons in the LCTs and opportunities to practice teaching lessons to one another. The LCT preservice workshop should demonstrate to TAs how they can teach in the target language, despite any preconceived notions that it is "too difficult" for Americans. By presenting a sample lesson, the LCT preservice workshop director can do much to dispel notions that might prevent TAs from using the target language in their introductory-level courses and help them understand the value of authentic input at every level of instruction. One teaching assistant in Russian at my own institution, a native speaker from Moscow, was excited to observe an introductory Russian lesson because, as he said, he simply could not imagine beginning a class from "nil" and moving rapidly into communicative activities in the target language with simple language and memorized material involving greetings and introductions. Mixed language groups of TAs drawn from the LCTs provide a marvelous opportunity for TAs to reexperience the learning of a foreign language (Garner, Geitz, Knop, Magnan & Di Donato, 1987) as they discover the joys of teaching one.

The preservice workshop is also the place to establish the importance of the affective domain of the foreign language classroom, to talk about the differences between teacher-student relationships in the United States and in the target cultures, and to discuss different kinds of instructional formats, such as pair work and small-group activities (Billson & Tiberius,

1989). We need to remind LCT TAs of the importance of our learners' psychological needs and the relationship between affective concerns and foreign language teaching methods and practices (Rivers, 1991), since it is difficult to learn in an atmosphere lacking in trust and security. Rivers (1980, p. 64) notes the enhanced importance of the affective domain for the foreign language classroom: "Since any genuine communication requires that one feel at ease in the situation, these [basic] needs [as described by A.H. Maslow, *Toward a Psychology of Being*, 1968] among students and between teachers and students affect the success of the communicative interaction, even apart from differing levels of language control." The LCT preservice workshop is the place to focus TAs' attention on these affective concerns precisely because learners tend to be least comfortable in the new and unfamiliar situation of the first day of an introductory-level foreign language class. This is especially true in the case of LCTs, whose cultures are so distant from the experiences of the American college student. Attention to the affective domain is especially important for target-native LCT TAs because their cultures have such different norms for student and teacher roles. If LCT TAs can come together as a group, it will be easier for them to discuss these cultural differences and come to grips with the norms of the American classroom than if they were left to their own devices or placed in a larger contingent of TAs in French, German, and Spanish, who are often either Americans or used to American culture. The discussion of affective concerns should not end in the preservice workshop, but it should certainly begin in this context in order to focus on these issues from the first hour of instruction.

The LCT preservice training should also provide TAs with the opportunity to deal directly with some of the cognitive concerns of language acquisition. All the teachers of languages with nonalphabetic scripts can learn firsthand the frustration encountered by American students when they are asked to hold back on the development of oral skills in order to develop writing. Frequently, native-speaker TAs in Chinese and Japanese seek to focus primarily on the instruction of the writing system in their teaching; after all, that is precisely what Chinese and Japanese students do in schools in China and Japan. But as Jorden and Walton (1987, p. 117) note, students in China and Japan are required to master the complicated writing systems of their native languages *only after* they have achieved a fairly solid mastery of the spoken language. TAs from Chinese and Japanese, languages with nonalphabetic scripts, and from Arabic and Russian, languages with non-

Roman alphabets, should come together for a preservice workshop in which they teach one another minilessons. In doing so, they would be able to address questions of sequencing instruction in listening, speaking, reading, and writing, which are problematic for languages with different alphabets and nonalphabetic scripts.

LCT TAs begin with the preservice workshop focused on the immediate "survival" needs for the first few days of instruction. LCT teacher training should continue with an in-service practicum focused on other problems and questions. LCT TAs can try out ideas for classroom activities on one another before taking those ideas into their classrooms. In many instances, these activities may be quite good, but a trial run in a friendly setting would help TAs to fine-tune their lesson with the help of their peers. In addition to providing TAs with ongoing instructional support, the practicum meetings are a model for collaboration among practitioners in the LCTs, a desirable goal in and of itself.

The LCT program of professional development should not consist solely of TA training (the preservice workshop and in-service practicum), but extend to TA *education,* a distinction made by Larsen-Freeman (1983) and Azevedo (1990). It is a mistake to limit the LCT professional development program to a preservice workshop lasting only a few days, for to do so is to convey the message that the answers to all the questions concerning the acquisition of these languages have already been found, and it is the TA's responsibility merely to "receive" this information from the course coordinator. It is also a mistake to limit the professional development program to a preservice workshop and an in-service methods course or courses, since this would also imply that teaching a foreign language is a skill that TAs can master in a very short period of time. This view of the processes of learning and teaching undermines long-term progress in the design and delivery of instruction, for it builds into our worldview a resistance to new information about language acquisition, new strategies for instruction, and new instructional materials to facilitate learning. The view of language teaching that considers the preservice workshop sufficient preparation for the foreign language classroom also devalues the importance of the work language teachers do in the classroom, making it comparable to simple transmission of information about language from instructor to learner. The message that we want to convey to our TAs is that learning and teaching go hand in hand and that learning and learning about teaching are lifelong processes. Accordingly, we should provide regular opportunities for TAs to meet and discuss the processes of learning and teaching in the context of the LCTs and their special needs.

TA Education: The LCT Methods Course

While the preservice workshop can be dedicated to the immediate needs of teacher training, it is the in-service methods course or courses (Lalande, 1991) that provides TAs with their teacher education. The course or courses could be taught by one or more faculty members from one of the departments whose students enroll in it. The methods course for graduate students is the subject of much discussion, at least among instructors of the more commonly taught languages. In examining the needs of a methods course for LCTs, it is useful to consider how foreign language teaching depends on certain attitudes, expectations, and modes of behavior between teacher and students. Through the methods course, we must help TAs understand these interpersonal and intercultural dynamics and from this understanding to learn appropriate and effective classroom techniques. For learning to teach constitutes entering a new culture, the land of individual students brought together in a classroom for the common purpose of acquiring a second language. In this sense we can view the methods course as a stepping-stone for TAs as they acquire the discourse and the culture of teaching. The framework of three of the more prominent theories about how learners acquire languages — acculturation theory, discourse theory, and cognitive theory, can therefore also be applied to how instructors learn and acquire the practice of teaching LCTs to Americans.

Acculturation/Pidginization Theory

According to the acculturation/pidginization theory of second language acquisition, learners acquire the second language as they become acculturated into the target culture. The difficulty of the process of acquisition is in direct relationship with the social and psychological distance between the native and target cultures. Therefore we should use teacher education to provide opportunities for our TAs to become integrated into the target culture of LCT teachers. This, of course, has implications for the relationship between methods instructors and methods students, which should be modeled on a collegial relationship between senior and junior colleagues, rather than a relationship between a master of erudition and an utterly hopeless novitiate. This might be a somewhat more comfortable relationship for the methods instructor, if he or she has lived in the United States for any length of time, than it might be for methods students from some of the cultures discussed in this study in which the relationship between teacher and student is very formal and the distance between them great. Methods instructors of students from these cultures need to address this issue directly in order to help their students feel that they are becoming LCT professionals.

The methods course should provide TAs with information about professional organizations, journals, and activities in their fields. TAs should become informed as soon as possible about the nature of the job market that awaits them, of professional organizations for teachers of foreign languages (and not only those to which their instructors belong), and of the kinds of conferences and workshops of interest to language teachers. It would be productive, in this sense, to require students to examine professional journals, not only those teaching their own target language(s), but also those concerned with other languages, as well as journals in applied linguistics (such as *Applied Linguistics* and *Language Learning*) and journals dedicated to issues concerning the foreign or second language teacher (such as the *ADFL Bulletin, Modern Language Journal, Foreign Language Annals,* and *TESOL Quarterly*). TAs should also become familiar with the newsletters and annual volumes published by such organizations as ACTFL and the Northeast Conference.

It might also be productive, in the context of this component of teacher education, to examine the history of foreign language education in the United States, in order to prepare students to understand the legacy of traditions and practices inherited from the days when Latin and classical Greek were taught as a mental exercise and to distinguish teaching practices based on this legacy from teaching practices based on more recent approaches to foreign language learning and teaching.

As an important part of the acculturation process, TAs in the LCT methods course should be given ample opportunity to observe teaching practices and be exposed to instructional materials in a wide range of languages, especially the more commonly taught languages and ESL. While it is true that one cannot simply take an excellent exercise, activity, or textbook in Spanish and "translate" it into an equally excellent exercise, activity, or textbook in Japanese, it is just as true that we do have much to learn from our colleagues in the more commonly taught languages. Teachers of the more commonly taught languages have significant professional advantages: larger enrollments (and thus more instructional materials), easier access to target culture communities (in Quebec and large Hispanic communities throughout the United States, for example), older traditions of foreign assistance to promote cultural activities and instruction (*Alliance française, Goethe Institut*), and more widespread instruction on the elementary and secondary level to support more research in learning and instruction processes.

For these and other reasons, colleagues in the more commonly taught languages have been able to produce a far greater number of textbooks of different kinds and at different levels than we in the LCTs can ever hope to do. While we need not slavishly copy from these books, we can learn a great deal from examining them. The methods course should provide students with opportunities to examine and compare instructional materials in the more commonly taught languages. LCT methods course instructors should consult reviews of textbooks in the professional journals and ask colleagues in French, German, and Spanish for their recommendations and examine these titles with their students.

The LCT methods course should not stop with the examination of instructional materials in their own target languages and the more commonly taught languages, but should involve a number of other activities and raise important questions. First, LCT TAs should be challenged to consider whether or not principles, methods, and strategies for foreign language instruction in the more commonly taught languages are, in fact, relevant for them. They should confront evidence supporting the notion that comprehensible authentic input and fluency activities promote the development of communicative skills in French, German, and Spanish (Brumfit, 1983; Dvorak, 1977; Rivers, 1986; Savignon, 1983; VanPatten, 1988, 1992a, 1992b), and debate whether and how the LCTs require different kinds of instructional approaches. The LCT methods course instructor should ask TAs to discuss how they learned their target language, if they are not native speakers, or how they learned English if they are target-native speakers, to discover what opportunities they lacked in their learning experiences (by comparison with experiences described by their peers), and whether they consider themselves to be typical of the learners they will encounter in their own classrooms. The course should require LCT TAs to visit and observe one another as well as their peers in French, German, and Spanish to determine whether or to what degree classroom activities and homework assignments used for the more commonly taught languages can be productive for the LCT classroom. This kind of observation, if properly prepared and undertaken, can promote teaching assistants' acculturation into the profession. It can also provide the "authentic input" that teachers need in order to refine their teaching skills.

How, then, should such observations take place when some teachers view this event as threatening? The methods course should provide TAs with a system for observation that makes it less intimidating. Some of the more effective observation systems are those described by Allen, Frolich, and Spada (1984) and the one by Fanselow (1977), called FOCUS, or "Foci for Observing Communications Used in Settings." One of the major features of Fanselow's system is that it allows the observer to record interaction without judging it or evaluating it. Teachers are then free to perform their own analyses of the interaction patterns and draw their own conclusions. The nonjudgmental collection of data is critical for the improvement of our understanding of the learning and teaching processes; we need to prepare teachers to engage in classroom-centered research, as described by Allwright (1983), in order to provide the groundwork for changes to come (Long, 1983, p. 281).

By preparing TAs to use this kind of observation system and by sending them out to observe one another, we give them the skills they need to understand the teaching act as practiced by others (whether successfully or not) and the skills they need to analyze their own teaching. LCT TAs empowered to analyze their own teaching practices will be able to continue their professional development as professors, drawing conclusions and implementing changes as their own professional philosophies evolve and as researchers make new discoveries about the nature of foreign language acquisition. Furthermore, when we help LCT TAs develop the ability to describe the teaching act as rigorously as the structures of the language can be described (Fanselow, 1977, pp. 18–19), we ultimately promote the view that foreign language learning and instruction are far from mechanical processes and are subjects worthy of scholarly research in their own right.

The skill of careful observation, then, is one that we need to impart to LCT TAs in order for them to realize their full potential as foreign language professionals in the immediate, pressing context ("What did I do yesterday that went well/poorly?") and in the context of their long-term professional growth. Furthermore, one might hope that LCT TAs, proficient in the use of an observation system with which they can analyze patterns in their own teaching practice, will ultimately be able to bring their teaching practice into agreement with their stated beliefs about the nature of teaching and learning foreign languages. In a study of the classroom interactions of teachers who were recent graduates of ESL programs and who professed a belief in communicative language techniques, it was shown that the classroom discourse of these instructors remained fundamentally in the realm of the display question (i.e., a question to which both parties know the answer). These teachers, who had had at least two years' experience by the time of the study, proved that what goes on in the classroom is not the same as what the instructor wants to occur or what the instructors necessarily believe or even desire to occur (survey reported by Long, 1983, pp. 285–87). LCT teachers who analyze their own teaching practice and make changes in their own classroom interaction should be able to embrace future innovations in instruction. The systematic observation of the teaching act should help LCT TAs understand the notions of authentic input and communicative output in the context of the LCT classroom. If LCT TAs observe one another using the target language to provide learners with authentic input and giving learners opportunities to use the target language for meaningful communication in the LCT classroom, they will be better prepared to bring these ideas to bear in their own teaching more consistently. A demonstration lesson in Spanish or French may not suffice to convince a beginning instructor of Japanese of the value of fluency activities in an introductory or intermediate Japanese classroom, but a demonstration lesson in Chinese or Arabic — in which the Japanese TA can participate as a learner — will be more likely to make a lasting impression and have an impact on that TA's own teaching.

Discourse Theory

As Schulz (1991b, p. 20) describes it, "discourse theory posits that learners develop competence in a second language not simply by absorbing input, but by actively participating in communicative interaction, i.e. by negotiating meaning and filling information gaps." This tenet of discourse theory is often put into practice by providing students with role-plays in which they use language to work through situations both realistic and typical of the target culture. For instance, students in a second-year Arabic class could be given a role-play in which they are assigned "to make a hotel reservation for yourself and a companion for the night of _____ at a Cairo hotel, but be sure the nightly rate for your room is under the equivalent of $100." Extending discourse theory of how students acquire language to how new TAs learn to teach suggests that the TAs need to practice teaching techniques actively. Thus, in learning to teach, TAs need opportunities to work through situations that are both realistic and typical of classroom teaching. For example: "You are the instructor of a second-year Arabic class at a state university with a class of 12 students (8 male, 4 female). Design and implement a classroom activity of 15 minutes' length in which students learn and practice using vocabulary and cultural formulas necessary for the topic 'hotel.' Anticipate and provide for any particular linguistic or cultural difficulties your students might encounter."

Because LCT TAs themselves may not have had communicative language learning experiences on which to base their teaching practice, it is especially important for the LCT methods course to model the behavior that TAs should demonstrate in their own teaching. As Freeman (1989, p. 29) notes, it is a misconception to believe that the graduate methods course can parallel in structure traditional courses in literature and linguistics, offering students a series of readings, lectures, presentations, and seminar papers. These kinds of assignments and projects will not lead to improved teaching practice.

Woodward (1991, p. 13) explains that methods course activities should be designed to provide teacher trainees with learning experiences that they can use in their classrooms and calls the inclusion of such activities "loop input." The content of the methods course activity is as important, therefore, as the process itself. Woodward provides an example of a methods course activity in jigsaw listening[3] in which TAs learn about such activities by experiencing one themselves. According to Woodward's model of loop input (1991, p. 43), TAs are better prepared to implement the practices described in the content of the methods course if these very same practices also constitute the process of the course:

> In loop input, the content is as much in the process of the session as is the handouts, texts, or trainer's talk. As mentioned earlier, it does take time and help for trainees to realize that answers to questions can be in what has just happened and not in the texts or in words coming from the trainer's mouth. Once trainees have become sensitive to the idea behind loop input, however, they begin to look for information everywhere within the session. Very little is lost and there is less boredom since the trainees search for signs of practice during the preaching.

Woodward (1991, p. 13) thus proposes that the methods course borrow the activity frame of the foreign language classroom, but that the frame be filled with content relevant to the methods course. In the context of the LCT methods course, TAs could design jigsaw reading lessons for one another, sharing information about features of their target cultures, such as the changing roles of women, for example, or gestures used for greetings and leavetakings, helping to make explicit the differences between the target and base cultures that others might not otherwise recognize.

Woodward's model of loop input is one important component of communicative interaction: TAs need to negotiate meaning and fill information gaps in order to acquire competence in the practice of communicative teaching. The other important component of this communicative interaction is the opportunity for TAs to design and implement teaching and learning activities in the context of the methods course. Knop's (1982) classic four-step lesson plan model of "overview, prime, drill, and check" can be productively applied to the methods course for each instructional unit (such as culture in the classroom and beyond, listening, reading, speaking and writing skills, fluency and accuracy, error correction, textbook comparison, assessment instruments, and so forth). The methods instructor can state the overview of the given instructional unit. The instructor can then prime the activity by ensuring that students have plenty of opportunities to observe and discuss the teaching act or feature in a variety of contexts including those with different languages and various teachers. In the drill or practice stage, the methods students should have opportunities to design and carry out lesson plans and to teach one another. Since the "students" in the class come from a variety of the LCTs, the TAs will face a group of novices in each microteaching segment. In the check stage, the TAs can carry out the same lesson (modified in view of experiences in the methods class) in their own language classrooms, record the lessons, and observe their own teaching, in order to assess their own performance. Loop input, combined with Knop's four-step lesson plan model, provides an excellent framework for the design of tasks and activities for TAs enrolled in the LCT methods course.

The loop input activities and the opportunities to plan and implement instruction, first in the safety of the methods course and later in the classroom, allow beginning TAs in the LCTs to practice problem solving in their own work and to help one another in the process. Celce-Murcia (1983, p. 98) cites problem-solving activities as the best means of bridging the gap between theory and practice that exists in many language teacher preparation programs.

The methods course instructor should design and implement activities that demonstrate not only solid teaching but also principles of second language acquisition in each of the four skills and in sociocultural proficiency. In so doing, the methods instructor provides LCT TAs with opportunities to participate in structured teaching and learning activities that they can ultimately use in their own classrooms.

Cognitive Theory

According to the cognitive theory of second language acquisition, learners must perform mental processes, analyzing the component subskills, before they can perform skill processes automatically. This means that learning can precede and promote acquisition. Teacher education should provide LCT TAs with ample opportunity to read about the development of the four modalities and sociocultural proficiency and about the use of technology and media in the foreign language classroom as they engage in the teaching and learning activities described above. Among the numerous articles, books, and anthologies available to meet this need, methods instructors for the LCTs might want to consider using R. Altman (1989), *The Video Connection;* Freed, ed. (1991), *Foreign Language Acquisition Research and the Classroom;* Nunan (1989), *Designing Tasks for the Communicative Classroom;* Omaggio (1986), *Teaching Language in Context: Proficiency-Oriented Instruction;* Omaggio, ed. (1985), *Proficiency, Curriculum and Articulation: The Ties That Bind;* Swaffar, Arens, and Byrnes (1991), *Reading for Meaning: An Integrated Approach to Language Learning;* Teschner, ed. (1991), *Assessing Foreign Language Proficiency of Undergraduates;* and Ur (1984), *Teaching Listening Comprehension.* It is particularly productive for LCT TAs to use works such as these when assessing instructional materials available in their own and other languages and when designing instructional materials to compensate for the deficiencies of their textbooks.

A number of authors have written on topics for the methods course, including Donahue (1980), Ervin and Muyskens (1982), Gilbert and McArthur (1975), Knop and Herron (1982), Lalande (1991), Murphy (1991), and Muyskens (1984). Almost all of these writers are primarily concerned with the more commonly taught languages. The methods instructor of a heterogenous group of TAs drawn from a number of LCTs will need to prepare opportunities for students to come to grips with issues relevant to these languages, such as the question of orality and literacy, the psychology that underlies reading processes in languages with fundamentally different alphabetic or nonalphabetic scripts (Horiba, 1990), the use of romanization (and different schools of romanization) to support speaking skills for languages with nonalphabetic scripts, the selection of a dialect for languages with a number of competing dialects or diglossia (such as Arabic) or of a dialect for foreigners (as exists in Japanese: see Jorden, 1986). LCT methods course instructors will certainly want to consider the presentation of what Jorden (1991, p. 384) calls "acquired culture" and "learned culture." She defines "acquired culture" as "the mindset, the patterns of behavior, generally outside the consciousness" of target natives who are generally not aware of such patterns, which are "often mistaken for universal human behavior," while "learned culture" consists of those cultural patterns consciously learned by both foreigners and native speakers of the target culture. LCT TAs should address the issue of American perceptions and prejudices concerning their target cultures and should discuss ways to dispel preconceived notions, cultural stereotypes, and clichés in their classrooms. The course can provide a framework for examining cultural notions of the measurement of time or the definition of friendship among adult men and women and gestures and behavior appropriate for various social contexts. LCT methods course instructors might want to consult works by Allen (1990), Jorden (1986, 1991), Jorden and Walton (1987), Lubensky and Jarvis (1984), Parkinson (1985), Rammuny (1989), Ryding (1991), Stansfield and Harman (1987), Stansfield and Hiple (1987), Thompson (1991), Thompson, Thompson, and Hiple (1988), and Walton (1989). TAs can discuss the unique features of their target languages and cultures and help one another determine the communicative value of each of these features.

The LCT methods course will profit from "break-out" sessions for each of the participating language groups so that each group can address some particular issue and then report to the larger group on its findings. For instance, a Russian group could discuss the communicative value of grammatical aspect or of prefixed verbs of motion and examine how these grammatical topics are presented in instructional materials to determine whether students' communicative needs are recognized and accommodated. A Chinese group could discuss different methods for teaching tones or characters and strategies for developing students' abilities to discriminate between them and recognize meaning in genuine communication. A Japanese group could brainstorm different ways of conveying to American students the important role played by levels of politeness and the use of certain gestures within the context of appropriate sociolinguistic registers.

Within each of the groups, nonnative speakers might ask target natives to discuss some of the more sophisticated nuances of linguistic features or to design and conduct advanced-level activities for them. Target-native TAs might ask the base-natives to address some part of Americans' perception of their target culture and to provide some examples of these perceptions from the popular media. After each series of break-out sessions, representatives from each of the languages can make brief presentations to the entire class, asking TAs in other languages for their impressions and input. These kinds of activities promote successful collaboration both within and among the different languages participating in the LCT methods course. By exposing all TAs to one another's target cultures and the particular teaching challenges of different target languages, the LCT methods course can help TAs understand issues in LCT instruction and better address the needs of their learners. When native-speaker TAs in Japanese struggle to understand some element of Egyptian or Russian culture or the concept of tone in Chinese, they are more likely to recognize and understand the problems their own students face in studying Japanese. This awareness helps prepare TAs to solve those problems or help their learners solve them as they select appropriate instructional strategies and design lessons and class activities. Furthermore, this sharing process will help LCT TAs understand the importance of authentic input, communicative activities, and cultural validity for their learners at every level of the instructional process, since they themselves will have observed these features in the instruction of teachers in the more commonly taught languages and the less commonly taught.

The break-out sessions described above also provide the context for the discussion of issues and the demonstration of activities for lessons conducted in courses other than the introductory-level class. LCT methods instructors should also consider topics and questions raised by Lalande (1991), especially the issue of teacher behaviors that promote the development of students' speaking skills beyond the sentence level. The LCT methods course should, therefore, devote some attention to types and characteristics of discourse and discourse strategies in each of the target cultures, the cultural norms that govern them, and means of using these kinds of discourse in the classroom. For instance, in any of the more commonly taught languages, one might consider using print and broadcast advertisements to develop reading or listening skills, yet until very recently the concept of the "advertisement" was virtually unknown in Russian culture. On the other hand, Russian cities were inundated with political slogans emblazoned on banners hung on buildings and across streets. Although target-culture natives generally ignored the banners and hardly noticed them, Americans visiting Russia were often struck by them and, much to the surprise of some of their hosts and guides, *wanted* to understand them. The Russian classroom could have provided students with the skills and tools to understand the slogans and their particular styles, as well as insight into why the Russians themselves ignored them. Now learners of Russian want and need to learn to make sense of the hand-made signs, placards, and posters that appear regularly at political demonstrations and rallies, a newly arisen form of discourse with its own linguistic characteristics.

To summarize, then, these three models of second language acquisition — acculturation, discourse, and cognitive theories — provide a solid foundation for the design of the goals, structures, and activities of the LCT methods course, the single most important opportunity during the course of graduate studies to provide LCT TAs with teacher education that will last them for their entire teaching careers. By focusing on the observation of the teaching act, teacher education provides LCT TAs with the skills and tools they need to assess their own instruction and implement changes in their teaching practices as needed.

LCT TA Supervision

Teacher training, in the form of preservice workshops and in-service practica, and teacher education, in the form of semester- or year-long methods courses, are the first two components of a professional development program for LCT TAs. The third component is TA supervision, the activities undertaken by the language instruction coordinator to guide LCT TAs toward improving their instruction. The nature of LCT TA supervision need not be distinct from supervision offered TAs in the more commonly taught languages. The LCT TA supervisor may supervise graduate students teaching a number of very diverse languages (e.g., in the case of a Department of Asian and Slavic Languages) or may supervise native-speaker TAs with ethnic hostilities toward one another (e.g., in the case of a Semitic Languages Department). LCT TA supervisors therefore may need time to develop some additional expertise to understand the nature of the languages and cultures taught by all of the TAs under their supervision.

LCT TA supervisors, who often have no formal training for their supervisory roles, should take care to use the supervision and observation/assessment processes to provide LCT TAs with information they can use to assess themselves, rather than prescribing "recipes" for instruction. Prescriptive approaches to professional development for TAs may be effective in a given instructional context, but in the long run they keep TAs in a position of dependence on outside authorities for the design and delivery of instruction. Supervisors should therefore use the observation/evaluation experience as yet another opportunity for TAs to participate in a process of discovery. The TAs themselves should lead this discovery process, whenever possible, analyzing the data of their classroom interactions and determining for themselves what patterns they can find in these data and what new strategies or activities they would like to explore. This approach relieves the supervisor of the responsibility of having all the answers to instructional problems by handing to the TAs the tools they need to understand and improve their own teaching practices.

It is critical for the observation process to be systematic and structured, as described above, in order for the TA to derive maximum benefit. Moreover, the TAs themselves must be given the opportunity to analyze their own teaching and come to their own conclusions, rather than be provided the conclusions of any "authority." This implies, of course, that the TA's teaching must be recorded in some way, such as in accordance with Fanselow's (1977) system described above. Meaning can only be discovered, not prescribed. Supervisory evaluation is prescription that denies TAs the possibility of solving problems for themselves, which deprives them of the independence they need to develop their own teaching styles and strategies. As Gebhard, Gaitan, and Oprandy (1987, p. 227) note, "teacher educators need to shift responsibility for decision making to classroom teachers, providing them with investigative skills and methodology for making decisions about what to teach."

The implementation of this approach for LCT TAs may require some effort on the part of the LCT TA supervisor, especially when working with target-native TAs from cultures that place high value on strict hierarchical structures and conformity. Supervisors working with such TAs will have to lead them to an understanding of this approach, rather than accede to what may be their explicitly stated desire for prescription. Gebhard (1990) suggests that the supervisor's role is not so much to evaluate the performance of TAs (unless, perhaps, their performance is so poor that the undergraduate students in their classes are at risk), but to help TAs observe their own teaching practices, recognize the patterns in their practices, interpret these patterns in accordance with theories of second language acquisition, and provide assistance in the exploration of new teaching behaviors. Supervision should provide LCT TAs with assistance in performing self-assessment: LCT TAs should have opportunities to observe themselves on videotape and to assess their own teaching practices after careful analysis of the video record. Supervisors should promote self-assessment as an integral part of reflection, a key component of teacher education. Without developing the capacity to reflect on teaching practice, TAs will not be able to adapt their teaching practices to changing circumstances in the future, and the one thing we can be certain of is that circumstances will change. TAs could be required to keep a journal for reflection and self-assessment on a variety of tasks at regular intervals so that they learn how to continue learning on their own upon completion of their studies (H. Altman, 1983). Providing a framework for reflection on practice, together with a system for observation of the teaching act, should instill in TAs the desire to continue to learn about teaching and learning long after the grades for the methods course have been posted. It is to be hoped that some of our TAs, excited by the study of learning and teaching processes, will go on to write dissertations on problems specific to the acquisition of the LCTs.[4]

In order to reduce the threat of supervisor observation for LCT TAs, faculty members trained in the chosen observation system may want to observe TAs in languages other than the ones they themselves teach. Thus, the LCT TAs — especially those who are not native speakers of the given target language — need not worry excessively about their own language during this kind of observation, which can be more easily focused on the teaching practices themselves. (The proficiency of nonnative speakers of the target language can be evaluated outside the context of TAs' classroom performance.) As the TAs mature during the course of their graduate studies, they should be given increasingly challenging teaching assignments and responsibilities and be asked to help younger TAs as they join the teaching program. Sprague and Nyquist (1989) offer some excellent suggestions for differentiated supervision of TAs that differs in style and substance depending on the needs and previous experience of those being supervised.

Conclusions: Working Together to Break Out of the Vicious Circle

The steps described here for implementing a professional development program for LCT TAs are not meant to represent a final product; instead, they are an interim measure. If we in the LCTs work together now to create programs such as those described above, we will be able to break out of the vicious circle and produce a generation of LCT specialists who are ready to do more than we have been able to do in the past. The ultimate goal is for enough of our departments in each of the LCTs to implement full-fledged degree programs in second language acquisition and foreign language pedagogy so that we can train language acquisition and instruction specialists in each of our fields, providing them with thorough graduate-level training in these disciplines. Graduates of the new programs would then take their places as the new generation of LCT teacher trainers and TA supervisors.

The only way for the LCTs to break out of the vicious circle of limited opportunities for professional development is for instructors of these languages to join together. A new organization, the National Council of Organizations of Less Commonly Taught Languages, has undertaken to help national teachers' associations, including the American Association of Teachers of Arabic, the Chinese Language Teachers Association, the Association of Teachers of Japanese, and the American Council of Teachers of Russian, work together to help solve problems afflicting all the LCTs.[5] The council is helping the teachers' associations collect data on the current state of instruction in their languages and address pressing issues such as guidelines for curriculum and materials design, professional development programs for teachers, and the uses of new technologies in the LCT classroom. The council has worked with the National Endowment of the Humanities to sponsor national summer institutes for the training of teachers in Russian, Japanese, and in Southeast Asian languages, and will soon sponsor teacher training for African languages.

We must implement effective programs of professional development for LCT TAs in order to retain students beyond the first year of instruction and to promote students' abilities to use the languages we teach. Some will argue that we cannot establish professional development programs in our institutions without first hiring LCT teacher educators, which is another vicious circle. We must refuse to fall into this trap and instead agree to work together, drawing upon one another's strengths, to provide our current TAs with the tools they need to become the next generation's teacher educators in our target languages. If we share the responsibilities of conducting the preservice workshop and the in-service practicum and methods course among LCT faculty members, none of us would have to teach an additional course more than once in two years. This additional course load is surely a small price to pay for a significant increase in the teacher preparation we offer our TAs. We can rely on some of the works cited above to help provide us with a framework for the design of methods courses and tasks and activities that would help our TAs acquire the skills they need to monitor their own instruction. Furthermore, in order to break out of the vicious circle we *can and must* teach methods courses even if we have never had the opportunity to take them ourselves. We can teach such courses by relying on our TAs to observe and question the teaching act and discover meaning themselves in the process. We must be ready for them to challenge us, for they *will* challenge our most basic assumptions about learning and instruction, assumptions we have used to design and implement instruction for years. The challenge, however, will be a healthy one, and will not necessarily lead to the rejection of all of our assumptions about foreign language acquisition and instruction. Those assumptions that withstand this challenge will be all the more valid in our eyes and in the eyes of our TAs.

The more commonly taught languages have been more successful than the LCTs in the more regular renewal of instructional materials and in the implementation of more permanent programs of professional development for TAs. One of the reasons for their relative success in these endeavors is the sheer numbers of their enrollments year after year. While we cannot hope to match their enrollments in the short term, we can take steps to solve these problems in our fields by coming together and working for common solutions. Over 135,000 students are enrolled in LCTs in American colleges, approximately one-third of the number of students enrolled in Spanish and one-half of those enrolled in French classes ("Foreign," 1991). These numbers should be sufficient to warrant the establishment of joint LCT professional development programs (teacher training, education, and supervision). In the context of collaboration in the establishment and administration of joint professional development programs, LCT teachers would have opportunities to discuss issues of singular importance to the learning and teaching of languages with "acquired cultures" (Jorden, 1991) far removed from the life experiences of American university students. Working together in professional development for our TAs, we can strive to come to some agreement about curricular design and instructional goals. Enrollments in each of the more commonly taught languages are now sufficient to support a wide range of instructional materials based on a variety of theories of second language acquisition and approaches to foreign language instruction. Enrollments in each of our languages have not, in the past, been sufficient to support this kind of range of materials, making it all the more important that we come to some agreement, within each of our fields, as to priorities for the development, design, and production of instructional materials.

In working together to create and implement professional development programs for TAs, therefore, we can more effectively promote the design and implementation of second language acquisition research. We need solid research in order to improve our understanding of the learning processes involved in acquiring the less commonly taught languages, to improve our instructional materials, and to improve our teaching practices. The National Council of Organizations of Teachers of LCTs must continue to receive federal and other funds in order to promote the collection of data on instruction in the LCTs and the collaboration of LCT specialists in institutions across the country. As Walton (1991, p. 182) comments, LCT professionals must become "proactive rather than reactive in expanding the vision of foreign language education in the United States." More LCT TA supervisors and coordinators should join the AAUSC to participate in our organization's ongoing discussion of issues related to the professional development of TAs. Swaffar (1989, p. 131) has said that "uncommon language learning represents a common cause." What is true of language learning is no less true of language teaching. We should agree to devote more time and energy to working together because only through collaboration can we advance the common cause of uncommon language teaching.

Notes

1. The author is grateful to Heidi Byrnes, Charles Hancock, and June K. Phillips for their help with this project at the 1991 MLA/NEH Summer Languages Institute, and to the Modern Language Association and the National Endowment for the Humanities for their support. The author is also grateful to Catherine Baumann of ACTFL, and to the following specialists for their help in assessing the current state of materials development, enrollments, and programs of professional development for TAs in Arabic, Chinese, Japanese,

and Russian, respectively: Roger Allen and Dilworth Parkinson; Richard Chi and Ronald Walton; Eleanor Jorden and Hiroko Kataoka; and Richard Brecht and John Caemmerer.

2. For this study, I interviewed at least two specialists in each of the less commonly taught languages examined here. These interviews, each lasting 30–45 minutes, were conducted by telephone in January 1992. Those specialists willing to be identified are named in note 1.

3. A "jigsaw" listening or reading activity involves a series of listening or reading texts on similar or related topics, which together make a "whole." Each student participating in the activity is assigned to listen to or to read only one of the texts and then must share the information gained from this text with the other participants in order to solve a problem or achieve some result or conclusion.

4. There were many fewer dissertations in foreign/second language acquisition of the less commonly taught languages than of the more commonly taught languages in 1990, perhaps in part because there are fewer graduate departments of less commonly taught languages where such dissertations are encouraged or even acceptable for the doctoral degree (Benseler, 1991, pp. 333–34).

5. The National Council is a task force under the auspices of the National Foreign Language Center in Washington, DC, and, as such, has a very limited membership. For more information, write: The National Foreign Language Center, 1619 Massachusetts Ave., NW, Washington, DC 20036.

Works Cited

Alatis, James E., H.H. Stern & Peter Strevens (Ed.). *Applied Linguistics and the Preparation of Second Language Teachers: Toward a Rationale.* Georgetown University Round Table on Languages and Linguistics 1983. Washington, DC: Georgetown University Press, 1983.

Allen, J.P.B., M. Frolich & N. Spada. "The Communicative Orientation of Language Teaching: An Observation Scheme." *On TESOL '83: The Question of Control.* Ed. R. Handscombe, A. Orem & B. Taylor. Washington, DC: TESOL, 1984: 231–52.

Allen, Roger. "Proficiency and the Teacher of Arabic: Curriculum, Course and Classroom." *al-'Arabiyya* 23 (1990): 1–30.

———— & Adel Allouche. *Let's Learn Arabic.* Unpublished manuscript. Philadelphia: University of Pennsylvania, 1988.

Allwright, Dick. "Classroom-Centered Research on Language Teaching and Learning: A Brief Historical Overview." *TESOL Quarterly* 17 (1983): 191–204.

Alosh, Mahdi. *Ahsalan wa-Sahlan.* Columbus: Ohio State University, 1989.

Altman, Howard B. "Training Foreign Language Teachers for Learner-Centered Instruction: Deep Structures, Surface Structures, and Transformations." In Alatis, Stern & Strevens, 1983: 19–25.

Altman, Rick. *The Video Connection: Integrating Video into Language Teaching.* Boston: Houghton Mifflin, 1989.

American Council on the Teaching of Foreign Languages (ACTFL). *Instructional Materials for the Teaching of Less Commonly Taught Languages.* Isabelle Kaplan, Project Director, Yonkers, NY: ACTFL Materials Center, n.d.

Andrews, Stephen. "Communicative Language Teaching — Some Implications for Teacher Education." *Perspectives in Communicative Language Teaching.* Ed. Keith Johnson & Don Porter. New York: Academic Press, 1983: 128–39.

Ariew, Robert. "The Textbook as Curriculum." *Curriculum, Competence and the Foreign Language Teacher.* Ed. Theodore V. Higgs. Skokie, IL: National Textbook Company, 1982: 11–33.

Azevedo, Milton M. "Professional Development of Teaching Assistants: Training versus Education." *ADFL Bulletin* 22, 1 (1990): 24–28.

Baker, Robert L. "The Ph.D. in Slavic Languages and Literatures: Does the Product Fit the Market?" *ADFL Bulletin* 12, 2 (1980): 40–43.

Belnap, R. Kirk. "Who's Taking Arabic and What on Earth for? A Survey of Students in Arabic Language Programs." *al-ʿArabiyya* 20 (1987): 29–42.

Benseler, David P. "Doctoral Degrees Granted in Foreign Languages in the United States: 1990." *Modern Language Journal* 75 (1991): 329–43.

Bernhardt, Elizabeth & Joann Hammadou. "A Decade of Research in Foreign Language Teacher Education." *Modern Language Journal* 71 (1987): 289–99.

Billson, Janet Mancini & Richard G. Tiberius. "Effective Social Arrangements for Teaching and Learning." *College Teaching: From Theory to Practice.* Ed. Robert J. Menges & Marilla D. Svinicki. New Directions for Teaching and Learning, no. 45. San Francisco: Jossey-Bass, 1989: 87–109.

Bragger, Jeannette D. "Materials Development for the Proficiency-Oriented Classroom." *Foreign Language Proficiency in the Classroom and Beyond.* Ed. Charles J. James. Lincolnwood, IL: National Textbook Company, 1985: 79–115.

Brumfit, Christopher J. "The Integration of Theory and Practice." In Alatis, Stern & Strevens, 1983: 59–73.

Celce-Murcia, Marianne. "Problem-Solving: A Bridge Builder between Theory and Practice." In Alatis, Stern & Strevens, 1983: 59–73.

Chaput, Patricia. "TA Training in Slavic Languages: Goals, Priorities, Practice." *Slavic and East European Journal* 35 (1991): 390–402.

Chi, Richard. "Observations on the Past, Present, and Future of Teaching Mandarin Chinese as a Foreign Language." *Journal of Chinese Language Teachers Association* 24, 2 (1989): 109–22.

Chism, Nancy Van Note & Susan B. Warner (Ed.). *Institutional Responsibilities and Responses in the Employment and Education of Teaching Assistants: Readings from a National Conference.* Columbus: Ohio State University Center for Teaching Excellence, 1987.

Devens, Monica S. & Nancy J. Bennett. "MLA Surveys of Foreign Language Graduate Programs, 1984–85." *ADFL Bulletin* 17, 3 (1985): 19–27.

Dien, Albert. "Survey of Chinese Language Teaching." *Journal of Chinese Language Teachers Association* 20, 1 (1985): 99–108.

Donahue, Frank E. "A Texas Model for TA Training." *Die Unterrichtspraxis* 13 (1980): 141–49.

Duff, Patricia A. & Charlene G. Polio. "How Much Foreign Language Is There in the Foreign Language Classroom?" *Modern Language Journal* 74 (1990): 154–66.

Dvorak, Trisha R. "Grammatical Practice, Communicative Practice, and the Development of Linguistic Competence." Ph.D. diss., University of Texas at Austin, 1977.

Ervin, Gerard. "A Training Program for New TAs in Russian." *Russian Language Journal* 35 (1981): 27–33.

_____ & Judith A. Muyskens. "On Training TAs: Do We Know What They Want and Need?" *Foreign Language Annals* 15 (1982): 335–44.

Fanselow, John F. "Beyond Rashomon — Conceptualization and Observing the Teaching Act." *TESOL Quarterly* 11 (1977): 17–41.

"Foreign Language Enrollments in US Colleges and Universities: 1990." *Modern Language Journal* 75 (1991): 425, 459.

Freed, Barbara F. (Ed.). *Foreign Language Acquisition Research and the Classroom.* Lexington, MA: D.C. Heath, 1991.

Freeman, Donald. "Teacher Training, Development and Decision Making: A Model of Teaching and Related Strategies for Language Teacher Education." *TESOL Quarterly* 23 (1989): 27–45.

Garner, Lucia C., Henry Geitz, Constance Knop, Sally Sieloff Magnan & Robert Di Donato. "Improved Training of Teaching Assistants through Interdepartmental Cooperation." Madison: University of Wisconsin, 1987. ERIC ED 279 210.

Gebhard, Jerry G. "Freeing the Teacher: A Supervisory Process." *Foreign Language Annals* 23 (1990): 517–25.

——, Sergio Gaitan & Robert Oprandy. "Beyond Prescription: The Student Teacher as Investigator." *Foreign Language Annals* 20 (1987): 227–32.

Gilbert, Claire P. & James F. McArthur. "In-Service Teacher Preparation of French Graduate Assistants: Design and Evaluation." *French Review* 48 (1975): 508–21.

Goodlad, John D. "A Study of Schooling: Some Findings and Hypotheses." *Phi Delta Kappan* 64 (1983): 465–70.

Gutiérrez, John R. "Making Better Use of the Native Teaching Assistant: Curricular Implications." *ADFL Bulletin* 19, 1 (1987): 28–29.

Herold, William R. "Gaps in the Preparation of Foreign Language Teachers." *Foreign Language Annals* 10 (1977): 617–22.

Horiba, Yukie. "Narrative Comprehension Processes: A Study of Native and Non-Native Readers of Japanese." *Modern Language Journal* 74 (1990): 188–202.

Jorden, Eleanor H. "On Teaching Nihongo." *Japan Quarterly* 33 (1986): 139–47.

——. "The Target-Native and the Base-Native: Making the Team." *Journal of the Association of Teachers of Japanese* 21 (1987): 7–14.

——. "The Use of Interactive Video in the Learning of Japanese." In Freed, 1991: 384–92.

—— & Mari Noda. *Japanese: The Spoken Language.* New Haven: Yale University Press, 1990.

—— & A. Ronald Walton. "Truly Foreign Languages: Instructional Challenges." *Annals of the AAAPSS* 490 (1987): 110–24.

Kataoka, Hiroko C. "A Pilot Study of Japanese Language Students at Three State Universities in the United States: Implications for Japanese Language Teaching Policy." *Journal of the Association of Teachers of Japanese* 20 (1986): 179–208.

Knop, Constance. "Overview, Prime, Drill, Check: An Approach to Guiding Student Teachers in Lesson-Planning." *Foreign Language Annals* 15 (1982): 91–94.

_____ & Carol A. Herron. "An Empirical Approach to Redesigning a TA Methods Course." *French Review* 55 (1982): 329–339.

Lalande, John F., II. "Advancing the Case for an Advanced Methods Course." In Magnan, 1991: 151–66.

_____ & Gerhard F. Strasser. "A Survey of International Teaching Assistants in Foreign Language Departments." In Chism & Warner, 1987: 251–62.

Larsen-Freeman, Diane. "Training Teachers or Educating a Teacher." In Alatis, Stern & Strevens, 1983: 264–75.

Launer, Michael K. "Can Aspect Be Taught?" *Russian Language Journal* 31, 108 (1977): 21–34 [Part 1]; 31, 109 (1977): 7–20 [Part 2].

Leaver, Betty Lou. "Review of *Elementary Ukrainian 1, Advanced Ukrainian 1, Ukrainian Vocabulary Supplement.*" *Modern Language Journal* 75 (1991): 280–82.

Lee, James & Bill VanPatten. "The Question of Language Program Direction Is **Academic**." In Magnan, 1991: 113–28.

Liskin-Gasparro, Judith E. "The ACTFL Proficiency Guidelines: A Historical Perspective." *Teaching for Proficiency, the Organizing Principle.* Ed. Theodore V. Higgs. Lincolnwood, IL: National Textbook Company, 1984: 11–42.

Long, Michael H. "Training the Second Language Teacher as Classroom Researcher." In Alatis, Stern & Strevens, 1983: 281–97.

Lubensky, Sophia & Donald K. Jarvis (Ed.). *Teaching, Learning, Acquiring Russian.* Columbus, OH: Slavica, 1984.

McCarus, Ernest N. "The Study of Arabic in the United States: A History of Its Development." *al-ʿArabiyya* 20 (1987): 13–27.

Magnan, Sally Sieloff (Ed.). *Challenges in the 1990s for College Foreign Language Programs.* AAUSC Issues in Language Program Direction 1990. Boston: Heinle & Heinle Publishers, 1991.

MLA Commission on Foreign Languages, Literatures, and Linguistics. "Resolutions and Recommendations of the National Conference on Graduate Education in the Foreign Language Fields." *ADFL Bulletin* 17, 3 (1986): 1–4.

Murphy, Joseph A. "The Graduate Teaching Assistant in an Age of Standards." In Magnan, 1991: 129–50.

Muyskens, Judith A. "Preservice and Inservice Teacher Training: Focus on Proficiency." *Teaching for Proficiency, the Organizing Principle.* Ed. Theodore V. Higgs. Lincolnwood, IL: National Textbook Company, 1984: 179–200.

National Foreign Language Center. *Survey of Japanese Language Instruction.* Washington, DC: National Foreign Language Center, 1991.

———. *Survey of Russian Language Instruction.* Washington, DC: National Foreign Language Center, in press.

Neu, Joyce. "In Search of Input: The Case Study of a Learner of Polish as a Foreign and Second Language." *Foreign Language Annals* 24 (1991): 427–42.

Nunan, David. *Designing Tasks for the Communicative Classroom.* Cambridge: Cambridge University Press, 1989.

Omaggio, Alice C. *Teaching Language in Context: Proficiency-Oriented Instruction.* Boston: Heinle & Heinle Publishers, 1986.

——— (Ed.). *Proficiency, Curriculum, Articulation: The Ties that Bind.* Middlebury, VT: Northeast Conference on the Teaching of Foreign Languages, 1985.

Packard, Jerome L. "High- versus Low-Pressure Methods of Chinese Language Teaching: A Comparison of Test Results." *Journal of Chinese Language Teachers* 24, 1 (1989): 1–18.

Parkinson, Dilworth B. "Proficiency to Do What? Developing Oral Proficiency in Students of Modern Standard Arabic." *al-ʿArabiyya* 18 (1985): 11–43.

Parrett, Joan L. "A Ten-Year Review of TA Training Programs: Trends, Patterns, and Common Practices." In Chism & Warner, 1987: 67–80.

Pons, Cathy R. "A Three-Phase Approach to TA Training: The Program for Associate Instructors in French at Indiana University." In Chism & Warner, 1987: 239–43.

Rammuny, Raji M. "Arabic Language Teacher Training Program." *al-ʿArabiyya* 22 (1989): 211–15.

Rava, Susan. "Training Teaching Assistants." *ADFL Bulletin* 19, 1 (1987): 26–27.

Rifkin, Benjamin. "Professional Training for Slavists: Priorities for the Next 30 Years." *Vision 2020.* Ed. Ray Parrott. Iowa City, IA: ACTR/AATSEEL, in press (a).

———. "The Communicative Orientation of Russian Language Textbooks." *Slavic and East European Journal,* in press (b).

Rivers, Wilga M. "Psychology and Linguistics as Bases for Language Pedagogy." *Learning a Second Language. Seventy-Ninth Yearbook of the National Society for the Study of Education* (Part 2). Ed. Frank Grittner. Chicago: University of Chicago Press, 1980: 44–66.

———. "Preparing College and University Instructors for a Lifetime of Teaching: A Luxury or a Necessity?" In Alatis, Stern & Strevens, 1983: 327–41.

_____. "Comprehension and Production in Interactive Language Teaching." *Modern Language Journal* 70 (1986): 1–7.

_____. "Psychological Validation of Methodological Approaches and Foreign Language Classroom Practices." In Freed, 1991: 283–94.

Ryding, Karin C. "LCTs: The Current Situation." *Language Teaching, Testing, and Technology: Lessons from the Past with a View toward the Future.* Georgetown University Round Table on Languages and Linguistics 1989. Washington, DC: Georgetown University Press, 1989: 114–21.

_____. "Proficiency Despite Diglossia: A New Approach for Arabic." *Modern Language Journal* 75 (1991): 212–18.

Samuel, Yoshiko Yokochi. "A Survey of the Status of Native and Non-Native Instructors of Japanese in Higher Education in North America." *Journal of the Association of Teachers of Japanese* 21 (1987): 133–147.

Savignon, S. *Communicative Competence: Theory and Classroom Practice.* Reading, MA: Addison-Wesley, 1983.

Schulz, Renate A. "TA Training, Supervision, and Evaluation: Report of a Survey." *ADFL Bulletin* 12, 1 (1980): 1–8.

_____. "Bridging the Gap between Teaching and Learning: A Critical Look at Foreign Language Textbooks." In Magnan, 1991a: 167–82.

_____. "Second Language Acquisition Theories and Teaching Practice: How Do They Fit?" *Modern Language Journal* 75 (1991b): 17–26.

Sprague, Jo & Jody D. Nyquist. "TA Supervision." *Teaching Assistant Training in the 1990s.* Ed. Jody D. Nyquist, Robert D. Abbott & Donald H. Wulff. New Directions for Teaching and Learning, no. 39. San Francisco: Jossey-Bass: 1989: 37–53.

Stansfield, Charles W. & Chip Harman. "ACTFL Proficiency Guidelines for the LCTs. A Familiarization Project for the Development of Proficiency Guidelines for LCTs." Washington, DC: Center for Applied Linguistics, 1987. ERIC ED 289 345.

_____ & David V. Hiple. "Design, Development and Dissemination of Information Materials and Instructional Sessions on 'Proficiency' Concepts for the LCTs. Final Report." Washington, DC: Center for Applied Linguistics, 1987. ERIC ED 295 458.

Stern, H.H. "Language Teacher Education: An Approach to the Issues and a Framework for Discussion." In Alatis, Stern & Strevens, 1983: 342–61.

Swaffar, Janet K. "Rethinking Roles: Western and Eastern Languages in the Foreign Language Academy." *Journal of Chinese Language Teachers Association* 24, 2 (1989): 123–34.

———. "Language Learning Is More than Learning Language: Rethinking Reading and Writing Tasks in Textbooks for Beginning Language Study." In Freed, 1991: 252–80.

———, Katherine M. Arens & Heidi Byrnes. *Reading for Meaning: An Integrated Approach to Language Learning.* Englewood Cliffs, NJ: Prentice-Hall, 1991.

Teschner, Richard V. (Ed.). *Assessing Foreign Language Proficiency of Undergraduates.* AAUSC Issues in Language Program Direction 1991. Boston: Heinle & Heinle Publishers, 1991.

Thompson, Irene. "Student Attitude and Achievement in Russian." *Russian Language Journal* 31, 109 (1977): 35–50.

———. "The Proficiency Movement: Where Do We Go from Here?" *Slavic and East European Journal* 35 (1991): 375–89.

———, Richard R. Thompson & David V. Hiple. "Issues Concerning the LCTs." *Second Language Proficiency Assessment: Current Issues.* Ed. Pardee Lowe & Charles Stansfield. Language in Education: Theory and Practice, no. 70. West Nyack, NY: Prentice-Hall, 1988. ERIC ED 296 612.

——— & Emily Urevich. *Reading Real Russian.* Englewood Cliffs, NJ: Prentice-Hall, 1991.

Ur, Penny. *Teaching Listening Comprehension.* Cambridge: Cambridge University Press, 1984.

VanPatten, Bill. "How Juries Get Hung: Problems with the Evidence for Focus on Form in Teaching." *Language Learning* 38 (1988): 243–60.

———. "Second Language Acquisition Research and Foreign Language Teaching, 1." *ADFL Bulletin* 23, 2 (1992a): 52–56.

———. "Second Language Acquisition Research and Foreign Language Teaching, 2." *ADFL Bulletin* 23, 3 (1992b): 23–27.

Walker, Galal L.R. "Intensive Chinese Curriculum: The EASLI Model." *Journal of Chinese Language Teachers Association* 24, 2 (1989a): 43–83.

———. "The LCTs in the Context of American Pedagogy." *Shaping the Future: Challenges and Opportunities.* Ed. Helen S. Lepke. Middlebury, VT: Northeast Conference on the Teaching of Foreign Languages, 1989b: 111–37.

———. "Gaining Place: The LCTs in American Schools." *Foreign Language Annals* 24 (1991): 131–50.

Walton, A. Ronald. "Chinese Language Instruction in the United States: Some Reflections on the State of the Art." *Journal of the Chinese Language Teachers' Association* 24, 2 (1989): 1–42.

_____. "Expanding the Vision of Foreign Language Education: Enter the Less Commonly Taught Languages." *Critical Issues in Foreign Language Instruction.* Ed. Ellen S. Silber. New York: Garland Publishing, 1991: 160–85.

Walz, Joel. "Is Oral Proficiency Possible with Today's French Textbooks?" *Modern Language Journal* 70 (1986): 13–20.

Wang, George C.Y. "Research on Teaching Chinese in Forty-Five Universities: Analysis of Survey Results." *Journal of Chinese Language Teachers Association* 24, 3 (1989): 101–13.

Woodward, Tessa. *Models and Metaphors in Language Teacher Training: Loop Input and Other Strategies.* Cambridge: Cambridge University Press, 1991.

Younes, Munther A. "An Integrated Approach to Teaching Arabic as a Foreign Language." *al-ʿArabiyya* 23 (1990): 105–22.

Young, John & Kimiko Nakajima. *Learn Japanese.* Honolulu: University of Hawaii Press, 1984.

Zimpher, Nancy L. & Suzan Yessayan. "An Overview of an Orientation Program for Graduate Teaching Associates at the Ohio State University." In Chism & Warner, 1987: 160–66.

The Seamless Web: Developing Teaching Assistants as Professionals

Marva A. Barnett and Robert Francis Cook
University of Virginia

The seamless web of our title is a metaphor for an academic life whose parts all fit together in ways that can be made visible, as good cloth is visibly warp and weft at once. The color of the cloth is, at first glance, the color of neither warp nor weft; but reflection and practice can make it possible, first, to see the cloth as a whole, and then to recognize how its appearance derives from how it was made. In the same way, what we call teaching and research, study and writing, thinking, arguing, and guiding group work are parts of a single enterprise, whether the practitioner be an undergraduate beginner, a graduate assistant, or a chaired professor.

Anything that teachers do well can be traced back to an intellectual principle; decisions about teaching are intellectual decisions. At the core, scholarly and teaching activities are very much the same, and we have something to gain by emphasizing that truth in our training programs. At first glance, it may seem paradoxical or sensationalistic to insist that teaching and research are not fundamentally different acts, but the alternative is to continue conceiving of our profession as a conventional yet arbitrary yoking of opposites. No one who thinks the link between teaching and research is arbitrary can present them in any fashion that has to do with the liberal arts, with critical analysis and independent thought, with any of the activities that departments and faculties hope to train students at all levels to do.

Our graduate students will experience their careers all at once: myths aside, we know they will be expected to "teach" and to "do research" simultaneously and to do both extremely well. They need not be frustrated by these expectations if they understand the very good reason why they are expected to live such a strenuous professional life. Our lives as scholars exemplify and manifest globally the activity often called "critical thought" for short, with its concomitant writing and self-criticism. Critical thinking is usually connected with courses of study, as a kind of "outcome"; but students can learn it only through teachers who embody it. Preparing for the profession means above all else preparing to embody the virtues of the active mind, and, in that largest frame, both "teaching" and "research" go without saying.

Scholarship as Teaching *and* Research

Arguments against the perception of teaching and research as separate are now becoming, in fact, rather numerous. Ernest Boyer (1990, p. 16), president of the Carnegie Foundation for the Advancement of Teaching, has recently summarized the link: "Surely scholarship means engaging in original research. But the work of the scholar also means stepping back from one's investigation, looking for connections, building bridges between theory and practice, and communicating one's knowledge effectively to students." Our basic premise is that teaching is genuinely a professional activity, one governed by the same rules of critical thought, intellectual honesty, and rigorously obtained knowledge as any other profession. The lower prestige of the teaching profession is an accident of fairly recent history; teaching has come to be associated, for some segments of the public and even for many educators, with details of practice rather than with principles based on that rigorously obtained knowledge. That association has not been good for teachers. Obviously, every profession has an essential body of practice, but the practice is justifiable *only* in terms of intellectual principles. Teachers cannot know what they are doing unless they know *why* in the broad sense that applies to all professions (cf. Azevedo, 1990).

It must be recognized that the view of scholarship as exclusively a research activity and of publishing as a pen-and-paper endeavor — and the concomitant acceptance of a dichotomy between research and teaching —

remain common throughout academia despite the best persuasive efforts of Booth (1981), Boyer (1990), and Jarvis (1988; 1991), among others. Most people can more easily maintain such a traditional view than ponder the sometimes subtle relationships between gaining and disseminating knowledge in very different contexts. In a day-to-day setting, rare are the associate or full professors willing to rock the professional boat that keeps them afloat; even rarer are assistant professors with the time to consider the broader implications of the work they do, implications that would carry them beyond the realities of the tenure-track, publish-or-perish bind they find themselves in. But graduate students, despite their familiarity with this dominant ethos, remember for a while their undergraduate experience and their interactions with stimulating professors. Early in their graduate careers they are still able to consider teaching, research, and scholarship from a fresh perspective.

Yet graduate teaching assistants (TAs) are in a divided position: at once students and teachers, intellectuals and low-paid hirelings. In departments where graduate students work as TAs, relatively familiar comments denote an inevitable tension. Some are framed as explicit criticisms:

- In a conversation with parents: "I certainly don't want my son to attend *that* university, where he'll be taught by TAs."
- In a student council meeting: "We're paying a lot to attend this university, and we shouldn't be taught by TAs."
- In the graduate student lounge: "The supervisor expects too much; she doesn't realize all the other work we have to do."
- In a conference between a graduate faculty member and a group of TAs: "Don't let those 202 exam committee meetings get in the way of your own work."
- In a graduate admissions committee meeting: "We can't be *too* selective in our admissions policy; after all, we do have to staff our required language courses."

We also hear more heartening comments:

- From deans of students: "The TAs in the Department of Any Language do a fine job of keeping us posted about students who are having problems."

- From undergraduate students: "I didn't plan to take any more French/
German/Italian/Spanish, but my TA was really great and got me
interested."
- From TAs: "It's the teaching that keeps me going in graduate school. It
makes a lot of sense."

For the sake of the undergraduates whom TAs teach and for the health of our
TAs, graduate students, and programs, we must deal with the contradictions
inherent in these disparate views of the same people doing the same job.

First, let us acknowledge that a staff whose members are simultaneously
students and teachers presents multiple dichotomies when its functions are
conceived narrowly. Departments with graduate language programs need
students in mutually supportive and dissimilar ways, both to keep alive
graduate programs and to teach basic language courses. Graduate faculty
frequently see these people primarily as budding scholars; moreover, some
faculty members were never TAs themselves, having pursued graduate study
in the halcyon, vanished days of generous fellowships. At the same time,
some administrators speak of TAs as though they were nothing but
functionaries who teach required or large undergraduate courses at a bargain
price. TAs themselves have relatively little power and often feel completely
powerless. Concurrently pursuing both solitary research and active communication with students, they face the standard academic dilemma, but rarely
realize how normal it is. They consider this conflict difficult (as indeed it is),
abnormal (which it is not in an academic setting), and temporary (little
realizing that it changes only slightly after the degree is in hand).

Now that we have acknowledged these conflicts, let us confront them.
As educators of graduate students, we must show them where they are going
and how they can succeed professionally and ethically in their chosen careers.
Most graduate students in our discipline complete degrees and become
educators themselves, whether as public or private high school teachers, as
members of college or university faculties, or as deans or other administrators. Simply giving our graduate students the tools of the discipline with little
indication about how to use them collegially and responsibly means that we
are doing only half the job, as the extramural colleagues who hire our
doctoral products know: "The beginning assistant professor of German
must often learn pragmatism on the job because many PhD-graduate
departments eschew it" (Van Cleve, 1987, p. 18). Or, as in Roger Soder's
graphic comment (cited in Mooney, 1990, p. A16): "In graduate school,

you'll hear, 'Don't let teaching get in the way of your dissertation.' What, then, has our budding young professor learned after seven years in the wilderness?" How can we best train graduate students for both their current and future roles?

A Required Professional Development Course

One solution has proven effective in our department: "Theories and Methods of Scholarship: Research and Teaching" (FREN 701). This professional development course is the mainstay of the TA training program in French at the University of Virginia, which also includes a week of hands-on practice teaching and orientation, follow-up workshops on specific topics, a year of careful supervision, peer observation (Barnett, 1983), videotaping of classes for self-analysis, and administrative opportunities for graduate students (see also TA program suggestions by Di Donato, 1983; Lee, 1987; Rivers, 1983; Waldinger, 1990). Theories and Methods of Scholarship combines two former one-hour practicum courses in teaching and bibliographic methods and is team taught by the specialists in second language acquisition and in medieval literature. Our departmental colleagues agreed that the one-hour practica too often impressed students as being afterthoughts, and they supported our experimental project of combining the two into a full-fledged course. (The team teaching, incidentally, causes no difficulties as to teaching load, since each year it counts as a full three-hour course for one of us.)

Thus, Theories and Methods of Scholarship began as an amalgamation of practicalities and immediately grew into a unique professional development course, neither a language-teaching methods course, nor a second language acquisition course, nor a bibliographic methods course, but rather a required course integrating all these aspects of the profession with ethics and with the broadest view of scholarship. We aim to prepare generalists in French studies. The course description notes the theoretical base for professional practicalities:

FREN 701:   THEORIES AND METHODS OF SCHOLARSHIP:
TEACHING AND RESEARCH

Offered yearly in the Fall semester. *Prerequisite:* Graduate standing. Required of all graduate students.

An introduction to the conceptual basis for research, writing, and teaching in French language, literature, and civilization. Exploration of the various disciplines pursued under the rubric of "French." Use of reference sources and the library; presentation of papers and articles in accepted style; the organization and presentation of French courses, especially the French language. Assignments include reference and bibliography exercises; readings and exercises on the teaching of language and literature; peer observations and analysis; and a final essay examination.

We present scholarship globally, as research and teaching together, with attention to theory and practice, general and particular, principles and goals, just as any other set of intellectual notions and their applications are properly taught. To offer the "language teaching practicum" and the "bibliography and research methods course" as one indissoluble whole is not merely to move toward banishing the trivial from these traditionally mechanical topics; it is to reveal their true nature as symbiotic components of the major intellectual enterprises we all work to further.

A three-credit-hour, graded course, Theories and Methods of Scholarship is required of all graduate students during their first or second year, normally during a semester in which they teach, regardless of their previous teaching experience. Exceptions are made only when a student has had a comparable initiation into all aspects of the course. The few graduate students who take the course before becoming TAs gain early insights that they can incorporate when they do teach, usually the following year. Requiring such a course is the first step toward developing graduate TAs as professional academicians, ethical scholars who make their ideas and analyses public both in the classroom and in writing.

By integrating ethics, research, and teaching, Theories and Methods of Scholarship explores truths of academic life, treats graduate students as the future professors they usually are, and makes some sense of the potentially divided nature of their position as both graduate students and TAs. Students in the course encounter and discuss each week their dual scholarly roles of researcher and teacher in the fuller professional, academic context. Their training is not only utilitarian — that is, a practicum in teaching and research methodologies — but also theoretical, including readings and discussions about such issues as ethical professional behavior, the interaction of research and teaching, and the role of the humanities in American education. (See Appendix A for details).

Objectives and Structure of Theories and Methods of Scholarship

How does this combining of practical and philosophical challenges translate into a course structure? We mix some joint presentations with very broad perspectives with classes that resemble what either of us might have done in a separate course. Matters sometimes left to the chances of conversation or "osmosis" are explicitly included. Problems in ethics and strategies for job seeking (and job keeping) are treated as part of the profession. Juxtaposing matters more commonly opposed stimulates and challenges both instructors and students. Fortunately, we are telling students their chosen profession is coherent, and they also entertain readily the course's guiding ethical notion: that we are not only at the service of ideas but at the service of people, students and the society that sends them to the university (Booth, 1981).

Theories and Methods of Scholarship introduces TAs to the profession of scholarly research and teaching in French language, literature, and civilization through a tripartite format: theory, practice, and ethics. Theoretical aspects of the course revolve not only around professional issues such as those cited above, but also around theories of second language acquisition and literary criticism. The former are taught for their intellectual value as well as for their importance in underpinning various methodologies; future professionals must know why the teaching techniques or methods they use are effective and must be prepared to progress as knowledge of the discipline advances (see Azevedo, 1990, p. 25). Theories of literary criticism are not so much taught (the responsibility of a separate course) as used for the purpose of illustration.

For example, during Week Ten of the course, when reading strategies are the topic of the day, we touch upon their relationships with general hermeneutic theory, with the interplay of expectation and recognition. The members of the class are reminded that sometimes as teachers they may be called upon to teach hermeneutics itself, as a topic, while other times they will teach elements of the reading process, depending on the moment; at no time, we suggest, can they afford to ignore what is known about the reading process. They can find out what is known by using the journals and reference works presented in other lessons, but not forgotten during Week Ten. In another context, we link teaching about culture to considerations of literature as an expression of culture that is simultaneously a case study in cultural understanding. Such discussion helps explain and justify the importance and prestige granted literary topics in the graduate curriculum. Discussion of the writing process, as it surfaces in elementary French courses, leads to the reminder that writing papers, briefs, reports, and essays is part of virtually all the jobs educated people do. If writing process theory is valid (the students are, after all, learning to judge such theories for themselves), the process is not confined to elementary teaching; it is the same process TAs themselves follow when they write required seminar papers and theses and the same process we follow (and they will follow) in communicating with colleagues in our disciplines through publication. This process is also either like, or related to, the processes by which literary works are created.

Even the arbitrary rules of MLA style, so often taught by rote as purely mechanical adjuncts to the scholar's real work, are brought before the class as examples of communicative convention. The students must learn the code sooner or later; but as they learn it, they also examine how it illustrates the intimate link many linguists postulate between arbitrariness and sharing (Saussure, 1922, pp. 104–08). Our syllabus, then, lists the topics of the day under familiar names, but the presentation of these topics regularly invites new associations.

The practical aspects of Theories and Methods of Scholarship are fairly standard: how to teach the four language skills and culture, as well as introductory literature; how to write and grade tests; how to correct students' errors; how to improve one's teaching; how to use standard bibliographies and journals of literature, language teaching, and linguistics; how to use the *MLA Style Manual;* how to write professionally, including abstracts; how to submit a paper for a conference or for publication (see the syllabus in Appendix A).[1] The practical aspects are also sometimes professional: an introduction to the *AATF Syllabus of Competence* (Murphy & Goepper, 1989) and discussion of its implications; case studies of teaching situations we use to elicit analyses of ethical dilemmas (see Appendix B); explanation of job searches, whether at the secondary or postsecondary level. Our mix of lecture and discussion works well, we think, to supply students with necessary information and to provoke them to think for themselves. We further encourage them to specify and test their own ideas through dialogue.

We have argued (following Booth, 1981) that the ethical aspects of the profession intertwine with theoretical and practical considerations. We have found that we must discuss ethics in a formal setting because, although we would like to believe that ethical behavior is transferred from professor to student automatically, we do not see evidence that such transfer happens regularly. In class, case studies have proven to be a forceful tool for promoting discussion of ethical issues (see Appendix B). So far, we have kept our case studies simple, asking students to state the problem(s) represented and to propose solutions. The ensuing debate often makes manifest the students' own value systems and allows them to consider, in a relatively safe atmosphere, controversial or intricate cases of cheating, sexual harassment, and other professional dilemmas they might eventually encounter in person. After discussing individual cases, students write a brief analysis of a preferred case, then rewrite the analysis in response to our comments. We are thus able to confirm their awareness of the issues involved, evaluate the breadth of their solutions, and inform their writing.

The integrated course format parallels our view of the profession: a back-and-forth movement in the topics treated and frequent contributions from both instructors on all subjects. For instance, as the syllabus shows, a class session focusing on writing leads to a session about the presentation of scholarly research and writing, which is followed by a hands-on session about evaluating students' compositions, which is succeeded by a class on the "hows" and "whens" of publishing and reading papers at professional meetings. Just as our professional lives put us at once on the creating and receiving ends of the writing process, this juxtaposition of teaching and doing scholarly writing gives our graduate students insights they might otherwise not gain until reaching assistant professor status. Because of this natural interaction, we find ourselves regularly returning to points made in a session ostensibly devoted to teaching when discussing research — and vice versa. We both contribute to all class sessions, despite the fact that most of the time one or the other of us officially assumes responsibility for teaching a particular topic. Because we both teach the first two sessions and then immediately alternate "official" control of each session, the students quickly adjust to our individual styles. They also profit from seeing that we do not always take the same position on issues and that frank debate is enlightening. In addition, evaluation of students' work is potentially more equitable when two instructors who have seen the same piece of work discuss its merits.[2]

The view that scholarship includes both teaching and research and that a scholar publishes in many ways is at the heart of our course, as the final exam essay section shows. In this largest part of the take-home exam, we always ask students to comment on a quotation within the context of Theories and Methods of Scholarship. For example:

Analyze the implications of the following remarks for the intertwined concepts of research and teaching. You may, of course, choose to agree with the author, to disagree, or both; you may also wish to point out areas for further exploration. Do not neglect either practice, principle, or ethics.

"My various societies thus allocate their resources and boost or hinder me in my scholarly endeavors. They support research about Chaucer or *Tristram Shandy* or Alcanter de Brahm because they have become somehow convinced, as we are convinced, that preservation of our literary culture is a good thing, that somehow literary culture graces or enhances their lives.

"It is obvious that they will do this allocating well only if we have managed to teach them how to do it. We scholars have taught, after all, in our role as teachers, every member of our society who carries much weight in society's allocations. And we continue to teach and thus to make our society, by the nature and quality of what we do; they learn from us whether or not to take our work seriously." (Booth, 1981, pp. 125–26.)

or

"The work of the professor becomes consequential only as it is understood by others. Yet, today, teaching is often viewed as a routine function, tacked on, something almost anyone can do. When defined as *scholarship,* however, teaching both educates and entices future scholars. Indeed, as Aristotle said, 'Teaching is the highest form of understanding.'" (Boyer, 1990, p. 23.)

Why would an expert, when asked to describe what professors do, describe teaching and scholarship in this way? In your essay, refer to any FREN 701 information that supports your answer.

Thus, we show regularly in specifics what the course's theme suggests: that research and teaching are not done by different people with different gifts, habits, and purposes, and that the topic of the moment is isolated from general principle only temporarily. Once one begins to think in this way, the possibilities of linking and comparison become almost too numerous, and it often requires discipline to avoid bringing up too many connections at once and thus throwing the class off track. Yet all of our presentations and remarks of this type have a single purpose: to make explicit the ordinary operations of the professional teacher's mind. These operations, and the training that permits them, are most effectively presented not as monads but as part of a seamless web of experience and action.

Is Such a Professional Course Really Necessary?

In contemplating the introduction of a course like Theories and Methods of Scholarship at another institution, one may anticipate specific criticisms that can be easily parried if colleagues are reminded of something they probably already know: that the traditional clichés do not really limit our disciplines to one or two activities. The main protest may be a reaction to the course's content: that this is a "vocational" course and therefore, by definition, not substantive enough, for it does not teach French or Spanish or German literature or culture per se. We object to such a definition of what is substantive and note the high intellectual level of *The MLA Introduction to Scholarship* (Gibaldi, 1992) and *The Academic's Handbook* (DeNeef, Goodwin & McCrate, 1988). This is an age of reflection and self-reflection, after all, and academics who accept the metahistorical and metacritical dimensions of scholarly discourse may well wish to reflect before they exclude the larger dimensions of professional life from the graduate curriculum.

That is all very well, some of our colleagues might say, but what has the intellect to do with elementary language teaching? Even if we break down the prejudice that separates scholars into "learner" halves and "teacher" halves, what can the teacher-learner do to prepare French 101 if not learn a set pattern — "methods," classroom management, "the book," *trucs et moyens?* That reaction implies, first, that second language learning is a static profession, and, second, that second language study has no intellectual content. We do not have to argue, for the readers of this collection, that the notion of a static "method" is hopelessly inaccurate. We do not have a small group of "methods" waiting to be mastered (and rejected, all but one); what we do have is only a type of inquiry: information to be gathered, investigations to be carried out, and endless decisions to be made. Every detail of the French 101 syllabus must be chosen deliberately, professionally, with all decisions under control, or else the syllabus is an accident.

It is a little harder to see how studying adjectival agreement and the names of cheese and bread at age 16 or 18 is an intellectual activity, and yet by nature it is. Even more than that, it is an adventure cognate with the adventure of diving into an unknown literature or an alien past. It means discovering language in a way no monolingual can, because it means discovering that one's native language, a fundamental constituent of personality, is not immanent. Rules of communication are neither inevitable nor absolute; they have a context and can be seen in a perspective. Many students discover this powerful reality more or less independently, but cannot necessarily name it. From our point of view, this discovery is only one form of contact with the foreign, and we do not have to talk about berets and baguettes to get across just how foreign another language is (Cook, 1977).

The intellectual challenge of accepting and finally manipulating something so very foreign becomes obvious to novice teachers once the nature of the challenge is made clear to them. After all, elementary sentences, like elementary chemical formulae or basic physics experiments, are not brought into the curriculum for their own sake, nor are they merely stepping-stones to real advanced study. They exemplify challenging mental problems: choices, pathways, the effect of prior knowledge and habits. That fact is written implicitly into every fill-in-the-blank exercise and should be explicitly present in the scholar-teacher's mind all the time. Only trained minds can manage to link why and what, principle and practice, while also managing the classroom. And so we openly invite our students in French 701 (and why not in French 101?) to avoid leaving the intellect at the door just because the topics of elementary-language-student discourse include such mundane matters as buying stamps. Buying stamps is not the only subject at hand; the subject is also the power and inevitability of language.

Another response to the antiprofessional stance is pragmatic and shifts the battleground a bit. Given the current assaults on higher education, and inquiries into its values and responsibilities (e.g., Bennett, 1984; Bloom, 1987; Sykes, 1988; Cheney, 1990; D'Souza, 1991), we know that the young scholars who complete our graduate programs cannot assume that academic practices will be accepted without reflection by outsiders. A course that deals in part with professionalism is not, therefore, superfluous any more than it is second rate; it is essential to our students' future professional health. Colleagues who realize that the reputations of departments and universities rest partly on the quality of their graduates recognize that sending well-rounded Ph.D.'s into the marketplace and hence into other institutions can only enhance our standing in the discipline. Departments granting doctorates need to respond to the demands of the marketplace. The views of state college and university chairs who attended a 1984 ADFL summer seminar are clear; they recommended that newly prepared Ph.D.'s have the following characteristics: versatility and a more generalist than specialist stance, near-native speaking ability, training in foreign language pedagogy, basic knowledge of linguistics and culture, the ability to teach a second language or area of concentration, training in professional ethics and protocol, preparation for the job market, and a comprehensive knowledge of English, including writing ability (Showalter, 1984).

Some colleagues may accept the idea that a course like Theories and Methods of Scholarship is both substantive and useful, but argue that teaching techniques and research methods are learned indirectly, without need of analysis, in the usual graduate literature, civilization, and linguistics courses. Those of us who train and supervise TAs and foster improved teaching know, rather, that instructors gain most through analyzing their own teaching practices with attention to experts' insights. Too often the learning about teaching that supposedly happens by osmosis when one takes a master teacher's course is vague, if not imaginary. Serious graduate students are conditioned to pay the greatest attention to subject matter and much less to teaching techniques or style — except when they find the latter annoying. Unreflective imitation, even of the best teachers, is not an adequate way to equip students to establish and maintain effective teaching practice. In any case, it may not always be the best teachers who are imitated.

With respect to research, graduate students are most likely to take their responsibilities as writers seriously if their departments give these matters serious — that is, explicit — attention. Although many members of graduate faculties may be uneasy with the situation, exposure to research protocols has for some time been the business of graduate schools. But a few faculty members still seem to expect students to leap into graduate school fully cognizant of the standard reference works in the discipline and capable of consulting them resourcefully. They request that students submit papers using the MLA's increasingly complex rules of documentation and assume that their request means something to neophytes. In fact, the level of bibliographic research required for graduate study is not that of undergraduate language and literature programs.

But the essence of why a course like Theories and Methods of Scholarship needs to exist and, in fact, to be required, grows from the larger questions that we have said graduate students and academics must consciously answer: What is the nature of scholarship? How must we act to be ethical researchers and teachers? In maintaining that teaching and research are inextricably linked to each other, what do we mean? In sum, what are the larger principles behind our practices as researchers and teachers? Perhaps, in the days of smaller graduate departments, questions like these were confronted, pondered, and answered over coffee or tea shared by a faculty mentor and a student protégé. Such a scenario (if it ever matched reality) has surely become rare today, but the quandaries remain. In a professional course, graduate students and their teachers must face these issues, sharing ideas, and reach at least temporary conclusions, expressed in their final essays.

Conclusion

In the light of four years' experience, we believe that Theories and Methods of Scholarship succeeds for both students and instructors. On the final anonymous evaluations, students have commented positively: "We're really lucky; as far as I know, we're the only department that has a course like this." Two second-year graduate students who had taught in high school before attending graduate school and who took French 701 before becoming TAs noted, "Last year we wondered how 701 could teach us anything new, but now we find it right on target." As the course has evolved, we, as instructors, have developed our own understanding of the true integration of the research and teaching aspects of our profession. Because both instructors attend all class meetings and discussion flows back and forth between "research" and "teaching," we see more connections and make them for and with the graduate students. By team teaching, we envision — and are tempted to tackle — teaching techniques different from those we have found comfortable. We tend to do our best in teaching this course: after all, our audience consists of graduate students, many of whom will soon become professors *and* valued faculty colleagues. We gain new insights into our own work from the different perspectives that a colleague with a different specialization brings to it. The integrated team teaching approach we take in this course leads to the type of scholarly discussions colleagues are supposed to have in the hallowed halls, but infrequently do. For a language program director who also happens to be a junior faculty member, having the opportunity to teach with a more advanced colleague whose specialty is literature or civilization can be a door to a greater mutual understanding between departmental colleagues. Experiences such as ours can help repair the "split community" many of us deplore (Rivers, 1983, p. 28).

Recent articles (Azevedo, 1990; Waldinger, 1990) show clearly that the language profession has made great strides toward taking elementary language teaching seriously, and there is good evidence that most departments are now paying more attention than ever to the training of future teachers, who in fact are actively teaching foreign languages even now. The next step is to put an end to the ghettoization implied in our profession's persistent tendency to treat language teaching as an isolated specialty (Dvorak, 1986). For most college teachers it is not a specialty; it is a regular and recurring responsibility. Those in more complex departments, who may not teach elementary language regularly, are every bit as responsible for what happens during the acquisition process as are the people who foster it; and they are, besides, dependent on the outcome when they teach "higher" courses in literature or civilization. The path to understanding that interdependent relationship is, in our view, a high road of theory rather than a low road of practice. Second language teaching uses particular materials and terms, but it is intellectually like all other teaching; it requires similar habits and similar mental equipment. Professors and administrators must know the language disciplines every bit as well as they know literary theory: that is, well enough to conceive the students' leap into the unknown as the leap it is. And where practice is concerned, we must not only recognize that language teaching is a form of applied linguistics, but agree that we have every reason to communicate that fact to graduate instructors.

We have a chance, early in graduate students' education, before they have engraved their opinions in stone, to help them integrate what may falsely appear to be very different axes of their current and future scholarly lives: that is, the introspective, sometimes necessarily narrow research that leads to new insights and the participatory, outward-looking sharing of the resultant knowledge that is teaching and writing at its best. A course like Theories and Methods of Scholarship can lead both departmental colleagues and graduate students to understand better the healthy interaction of research and teaching that is the mark of a true scholar and to realize that in the academic profession we expect competence and have need of inspiration in teaching and administration, as well as in publishing. Those of us who would design courses such as Theories and Methods of Scholarship can play a vital role in professionalizing the future professoriate, and we must make the most of it.

Notes

1. Clearly, Theories and Methods of Scholarship is not a standard language-teaching methods course; it accomplishes both more and less. Our inclusion of research and reference techniques and consideration of the ethics of publication, for instance, preclude our spending as much class time discussing teaching techniques and methods as one can in a three-hour methods course. With this trade-off, however, we lose nothing: the synthesis of teaching and research enhances both in the eyes of our students; we have more time for all aspects of the course than we had with our separate one-hour practica; ongoing workshops expand upon topics introduced in FREN 701; and finally, we also offer FREN 703, Methods of Teaching College French, upon students' request (see Lalande, 1991, for support of a similar course).

2. Shared evaluation, like shared teaching, has benefits beyond the scope of this chapter. Suffice it to say that arguing for the grade one wants to give, with reference to the text of the student's paper or exam, calls upon and makes explicit for us the scholarly virtues of accuracy, logic, and attentiveness.

Works Cited

Azevedo, Milton M. "Professional Development of Teaching Assistants: Training versus Education." *ADFL Bulletin* 22, 1 (1990): 24–28.

Barnett, Marva A. "Peer Observation and Analysis: Improving Teaching and Training TAs." *ADFL Bulletin* 15, 1 (1983): 30–33.

Bennett, William J. *To Reclaim a Legacy: Report on the Humanities in Higher Education.* Washington, DC: National Endowment for the Humanities, 1984.

Bloom, Allan. *The Closing of the American Mind.* New York: Simon & Schuster/ Touchstone, 1987.

Booth, Wayne. "The Scholar in Society." *Introduction to Scholarship in Modern Languages and Literatures.* Ed. Joseph Gibaldi. New York: Modern Language Association, 1981: 116–43.

Boyer, Ernest L. *Scholarship Reconsidered: Priorities of the Professoriate.* Lawrenceville, NJ: Princeton University Press, 1990.

Cheney, Lynne. *Tyrannical Machines: A Report on Educational Practices Gone Wrong and Our Best Hopes for Setting Them Right.* Washington, DC: National Endowment for the Humanities, 1990.

Cook, Robert Francis. "Foreign Language Study and Intellectual Power." *ADFL Bulletin* 8, 4 (1977): 6–9.

DeNeef, A. Leigh, Craufurd D. Goodwin & Ellen Stern McCrate (Ed.). *The Academic's Handbook.* Durham, NC: Duke University Press, 1988.

Di Donato, Robert. "TA Training and Supervision: A Checklist for an Effective Program." *ADFL Bulletin* 15, 1 (1983): 34–36.

D'Souza, Dinesh. *Illiberal Education: The Politics of Race and Sex on Campus.* New York: Free Press, 1991.

Dvorak, Trisha R. "The Ivory Ghetto: The Place of the Language Program Coordinator in a Research Institution." *Hispania* 69 (1986): 217–22.

Gibaldi, Joseph (Ed.). *Introduction to Scholarship in Modern Languages and Literatures.* 2nd ed. New York: MLA, 1992.

Jarvis, Donald K. *Junior Faculty Development.* New York: MLA, 1991.

_____. "Junior Faculty Development and Language Department Quality." *ADFL Bulletin* 19, 3 (1988): 32–37.

Lalande, John F., II. "Advancing the Case for an Advanced Methods Course." *Challenges in the 1990s for College Foreign Language Programs.* Ed. Sally Sieloff Magnan. AAUSC Issues in Language Program Direction 1990. Boston: Heinle & Heinle Publishers, 1991: 151–66.

Lee, James F. "Toward a Professional Model of Language Program Direction." *ADFL Bulletin* 19, 1 (1987): 22–25.

Mooney, Carolyn J. "Higher–Education Conferees Applaud Carnegie Plan to Broaden the Definition of Faculty Scholarship." *Chronicle of Higher Education,* 11 April 1990, pp. A1, A16.

Murphy, Joseph & Jane Black Goepper (Ed.). *The Teaching of French: A Syllabus of Competence.* The Report of the Commission on Professional Standards, the American Association of Teachers of French. *AATF National Bulletin* 14 (October 1989). (Special issue.)

Rivers, Wilga M. "Preparing College and University Instructors for a Lifetime of Teaching: A Luxury or a Necessity?" *ADFL Bulletin* 15, 2 (1983): 23–29.

Saussure, Ferdinand de. *Cours de linguistique générale.* 2nd ed. Paris: Payot, 1922.

Showalter, English. "What Departments Look for in New PhD's." *MLA Newsletter* 16, 3 (1984): 3–4.

Sykes, Charles J. *ProfScam: Professors and the Demise of Higher Education.* Washington, DC: Regnery Gateway, 1988.

Van Cleve, John. "Graduate Study and Professional Responsibilities: Bridging the Gap." *ADFL Bulletin* 18, 2 (1987): 18–19.

Waldinger, Renée. "Training PhD Students to Teach in College." *ADFL Bulletin* 22, 1 (1990): 20–23.

Appendix A

Syllabus for Theories and Methods of Scholarship

FREN 701: THEORIES AND METHODS OF SCHOLARSHIP:
RESEARCH AND TEACHING

(Required; 3 credit hours; meeting 2½ hours per week. Fall 1991: Mondays/
Wednesdays, 1:00–2:15. One topic each meeting.)

[NOTE: Brackets indicate information not on students' copies.]

WEEK ONE (September 2, 4)

Joint Introduction to All Aspects of the Course: Learning and Teaching.
[What the course is and why it is needed.] (Joint presentation.)

READ: *Academic's Handbook,* preface and section 1 ("The Academy and
the Academic").

The Concept of Proficiency as a Model.

READ: Omaggio, ch. 1–2; also, pp. 337–41 ("The Structure of the
ACTFL/ETS Oral Proficiency Interview").

WEEK TWO (September 9, 11)

Examine Reference Sources in Print Form. Major bibliographies, encyclo-
pedias, and manuals in French studies: form and content.

The AATF Competencies: What does language teaching entail?

DUE: Be prepared to discuss the AATF competencies. How well do the
undergraduate programs you know help student to reach the
basic level of competence?

WEEK THREE (September 16, 18)

Electronic Reference and Bibliographical Sources.

Ethics of the Profession, 1. (Joint presentation.)

READ: *MLA Newsletter* list of ethical concerns in colleges.

READ: Case studies, to be discussed in class.

RECOMMENDED READING: *Saints and Scamps,* ch. 5.

WEEK FOUR (September 23, 25)

The Preparation of Scholarly Research and Writing, 1: Bibliographical access to sources in language, literature, and civilization: general considerations. (Using the reference handlist [over 30 pages long].)

DUE: First (brief) reference exercise.

Testing (Written and Oral); Giving Feedback.

READ: Omaggio, ch. 8; be able to define the terms in #1, p. 354; prepare #7, p. 355, for discussion.

DUE: Case study analysis (2 pages): Rough Draft.

WEEK FIVE (September 30, October 2)

The Preparation of Scholarly Research and Writing, 2: Reference and verification. [Why the scholar's habits are both useful and important.]

Teaching Writing.

READ: Omaggio, ch. 6; prepare #3, p. 269, for discussion.

DUE: A quiz you might use in class.

WEEK SIX (October 7, 9)

The Presentation of Scholarly Research and Writing, 1: Thesis and dissertation writing, publication, and paper-giving: WHY?

READ: *Academic's Handbook,* section 5 ("Publishing Research"), with special attention to the sections by Budd and by Rowson.

DUE: Second (brief) reference exercise.

DUE: Final text of case study analysis.

Evaluating Compositions. Peer Observation.

DUE: Composition assignment; graded compositions; discussion of criteria.

[Here is the assignment as distributed:]

Explain in writing the way in which you will assign a future contextualized composition topic to your FREN 101, 102, 201, or 202 students. (If you are not currently teaching, imagine that you are working with students at one of these levels. Take a look at the appropriate textbook.) Give as many details as necessary for us to understand how the presentation/assignment will work in class. Include any handouts you will use. Be sure to consider and include the following also:

- Prewriting activity: brainstorming for vocabulary and/or topic and or organization; providing a model; providing a context.
- Logical, realistic framework for the composition.
- Will you give the students a choice of topic?
- How will you advise them to revise their first draft *before* handing the composition in?
- What will you tell them about how the composition will be evaluated?

Along with this lesson plan and assignment, give us the details of how you will evaluate this composition: percentages or relative weight of different aspects of the composition.

READ: Explanation of the peer observation system.

WEEK SEVEN (October 14 [Fall Break], 16)

The Presentation of Scholarly Research and Writing, 2: Publication and paper-giving: HOW? WHEN?

WEEK EIGHT (October 21, 23)

Journal Reviews: How can journals on second language acquisition and language teaching help you in your present and future academic career?

DUE: Be prepared to present one language teaching/linguistics/literature journal to the class, answering the questions previously distributed. Hand in your written review of another journal.

[Here is the assignment as distributed:]

To become familiar with journals in the field of second language acquisition, teaching of literature, language pedagogy and methodology, and applied linguistics, study two of the journals in the list you received [a list of nine journals in second language acquisition, foreign language teaching, and applied linguistics]. Decide how useful you think the journals will be to you as you continue your career and why. Consider the questions below for each of the journals you choose, and integrate answers to them into a professionally written summary. Think beyond your years as a graduate student.

How frequently does the journal appear?

What kinds of articles or items are included?

What is the general focus of the journal?

For whom are they written?

What percentage of them would be of use or interest to you now *and* during your future professional life? Why?

Is the journal published by an association? Is this an advantage? Should you join the association? Why or why not?

Does the journal carry advertising? How much?

Will the advertising be useful to you? Why or why not?

For one journal, type your summary as an essay to be handed in (1–2 pages). Be prepared to present both journals to your classmates on October 21. That day we will discuss as many different journals as possible.

MLA Style, Hands-on Session. Discussion of the MLA Introduction to Scholarship: Lehmann on linguistics, Tanselle on textual criticism.

EXAMINE: The *MLA Style Manual.*

DUE: A note of peer observation groups and first meeting date.

WEEK NINE (October 28, 30)

Discussion of the MLA Introduction to Scholarship: Lewalski on historical scholarship, Lipking on criticism.

Error Correction.

READ: Omaggio, ch. 7; be able to define the terms in #1, pp. 304–5, and prepare #5, p. 305, for discussion.

WEEK TEN (November 4, 6)

Teaching Reading. Reading Process Theory.

READ: Omaggio, ch. 3; prepare #1, pp. 117–18, for discussion.

MLA Style, Hands-on Session.

EXAMINE: *MLA Style Manual.*

WEEK ELEVEN (November 11, 13)

Listening Comprehension; Using Videotapes; Conversation Classes.

READ: Omaggio, ch. 4.

DUE: Reading comprehension activity (Omaggio, p. 173, #5)

Details of MLA Style.

DUE: Error correction assignment.

Receive: Take-home final exam (due December 11 at 5:00 P.M. in Mr. Cook's mailbox in Cabell 329).

WEEK TWELVE (November 18, 20)

Culture and Civilization in the Language Course; Ethical Implications of Teaching Culture.

READ: Omaggio, ch. 9; prepare #3 and #4, pp. 403–4, for discussion.

REREAD: Culture section of AATF Syllabus of Competence.

DUE: Listening Comprehension Activity (Omaggio, p. 173, no. 4).

Discussion of the MLA Introduction to Scholarship: Hernadi on literary theory.

DUE: Peer observation reaction forms.

WEEK THIRTEEN (November 25, 27)

Ethics of the Profession, 2. (Joint presentation.)

READ: Booth on the scholar in society.

READ: *Academic's Handbook,* section 3, "Teaching and Advising."

RECOMMENDED READING: *Saints and Scamps,* ch. 2 and 3.

Current Second Language Acquisition Theory and Research. Reading and understanding research articles; integrating theory and method into your own teaching.

DUE: Two journal article abstracts; be prepared to present a three-minute summary of each in class.

[Here is the assignment as distributed:]

Write summaries of and reactions to one article from each of two different professional journals (see sample abstract [one student's excellent work from a previous semester]). One of the articles you choose must report an experiment on some aspect of second language acquisition/learning; the other may be classroom-oriented, theoretical, or also research-based. Each summary/reaction must be limited to one 8½ × 11" sheet of paper and typed.

Both written abstracts are due on *November 27.* Be prepared to present at that time a three-minute oral summary of each article and your reactions to them.

DUE: A cultural activity you can use in the future. See Omaggio, #5, p. 404.

READ: Omaggio, ch. 5. Prepare #2, p. 217, for discussion.

WEEK FOURTEEN (DECEMBER 2, 4)

Getting a job — MLA *Career Guide,* MLA job list, *Chronicle,* departmental files, CV, conferences, letters of application, interviews. (Joint presentation.)

READ: *Academic's Handbook,* section 2.

DUE: MLA Style exercise (December 2).

READING LIST

Required:

Achtert, Walter S. & Joseph Gibaldi. *The MLA Style Manual.* New York: MLA, 1985.

DeNeef, A. Leigh, Craufurd Goodwin & Ellen Stern McCrate (Ed.). *The Academic's Handbook.* Durham, NC: Duke University Press, 1988.

Gibaldi, Joseph (Ed.). *Introduction to Scholarship in Modern Languages and Literatures.* New York: MLA, 1981. [Replaced by the 1992 edition.]

Omaggio, Alice C. *Teaching Language in Context: Proficiency-Oriented Instruction.* Boston: Heinle & Heinle Publishers, 1986.

Recommended:

Cahn, Steven M. *Saints and Scamps: Ethics in Academia.* Totowa, NJ: Rowman, 1986. (On reserve in Clemons Library.)

Cook, Claire K. *Line by Line: How to Edit Your Own Writing.* Boston: Houghton Mifflin, 1985. (Sometimes cited as "The MLA's Line by Line.")

Williams, Joseph C. *Style: Ten Lessons in Clarity and Grace.* New York: Scott Foresman, 1989.

WORK LOAD AND GRADE COMPONENTS:

- Participation in discussions (15%)
- Short written assignments (15%)
- Journal article abstracts and analysis (10%)
- Two or three reference library-use exercises (20%)
- An MLA Style exercise (10%)
- The final exam (30%)

The FINAL EXAM is to be taken home. It will include:

1) Identification questions (with an emphasis on concepts in language teaching).

2) An exercise in the application of the rules of MLA Style (writing entries for previously unseen books and articles.) The *Manual* may NOT be consulted during this exercise.

3) A question requiring the description of a strategy for solving a research problem.

4) An essay on the general topics of the course: teaching and learning, principles and practice; their relationships within our profession.

Appendix B

Case Studies: Introduction and Samples

The case study method educates, in principle, by presenting imaginary situations that are more important to talk about than to solve. Indeed, that is the way the cases proposed reflect reality: they are usually complex, presenting dilemmas, not calling forth formulas. The problems raised may never appear in your futures in the form they take here, but the principles will return.

It will be helpful to organize your thoughts about the cases around a few basic questions. You may, of course, reorder or replace the ones we propose here. We suggest these questions as valuable for each of the following cases. You will use them to organize your analysis of the case you choose to write about, and we will use them to organize our discussion.

1) What is the nature of the problem? Define the issues raised and locate the horns of the dilemma.

2) What additional information might the characters ideally wish to have before acting?

3) What are the ethical and professional responses you would recommend for the principal character?

4) What are the limits of possible action the character faces in the search for a solution?

1.

Mara Wisniewski cannot at first believe her ears. Yet the words come again. In the third week of the course, the theoretical introduction is over, and the professor is speaking of the nature of the learning process in general. She hears him say, "It is, of course, well known that not all population groups have the same learning characteristics. I will take as an example Polish people. They are slow learners and poorly equipped to grasp certain tasks. The classic examples are changing a light bulb and popping popcorn; these will be familiar to all of you."

Mara is barely aware of the sentences on the cognitive aspects of light-bulb changing that follow. Only the conclusion strikes her with renewed force: "We must keep in mind, therefore," the professor states, "that Poles as a group score low on standardized measures of intelligence and achievement for the reasons just given."

What does Mara write in her notebook? What does she do at the end of the class? The next day? In short: how does she approach the intellectual and ethical problem of thinking about what she has heard?

2.

Jack Straw, super TA, leaps into action on the first day of class, reading the roll with gusto, associating names and faces, making even this routine act a form of relationship with his new group of FREN 201 students. Near the middle of the roll, he reads out a name of familiar aspect: Thomas Levéreux. "Here's one I won't have to use my fake French accent on," he thinks; "no more 'Couques' or 'Barresnettes'; this one's a piece of cake."

"/to mA lə ve rø/," intones Straw. There is no response (although every student called to that point has replied at once). "/lə ve rø/," he repeats patiently.

There is a stirring at the back of the room. A young man frowns. "Monsieur Levéreux?" asks Jack. This time the response is immediate. "*Lever*oh. I don't know what you said, but my name's *Lever*oh, *that's* how you pronounce my name." The frown remains; how does Jack reply?

3.

Harry Friendly looks up from the 101 papers he is grading to see Jennifer Lerner standing in his doorway. He is glad she has come to him for advice again; it makes him think that what he told her about her course selection must have been useful. Only she is pale, and her eyes are rimmed with pink.

"Can I talk to you about something?" she asks.

"Come in, Jennifer," he says; "I haven't seen you since you finished my 101 last semester. How is 102 going?"

"Not good at all," she replies at once.

"Tell me what's up."

"Well, you know I wanted to be a French major. But I just don't understand what is going on in 102. I just got back a D on the third quiz. It's the TA, Stanley. He seems so snappish, and if we make a mistake, he just sneers at us, and I study for hours and never recall anything, and all my friends feel the same way, and I used to love French and always get As, and I can't be a French major if I don't do well in 102." (You may supply further comments.)

There is a good chance Harry has never heard anything of the sort about Stanley before. He has perhaps 10 or 15 seconds to give a correct and meaningful reply without appearing stumped or evasive. What are some of the things he might say or ask?

4.

In the convention hotel, Luke S. Walker sits down to dinner with a feeling of satisfaction. His paper on prethinking strategies in the foreign language classroom went well; the drive down with his supervisor, Helen Troy, was enlivened by discussion of everything from the weather to new language lab equipment. Now, as Helen Troy sits down across from him, he anticipates a valuable discussion of the day's events.

Yet Troy's remarks on the reception given Walker's paper are perfunctory. She seems distracted, eye contact is difficult; she speaks again and again of frustration, then of loneliness. Her gestures and the tilt of her shoulders seem unfamiliar.

Then dinner is nearing its end, and, to his surprise, she places her hand on Luke's, saying, "Why don't we go up to my room and talk about these things over a drink, in a place where we can be more private?"

Do we need to set a question on this one?

Beyond the Methods Course: Designing a Graduate Seminar in Foreign Language Program Direction

Keith Mason
University of Virginia

Teaching assistants (TAs) of foreign languages (FLs) often attend an orientation workshop before teaching their first college FL classes, and they may also be required to take a course in FL methodology during their first term of teaching.[1] In fewer cases do FL departments provide additional coursework in methodology for graduate students who wish to gain further knowledge. Many FL TAs with graduate degrees secure positions in academia as language program directors (LPDs), which require them to supervise basic, intermediate, or advanced language courses even though they had no specific coursework to prepare them for this task. Experienced TAs are often appointed as course directors while working toward their graduate degree, but receive little additional training to meet the new challenges that await them. In terms of professors serving as LPDs, Dvorak (1986, p. 217) states, "Basic language programs are not new, of course, and the use of TAs to staff them is no innovation. What is relatively recent is the search for someone *specially trained* to direct them." The type of training that a student receives in a general supervision course in a school of education may not be adequate preparation. Many of the concerns of LPDs are not shared by supervisors of programs in mathematics, science, English, or history. Our TAs need more than a methods course, especially if they plan on securing a teaching position in today's job market. Not all of our TAs secure positions as LPDs, but most teach language at some level. Therefore, they need high-quality training in pedagogy, and future LPDs need special training in FL program administration.

Some of our graduate students in literature, linguistics, and applied linguistics will be required to coordinate at the beginning of their appointment as assistant professors, and others often continue to coordinate later. Many scholars who have received Ph.D.'s in literature or in theoretical linguistics have turned to coordinating FL programs and supervising TAs (Teschner, 1987). Sprague and Nyquist (1989, p. 37) point out that "few faculty members set as a career goal the supervision of graduate teaching assistants (TAs). Typically, a faculty member volunteers or is drafted into such a position." They add that such a faculty member must possess a specialized set of leadership skills in three areas: as managers, professorial models, and mentors. Dvorak (1986, p. 222) states that individuals trained in language learning and teaching are attracted to the possibility of designing and directing an effective language program. These individuals could profit from more professional preparation for their tasks.

The position of LPD is multifaceted: the LPD must serve as a teacher, linguist, methodologist, editor, curriculum planner, counselor, psychologist, placement officer, organizer, arbiter, personnel director, supervisor, quality control worker, and evaluator.[2] The LPD has contact with many students: those enrolled in the basic-level courses, undergraduate minors and majors, graduate students, teaching assistants, and, in some universities, lecturers. Learning how to direct FL programs is an additional skill that graduates must master and utilize if they are to meet the challenges of running a basic-level language program. Such training is important because it allows TAs to view the teaching and learning process from a different perspective; and it provides them with professional preparation that will help qualify them to be LPDs. As Lee and VanPatten (1991, p. 116) state, "The support staff of course supervisors (graduate students, lecturers, or junior faculty) should be capable, talented, and well-trained." And it is members of the support staff that often serve as LPDs after becoming professors. This chapter presents a rationale and proposal for a special graduate seminar for foreign language program direction (FLPD) that would provide interested graduate students with additional professional preparation and expertise. While the course would not be suitable for all graduate students, it would be beneficial for individuals who believe they will coordinate language courses in the future. The course could also include segments devoted to supervising study-abroad programs, basic-level programs, advanced-level language course sequences, summer language institutes, and college language dormitories or houses.

This chapter is addressed to LPDs and professors who would offer a course in FLPD in academic institutions with graduate FL programs. In the subsequent sections of this chapter, we shall look at the following important areas essential to a course in FLPD: a rationale, its objectives, course content, materials, assignments, and an experimental independent study or seminar.

Rationale

Convincing our colleagues of the need for specialized training in directing skills is undoubtedly a challenge. Unpublished minutes from a 1985 meeting of the CIC (Committee on Institutional Cooperation: the Big Ten Universities and the University of Chicago Coordinators' Meeting) describe the main problem:

> At many institutions in the country, junior faculty members are required to do coordination during their first few years on the job, even though they may have a degree in literature. The implication seems to be that some colleagues do not recognize foreign language education as a legitimate field in its own right, but believe that virtually anyone can coordinate lower division courses without specialized training. (Cited in Teschner, 1987, p. 34.)

The feasibility of including a course in FLPD certainly requires consideration. The person who would teach such a course would be the LPD, who is already heavily burdened with many responsibilities in the FL program (see Dvorak, 1986, and Lee and VanPatten, 1991a, for detailed discussions). FL graduate students need to be better prepared to undertake a wide variety of duties within the foreign language department, including coordinating basic- and intermediate-level courses and supervising and evaluating TAs. It makes sense to add a course like the one described and defended here to the graduate FL curriculum in order to help our students meet the challenges of the future.[3]

Teschner (1987) discusses the professional preparation and background of 154 lower-division LPDs. He addresses the fields in which directors wrote their doctoral dissertation and the areas in which they publish journal articles and present conference papers. He reports that 59% of LPDs surveyed wrote their dissertation in literature, 19% in theoretical linguistics, and 14% in educational linguistics. Of the LPDs surveyed, 40% publish on literature, 14% publish on educational linguistics partially (one- to two-thirds of their publications), and 19% publish exclusively on educational linguistics (two-thirds to 100%). A small number of directors (12%) publish exclusively on theoretical linguistics. Of those surveyed, more directors with a linguistics background were attracted to publishing in educational linguistics than were directors with a literature background (p. 30). Teschner states: "We now know that while only about 15% of all eventual French, German and Spanish LD (lower division) directors write dissertations on educational linguistic topics, higher percentages of them come to publish and speak on those topics as their careers develop" (p. 34). The statistics provided by Teschner are enlightening. Some of our students enrolled in literature and theoretical linguistics courses are destined to serve as LPDs and publish in applied linguistics. More coursework needs to be implemented to help prepare them for this future.

A course in FLPD could be offered using several options. One possibility would be a seminar course meeting at least once every week during a regular academic semester or quarter. Another option would be to hold a colloquium with invited faculty from various language departments open to interested graduate students, preferably the term before a TA would begin directing courses. This option would be possible only in institutions where TAs have the opportunity to coordinate basic-level courses. Yet another possibility would be to have a summer course or an intensive summer seminar. Still another possibility would be to create an independent study course in which one TA worked alone with a professor.

Lalande (1991a) provides a rationale for offering an advanced methods course in that the beginning methods course is in some places designed to meet immediate "survival needs" of new TAs. Where this is the case, the beginning methods course is often too basic to provide an adequate amount of information for experienced TAs. Lalande also points out how many methods courses combine both undergraduate and graduate students, thus limiting the possibilities for a challenging, advanced-level treatment of methods.

A distinction between training and education in terms of the professional development of teaching assistants is made by Azevedo (1990). Training entails preparing instructors for their immediate departmental tasks. Azevedo believes that this task is crucial, but that a fully integrated development program "must not only *train* instructors for the present but also *educate* them for their future work as full-fledged faculty members" (p. 25, original emphasis). The FLPD seminar would need to address both training and education by preparing TAs serving as LPDs for their immediate duties as well as educating them for potential areas in which they will work and publish in a full-time career in a FL department.

At present, methodology receives very little coverage in the graduate school curriculum as evidenced by a survey conducted by Di Pietro, Lantolf, and Labarca (1983). They report that 73% of all coursework in FL graduate programs is in literature and literary criticism, 12% in linguistics, and a mere 3% in pedagogy. This imbalance could easily be remedied by including the following in graduate programs of study: (1) basic methods course during the first semester of teaching; (2) a second methods course during the TA's third year following Lalande's recommendation; (3) a linguistics course (Murphy, 1991, p. 137); and (4) a seminar in supervising foreign language instruction when TAs are appointed as course directors or for any TA desiring more specific professional preparation. Do our students truly want or need to take mostly literature or linguistics courses to the exclusion of more pedagogical courses, or are they interested in more applied linguistics coursework? Perhaps if we ask our graduate students what *they* want and need in terms of coursework, we will discover that they are interested in more coursework that focuses on teaching.

By analyzing the *MLA Job Information List,* Dvorak (1986, p. 222) found that an increasing number of universities are searching for LPDs. Regarding the use of experienced graduate students as course directors, Dvorak (1986, p. 222) states, "This represents an excellent opportunity for experience in program administration." Azevedo (1990, p. 26) declares: "Insights TAs acquire as course leaders may enhance their future eligibility for positions requiring duties like those of a course supervisor." He adds: "A professional does not spring into existence on receiving the doctorate but, rather, develops through habitually exchanging ideas with more experienced colleagues and, above all, by meditating on the nature and means of our calling as educators" (p. 28). An analysis of the October 1991 *MLA Job Information List* shows that out of a total of 606 foreign language positions listed, 72 or

12% called for the coordinating of language courses ("Number," 1992). This means that almost one-eighth of all positions require coordinating skills. Are our graduate-level FL programs preparing job candidates to be coordinators?

Lee (1987, p. 22) emphasizes the pivotal position of the LPD in any FL department: "How this person performs the job influences the lives of graduate teaching assistants and of all the undergraduate students enrolled in the language program." He stresses that the language coordinator should not be viewed as the "low person on the totem pole" but rather as having "the responsibility of a professional" (p. 23). Sadow (1989) briefly describes LPDs' activities and their contributions within FL departments. His essay is addressed to colleagues in literature and linguistics who may not know precisely what being a methodologist entails. Dvorak (1986) confronts the principal problems of being the language coordinator in a research institution and Lee and VanPatten (1991a) view FLPD as "academic." The use of this term means that the LPD should be regarded as an expert within academia in the same manner that scholars in literature and linguistics are regarded. They stress the importance of tenure-track appointments for LPDs, reasons not to expect a reduced publication requirement for LPDs, and a proposal for integrating the LPD gradually into a FL department.

Courses designed to train LPDs should be recommended for qualified TAs who have been appointed by the LPD to coordinate a course or courses in the basic-level program. Naturally, the situation differs according to academic institution. In some universities (for example, the University of Illinois and the University of Virginia), TAs run an entire course and are course coordinators while still graduate students. In other institutions, the opposite is true; TAs receive little or no experience as course coordinators. Therefore, the FLPD seminar would vary according to where it was offered. In any case, many graduate students studying languages are interested in practical professional preparation; they could utilize training in FLPD immediately when appointed as course coordinators while attending graduate school and after graduation upon securing a tenure-track position at a college or university. Shumway (1990) discusses enrollments in language compared with those in literature and civilization using figures from his own department, Spanish and Portuguese, at Yale University. He finds that over 85% of students were enrolled in language courses versus approximately 18% in literature and civilization courses. In the context of the undergraduate FL curriculum, Woloshin (1983) also points out that at the University of Maryland, Baltimore Country, 80% of students in the Department of

Modern Languages and Linguistics are enrolled primarily in language courses. With these statistics in mind, we must insist upon professional training and special coursework to prepare individuals who are or will become directly involved with language courses or entire sequences of language courses at various levels, such as the LPD. In Spanish at the University of Virginia, we have 41 TAs, who teach 50 or more sections of basic-level courses, and approximately 1,250 enrollments during each fall term, which is almost 10% of all undergraduate students enrolled at the university. My position as LPD makes me responsible for all the TAs and undergraduate students involved in the program. In many institutions the FLPD is responsible for many more students. This responsibility makes TA training absolutely imperative.

Course Content

A course in FLPD could carry from one to three semester credits, depending on the time available and the amount of work required. A three-credit seminar would allow for the most comprehensive coverage. It would be of the utmost importance to have an extensive reading list, tests, and a substantial term paper, in addition to other, smaller assignments. If it were not designed as a rigorous course, it would be viewed as too easy, which must be avoided if it is to be considered scholarly by both students and colleagues.

A course on FLPD would need to address many important areas in order to provide a comprehensive overview of what the LPD of a FL program does. These areas would include the following: (1) current theories in methodology and applied linguistics; (2) text and materials selection; (3) materials development; (4) course design, syllabus design, and curriculum planning; (5) testing (including oral testing and placement testing); (6) information on training new teachers and teacher staff development; (7) evaluating teachers' classroom performance; (8) program evaluation; (9) placement of students in appropriate levels; (10) advising TAs and undergraduate students; and (11) the use of video, computers, and other technologies in teaching foreign languages. Other topics could be covered; they will be discussed later in the section "An Experimental Independent Study or Seminar." The appendix presents a sample course syllabus for FLPD.

A course in FLPD is feasible because of high-quality research that is being published. The number of publications in applied linguistics, second language acquisition, and foreign language methodology is steadily increasing. Indeed, theories of second language acquisition have changed substantially in the past five years. This increase further justifies coursework in which students would read and analyze current research. Future LPDs would benefit from the ability to apply research findings and conduct their own classroom research.

While it is beyond the scope of this chapter to provide a detailed review of materials that address FL methodology, teaching the four skills, and language testing, mention of key sources in language pedagogy should be considered by the LPD in training and included in coursework. The content of the FLPD course depends, of course, on what is taught in the required methods course. Many of these materials have appeared in the last five years and may be readily used in a course in FLPD.[4] The manual by Lee (1989) deserves primary attention, since it was written with LPDs and TAs in mind. By giving a detailed description of instruction in Spanish and Italian at the University of Illinois at Urbana-Champaign, Lee covers the many practical concerns and problems (with solutions) of the basic-level FLPD. He divides his guide into a section for course directors and TA trainers and one for TAs. The important issues that he addresses include the roles of TAs, course supervisors, and the director of basic language instruction; communication between the director and students in the basic courses; TA training, communicative language teaching; classroom management; and syllabi and lesson plans. Chapter 7, "What a Director of Basic Language Instruction Should *Not* Hear," presents problematic interchanges between basic-level students, TAs, and directors and how to avoid them. It also helps characterize exactly what the director of basic language instruction does in addition to duties of coordinating, namely, publishing, presenting papers at conferences, teaching, and participating in committee meetings. This text is very useful for LPDs in training and should be required reading because of its practical treatment of the subject.

Other materials appropriate for a course in FLPD include several series of books published by Cambridge University Press: Cambridge Applied Linguistics, New Directions in Language Teaching, Cambridge Language Teaching Library, and Cambridge Handbooks for Language Teachers. For example, Dubin and Olshtain (1986), as well as Yalden (1987), discuss course design, especially in terms of the communicative framework. Books by Chaudron (1988) and Nunan (1988) address classroom-based research and the learner-centered curriculum, respectively. Richards (1990) addresses the four language skills, methods, curriculum development, and content-based language instruction. A collection of articles dealing with second language teacher education is found in Richards and Nunan (1990). Key articles in this collection include studies by Gaies and Bower, Gebhard, Fanselow, and articles on the practicum, self-observation in teacher development, case studies, teachers and learners in the classroom, and issues and approaches in teacher education. A new collection, edited by Rivers (1992), deals with many aspects of teaching languages in college. Two recent collections of articles in second language acquisition research have appeared (O'Malley & Chamot, 1990; Gass & Schachter, 1989). Johnson (1989) addresses the second language curriculum in the Cambridge Applied Linguistics series. Richards (1984) addresses language curriculum development and should be considered by the instructor of the FLPD course in planning the syllabus.

Sources in language testing may not get attention in the first-level methods course due to time limitations. Lado (1961) and Oller (1979) are standard language testing manuals. Lado's treatment is very traditional and reflects the audiolingual method, but should be analyzed as a point of departure with which to compare more current FL testing models. Oller (1979) includes a more pragmatic and communicative focus to language testing. Several texts on language test preparation were published in the 1980s: Cohen (1980), Finocchiaro and Sako (1983), Carroll and Hall (1985), Henning (1987), Underhill (1987), and Hughes (1989). Oller (1983) offers a collection of articles within a more theoretical framework. A two-part article by Skehan (1988, 1989) about language testing treats important theoretical and practical issues. The 1991 AAUSC Annual Volume entitled *Assessing Foreign Language Proficiency of Undergraduates* (Teschner, 1991) treats many aspects of language testing and aptitude. Specifically, key issues in language testing include placement (Heilenman, 1991; Wherritt, Druva-Rush & Moore, 1991), language test design (Hammerly, 1991), exit requirements (Fleak, 1991), task-based and process-oriented testing (Magnan, 1991b), and testing of reading (Lee, 1991), speaking (Ballman, 1991), and listening (Bacon, 1991). Walz (1991) addresses published tests that are part of French textbook packages. Attention to ancillary materials developed by textbook publishers is rare in research literature and needs to be addressed further for all modern languages. Generalities about language testing are treated in studies by Nuessel (1991), Hagiwara (1991), and Bernhardt and Deville (1991); all of the readings in this volume are ideal for the LPD in training.

A nine-book series, known as the "Program Evaluation Kit," is useful to the FLPD (Fitz-Gibbon, Taylor & Morris, 1987a & b; Henerson,

Morris & Fitz-Gibbon, 1987; Herman, Morris & Fitz-Gibbon, 1987; King, Morris & Fitz-Gibbon, 1987; Morris, Fitz-Gibbon & Freeman, 1987; Morris, Fitz-Gibbon & Lindheim, 1987; Patton, 1987; Stecher, 1987). The series addresses all aspects of educational programs and includes the following: focusing an evaluation, an evaluator's handbook, measuring attitudes, qualitative methods in evaluation, communicating evaluation findings, assessing program implementation, analyzing data, measuring performance and using tests, and designing a program evaluation. While the kit does not relate specifically to foreign language programs, it has much information that the LPD can utilize in designing a basic-level language program and a method for evaluating instruction and course design.

Assignments

Course assignments required of students in a course on FLPD could include the following: observing several classes and writing formal evaluations, writing recommendations for future employment, making a comparative analysis of textbooks for one or several languages, reviewing a book in applied linguistics, writing a critical essay comparing several researchers' views on a controversial topic in FL learning and teaching, creating a syllabus for a specific course, designing an evaluation form for teacher performance or for program evaluation, writing a rationale for the goals of a basic-level FL program, drafting a test that reflects current thoughts on FL testing, formulating criteria for placing students at different levels, and investigating areas within FLPD in which more research is needed. The following sections outline more specifically the assignments that could be completed by students in a course in FLPD.

Program Rationale

Write a rationale for a basic-level language program. What are the goals of the sequence of courses? What materials will be used? What approach or method of language teaching will be used?

Comparison of Three Approaches/Methods

Choose three methods or approaches to language teaching and learning. Compare them and state the benefits and drawbacks of each. Use the books by Larsen-Freeman (1986) and Richards and Rodgers (1986) for background information about FL methods and approaches.

Textbook Review

Do a comparative review of five textbooks of the same level using a checklist as a guide (Omaggio, 1986, and Savignon, 1983). Which text is the best one in your estimation? Why? Be specific in your conclusion of why you would select one of the five texts.

Teacher Evaluation Form

Develop a form for evaluating a FL class. Use Omaggio (1986, pp. 468–72) and Fitz-Gibbon & Morris (1987b) as guides.

Test Preparation

Using Omaggio (1986, pp. 450–67), design a chapter test for a beginning-level language course. All items should be contextualized and you should include grammar, vocabulary, reading comprehension, listening comprehension, and a composition.

Materials Development

Develop materials for teaching target-language grammatical structures or vocabulary using pictures, line drawings, or cartoons from magazines and newspapers. Write a detailed lesson plan showing how you would integrate the materials into your teaching.

Placement of Students

How does one place students into the appropriate level in a FL course sequence? Contact three academic institutions and find out how they place language students. Write a two-page document summarizing their criteria for placement. Include high school preparation, other language study, and scores on achievement/placement exams when applicable.

Syllabus Design

Design two syllabi for any basic-level language course: one for instructors and one for students. Include textbook information, weekly class assignments, the importance of the four skills, testing (including oral testing), lab and workbook requirements, grade breakdowns, and so on. Collect syllabi from colleagues to use as a guide.

Professional Literature in FL Methodology

Browse through the library for applied linguistics and methodology texts and journals. What journals are essential for the FL methodologist or program director? Compile a list of these journals. What are the issues commonly addressed in these journals for the past five years? Analyze several FL methodology texts.

Class Observations

Observe two language classes at different levels. Write up the evaluation using forms that you have devised. Do it as if you were evaluating a class as an LPD. A follow-up meeting between evaluator and teacher will be simulated once you complete this assignment. Samples of completed evaluation forms are available to help guide you.

Video Observations

Videotape two language classes at different levels. Write up the forms the way you would if you were evaluating a class as LPD. A follow-up meeting between evaluator and teacher will be simulated once you complete this assignment.

Videorecording has been used in teacher training and deserves particular attention in a course in FLPD. In their discussion of video in the context of technology for language learning and teaching, Furstenberg and Morgenstern (1992) point out the distinction between video viewing and videorecording: commercial video programs, satellite, or telecast taping may be used as pedagogical materials with students, or the teacher may use the videotape process to evaluate instruction. Franck and Samaniego (1981) describe videotape as a feedback device for self-analysis and confrontation of one's own teaching and outline a clear technique for using video in the supervision of TAs. Additionally, teachers find video feedback effective in making them aware of the amount of target language used in class, how much the teacher monopolizes class time, the effectiveness of drilling techniques, and the effectiveness of grammar explanations (Franck & Samaniego, 1981, p. 274).

Franck and Samaniego admit that some TA supervisors have qualms about utilizing video in TA supervision. They explain, however, that this reluctance is often allayed by the assistance of their Teaching Resource

Center staff. By receiving external support, LPDs do not have to deal with all aspects of using video; they may consult with professionals to assist them.

Smith (1973) offers clear guidelines on how to use videotape recording in instructor supervision and evaluation. These guidelines include procedures on how to critique the videotaped classes and sensible recommendations about who may see the tapes and the ethics of retaining videotaped classes for future use.

An Experimental Independent Study or Seminar

In the summer of 1991 I offered an independent study in FLPD to a graduate student in Italian. Requirements included readings from many of the works I have cited and assignments I have discussed in this chapter.

New courses are by nature experimental, and it is often beneficial to try them out first as independent studies or in a seminar slot. The benefits of experimenting are substantial; instructors receive feedback from students so that when they offer the course a second time, any problem areas in terms of readings, assignments, or class setup will have been ironed out. Since giving the independent study, I have had several graduate students express interest in a course in FLPD.

As the instructor of FLPD, I must evaluate the success of the course. While I was satisfied with what we did cover, several areas could have been treated, but were not. Undoubtedly, some topics may have been overlooked because it was the first time I offered the course and it was an independent study with only one student. Additional topics that could be implemented into the FLPD course include the legal ramifications of teaching, such as the right to privacy, academic dishonesty, sexual harassment, and learning disabilities. Also helpful would be the treatment of directing study-abroad programs and language-interest houses, since both these contexts require individuals who possess administrative skills.

One important part of teaching that could not be ascertained from the independent study offering of FLPD was how effective the class discussions would have been with more than one student enrolled. Both instructors and students would benefit more from in-class discussions, especially when controversy is an issue. The instructor would undoubtedly need to develop strategies to lead successful discussions of the course themes.

In terms of the assignments (described above in the section "Assignments"), they worked out well overall, but may have been too directive.

Several of the assignments could be relatively open-ended, especially the term paper and the program rationale. Of course, the danger of open-ended assignments is that students will stray and not complete the work adequately. A remedy is to require students to submit outlines and drafts beforehand to check their progress. Upon offering the FLPD seminar again, I will modify the syllabus and assignments to create a more comprehensive treatment of topics and make the assignments more challenging for students.

Summary and Conclusions

Few, if any, courses are offered within the regular graduate FL program that are designed to train TAs to supervise foreign language instruction. This omission may be explained by a refusal to accept the importance of pedagogy in FL departments and a lack of recognition of employment opportunities. This nonacceptance must change. A lack of respect and understanding exists concerning what the LPD is and what the LPD does. The MLA Job Information List has shown that there are many positions for LPDs. Today, many high-quality books and articles are available for teaching courses in FLPD and more research will most certainly continue to be published. This research needs to be recognized in the FLPD seminar.

Di Pietro, Lantolf, and Labarca (1983) have shown that FL departments throughout the United States offer only a minimal number of courses at the graduate level in pedagogy, compared with a great abundance in literature and literary criticism, and a moderate-to-low number of courses in linguistics. A course in FLPD would certainly help better prepare our future colleagues. Courses in supervision offered in education departments provide useful information to future teachers, but they are not specific enough to meet the needs of the LPD in training.

In summary, the following observations and recommendations about preparing TAs to direct FL programs may be made:

1) We must bring FL coordinating skills to the graduate-level curriculum by offering a course in FLPD. We who presently coordinate would have benefited greatly from such training; coursework in supervising FL programs is not simply an issue of methodology, but also of administration, testing, evaluating, counseling, and directing personnel. We need to recognize coordinating skills as a valuable learning experience for graduate students in training for careers as professors and language teachers.

2) We should look to the future and strive to create programs comprising a sequence of courses designed specifically to prepare individuals to be LPDs.

3) We must continue to publish research concerning the supervision of language programs so that FLPD will advance as a subfield within applied linguistics.

We must look to the future in preparing our TAs for positions in FL departments. We should include students of literature, linguistics, and applied linguistics, all of whom may secure positions as FLPDs. The methods course is extremely useful for teachers in training; however, individuals who find themselves directing FL programs would be better equipped to coordinate if they had coursework that helped them view FL programs not only from an instructional perspective, but from an administrative one as well. For this reason, we must look beyond the methods course and design graduate seminars that train individuals as LPDs. It is truly becoming more the rule than the exception for our graduate students to be involved in supervising TAs and in directing language courses or programs.

Notes

1. I wish to thank Marva Barnett, Kenneth Chastain, and Carla Tchalo for their comments on earlier drafts of this chapter. Special thanks to Jeffrey Bersett, Elizabeth Castleman, Campbell Lewis, Ian Pallini, Albert Shank, and Kevin Vandergrift. I alone remain responsible for any imperfections in this final version.

2. See Jarvis (1991) on junior-faculty development and the importance of balancing teaching and research. See also Barnett and Cook in this volume.

3. The works cited in this chapter are appropriate readings for a course or seminar on FLPD. Several books in combination with a selection of articles would ideally provide an adequate amount of professional literature to be read and discussed by the instructor and students. An experimental course in FLPD could easily be tested in the seminar slot that many graduate FL programs already include in their course offerings.

4. For an extensive bibliography of materials for TA training and development, see Benseler and Cronjaeger (1991a).

Works Cited

Azevedo, Milton M. "Professional Development of Teaching Assistants: Training versus Education." *ADFL Bulletin* 22, 1 (1990): 24–28.

Bacon, Susan M. "Assessing Foreign Language Listening: Processes, Strategies, and Comprehension." In Teschner, 1991: 205–20.

Ballman, Terry L. "The Oral Task of Picture Description: Similarities and Differences in Native and Nonnative Speakers of Spanish." In Teschner, 1991: 221–31.

Benseler, David P. & Christine Cronjaeger. "The Preparation and Support of Graduate Teaching Assistants in Foreign Languages: A Bibliography." In Magnan, 1991a: 207–32.

Bernhardt, Elizabeth B. & Craig Deville. "Testing in Forcign Language Programs and Testing Programs in Foreign Language Departments: Reflections and Recommendations." In Teschner, 1991: 43–60.

Carroll, Brendan J. & Patrick J. Hall. *Make Your Own Language Tests. A Practical Guide to Writing Language Performance Tests.* Oxford: Pergamon Press, 1985.

Chaudron, Craig. *Second Language Classrooms.* New York: Cambridge University Press, 1988.

Cohen, Andrew D. *Testing Language Ability in the Classroom.* Rowley, MA: Newbury House Publishers, 1980.

Di Pietro, Robert J., James P. Lantolf & Angela Labarca. "The Graduate Foreign Language Curriculum." *Modern Language Journal* 67 (1983): 365–73.

Dubin, Fraida & Elite Olshtain. *Course Design: Developing Programs and Materials for Language Learning.* New York: Cambridge University Press, 1986.

Dvorak, Trisha R. "The Ivory Ghetto: The Place of the Language Program Coordinator in a Research Institution." *Hispania* 69 (1986): 217–22.

Fanselow, John F. "'Let's see': Contrasting Conversations about Teaching." In Richards & Nunan, 1990: 182–97.

Finocchiaro, Mary & Sydney Sako. *Foreign Language Testing. A Practical Approach.* New York: Regents Publishing, 1983.

Fitz-Gibbon, Carol Taylor & Lynn Lyons Morris. *How to Analyze Data.* Newbury Park, CA: Sage Publications, 1987a.

———. *How to Design a Program Evaluation.* Newbury Park, CA: Sage Publications, 1987b.

Fleak, Ken. "Using an Exit Requirement to Assess the Global Performance of Undergraduate Foreign Language Students." In Teschner, 1991: 115–34.

Franck, Marion R. & Fabián A. Samaniego. "The Supervision of Teaching Assistants: A New Use of Videotape." *Modern Language Journal* 65 (1981): 273–80.

Furstenberg, Gilberte & Douglas Morgenstern. "Technology for Language Learning and Teaching: Designs, Projects, Perspectives." *Teaching Languages in College: Curriculum and Content.* Ed. Wilga M. Rivers. Lincolnwood, IL: National Textbook Company, 1992: 117–40.

Gaies, Stephen & Roger Bowers. "Clinical Supervision of Language Teaching: The Supervisor as Trainer and Educator." In Richards & Nunan, 1990: 167–81.

Gass, Susan M. & Jacquelyn Schachter. *Linguistic Perspectives on Second Language Acquisition.* New York: Cambridge University Press, 1989.

Gebhard, Jerry G. "Models of Supervision: Choices." In Richards & Nunan, 1990: 156–66.

Hagiwara, M. Peter. "Assessing the Problems of Assessment." In Teschner, 1991: 21–42.

Hammerly, Hector. *Synthesis in Language Teaching. An Introduction to Linguistics.* Blaine, WA: Second Language Publications, 1986.

_____. "Two Philosophies of Language Program and Language Testing Design." In Teschner, 1991: 61–78.

Heilenman, L. Kathy. "Self-Assessment and Placement: A Review of the Issues." In Teschner, 1991: 93–114.

Henerson, Marlene E., Lynn Lyons Morris & Carol Taylor Fitz-Gibbon. *How to Measure Attitudes.* Newbury Park, CA: Sage Publications, 1987.

Henning, Grant. *A Guide to Language Testing.* Cambridge, MA: Newbury House Publishers, 1987.

Herman, Joan L., Lynn Lyons Morris & Carol Taylor Fitz-Gibbon. *Evaluator's Handbook.* Newbury Park, CA: Sage Publications, 1987.

Hughes, Arthur. *Testing for Language Teachers.* Cambridge: Cambridge University Press, 1989.

Jarvis, Donald K. *Junior Faculty Development: A Handbook.* New York: Modern Language Association, 1991.

Johnson, Robert Keith (Ed.). *The Second Language Curriculum.* New York: Cambridge University Press, 1989.

King, Jean A., Lynn Lyons Morris & Carol Taylor Fitz-Gibbon. *How to Assess Program Implementation.* Newbury Park, CA: Sage Publications, 1987.

Lado, Robert. *Language Testing: The Construction and Use of Foreign Language Tests.* New York: McGraw-Hill, 1961.

Lalande, John, II. "Advancing the Case for an Advanced Methods Course." In Magnan, 1991a: 151–66.

Larsen-Freeman, Diane. *Techniques and Principles in Language Teaching.* New York: Oxford University Press, 1986.

Lee, James F. "Toward a Professional Model of Language Program Direction." *ADFL Bulletin* 19, 1 (1987): 22–25.

———. *A Manual and Practical Guide to Directing Foreign Language Programs and Training Graduate Teaching Assistants.* New York: Random House, 1989.

———. "On the Dual Nature of the Second-Language Reading Proficiency of Beginning Language Learners." In Teschner, 1991: 187–204.

——— & Bill VanPatten. "The Question of Language Program Direction Is Academic." In Magnan, 1991a: 113–27.

Magnan, Sally Sieloff (Ed.). *Challenges in the 1990s for College Foreign Language Programs.* AAUSC Issues in Language Program Direction 1990. Boston: Heinle & Heinle Publishers, 1991a.

———. "Just Do It: Directing TAs toward Task-Based and Process-Oriented Testing." In Teschner, 1991b: 135–62.

Morris, Lynn Lyons, Carol Taylor Fitz-Gibbon & Marie E. Freeman. *How to Communicate Evaluation Findings.* Newbury Park, CA: Sage Publications, 1987.

———, Carol Taylor Fitz-Gibbon & Elaine Lindheim. *How to Measure Performance and Use Tests.* Newbury Park, CA: Sage Publications, 1987.

Murphy, Joseph A. "The Graduate Teaching Assistant in an Age of Standards." In Magnan, 1991a: 129–49.

Nuessel, Frank. "Foreign Language Testing Today: Issues in Language Program Direction." In Teschner, 1991: 1–20.

"Number of Positions Advertised in MLA's *Job Information List* Continues to Decline." *MLA Newsletter* 24, 1 (Summer 1992): 12–16.

Nunan, David. *The Learner-Centred Curriculum.* New York: Cambridge University Press, 1988.

Oller, John W., Jr. *Language Tests at School.* London: Longman, 1979.

_____ (Ed.). *Issues in Language Testing Research.* Rowley, MA: Newbury House Publishers, 1983.

Omaggio, Alice C. *Teaching Language in Context: Proficiency-Oriented Instruction.* Boston: Heinle & Heinle Publishers, 1986.

O'Malley, J. Michael & Anna Uhl Chamot. *Learning Strategies in Second Language Acquisition.* New York: Cambridge University Press, 1990.

Patton, Michael Quinn. *How to Use Qualitative Methods in Evaluation.* Newbury Park, CA: Sage Publications, 1987.

Richards, Jack C. "Language Curriculum Development." *RELC Journal* 15 (1984): 1–29.

_____. *The Language Teaching Matrix.* New York: Cambridge University Press, 1990.

_____ & David Nunan. *Second Language Teacher Education.* New York: Cambridge University Press, 1990.

_____ & Theodore Rodgers. *Approaches and Methods in Language Teaching. A Description and Analysis.* New York: Cambridge University Press, 1986.

Rivers, Wilga M. (Ed.). *Teaching Languages in College: Curriculum and Content.* Lincolnwood, IL: National Textbook Company, 1992.

Sadow, Stephen A. "Methodologists: A Brief Guide for Their Colleagues." *ADFL Bulletin* 21, 1 (1989): 27–28.

Savignon, Sandra J. *Communicative Competence: Theory and Classroom Practice.* Reading, MA: Addison-Wesley, 1983.

Shumway, Nicolas. "Language Teaching in Literature Departments: Natural Partnership or Shotgun Marriage?" *ADFL Bulletin* 21, 3 (1990): 40–43.

Skehan, Peter. "Language Testing, Part 1." *Language Teaching* 21 (1988): 1–11.

_____. "Language Testing, Part 2." *Language Teaching* 22 (1989): 1–13.

Smith, Ronald E. "Video Tape Recording in Instructor Supervision and Evaluation." *Foreign Language Annals* 6 (1973): 523–24.

Sprague, Jo & Jody D. Nyquist. "TA Supervision." *Teaching Assistant Training in the 1990s.* Ed. Jody D. Nyquist, Robert D. Abbott & Donald H. Wulff. San Francisco: Jossey-Bass, 1989: 37–53.

Stecher, Brian M. & W. Alan Davis. *How to Focus an Evaluation.* Newbury Park, CA: Sage Publications, 1987.

Teschner, Richard V. "A Profile of the Specialization and Expertise of Lower Division Foreign Language Program Directors in American Universities." *Modern Language Journal* 71 (1987): 28–35.

_____ (Ed.). *Assessing Foreign Language Proficiency of Undergraduates.* AAUSC Issues in Language Program Direction 1991. Boston: Heinle & Heinle Publishers, 1991.

Underhill, Nic. *Testing Spoken Language. A Handbook of Oral Testing Techniques.* Cambridge: Cambridge University Press, 1987.

Walz, Joel. "A Survey and Analysis of Tests Accompanying Elementary French Textbooks." In Teschner, 1991: 163–86.

Wherritt, Irene, Cynthia Druva-Rush & Joyce E. Moore. "The Development of a Foreign Language Placement System at the University of Iowa." In Teschner, 1991: 79–92.

Woloshin David J. "The Undergraduate Curriculum: The Best and the Worst." *Modern Language Journal* 67 (1983): 356–64.

Yalden, Janice. *Principles of Course Design for Language Teaching.* New York: Cambridge University Press, 1987.

Appendix

Sample Syllabus

Fall 1992

Directed Research

FOREIGN LANGUAGE PROGRAM DIRECTION

Course Syllabus

Professor: Keith Mason

Course Objectives:
A course in Directing Foreign Language Programs needs to reflect the many important areas that a director or coordinator of FL program is required to know. The following areas will be addressed: (1) theories in methodology and applied linguistics; (2) text and materials selection; (3) materials development; (4) course and syllabus design and curriculum planning; (5) testing, including oral testing and placement testing; (6) information on training new TAs and teacher staff development; (7) evaluating teacher's classroom performance; (8) program evaluation; (9) placement of FL students; and (10) the director as an adviser to TAs and undergraduate students.

Course breakdown:

Written Assignments:	30%
Class observations and simulated follow-up:	15%
Two Exams:	20%
Term paper:	20%
Attendance/participation:	15%

Week of:	Class Topics:	Readings and Assignments:
Aug. 31	Introduction; The Language Program Director (LPD); Designing a FL program	Dvorak, Lee & VanPatten, 1991; Lee, 1987; Lee, 1989 (Chs. 1–4)
Sept. 7	What does the LPD do? Problems of being the LPD/The LPD as a professional	Lee, 1989 (Chs. 5–7); Johnson (whole book); Richards, 1984
Sept. 14	Designing a FL program: Curriculum and syllabus design	Richards, 1990 (Chs. 1–4); Program rationale essay
Sept. 21	Methods and approaches in language learning and teaching	Richards, 1990 (Chs. 5–8)
Sept. 28	Methods and approaches in language learning and teaching	Larsen-Freeman, 1986 (whole book)
Oct. 5	Methods and approaches in language learning and teaching	Assignment comparing three methods/approaches
Fall Break	No class	
Oct. 19	Materials development/text selection	Textbook review; Skehan, 1988, 1989

Week of:	Class Topics:	Readings and Assignments:
Oct. 26	Language testing	Underhill, 1987 (whole book) Exam 1
Nov. 2	Language testing	Henning, 1987; language test assignment; Gebhard, 1990
Nov. 9	Evaluating instruction: Watching videos and completing formal evaluations	Submit completed evaluation forms
Nov. 16	Placement and advising	Furstenberg and Morgenstern, 1992
Nov. 23	Technology for language learning	Term paper due
Nov. 30	Learning disabilities and language learning	Exam 2
Dec. 11	Individual presentations on term papers	

What TAs Need to Know to Teach According to the New Paradigm

Charles J. James
University of Wisconsin–Madison

Teaching assistants (TAs) in the 1990s need to be able to (1) teach discourse strategies, (2) give personalized yet focused speaking and writing assignments, (3) set and guide partner work, (4) encourage interactive reading strategies, and (5) integrate authentic audio and video material into the language classroom. In short, they have to be able to operate within the "new paradigm in language learning," as outlined by Swaffar, Arens, and Byrnes (1991). The "new paradigm" contains many different aspects, but in terms of learning materials and teaching techniques that apply directly to TA-taught classes, the authors (p. 12) list the following principles (the additions in brackets are mine):

1) Personalized language [should be developed in each learner.]
2) Authentic texts [should be used] as a basis for oral [and] written work as well as reading[.]
3) [G]rammar [must be] linked to meaning in a sentence as well as to meaning in paragraphs and discourse[.]
4) Grammar rules [should be] learned by students mainly as independent activity [primarily] outside of class[.]

5) Most of class time [should be] devoted to contextual practice cued by situational variables[.]

6) [The] distinction [should be made] between actively-used and comprehended words [, that is,] vocabulary understood and cued in L2 context.

On the surface, most TAs can readily espouse these principles; indeed, they sound self-evident. At the same time, a number of practical considerations need to be addressed in order to help TAs translate these principles into classroom activities.

TAs love to read. They also love to lecture. And talk. And question. And argue. And experiment. And above all, develop routines and maintain "satisfactory progress." After all, they are still students themselves and have responsibilities for their own academic development that at times conflict with their duties as teachers. For this reason, I have compiled a bibliography of practical reference works that should help them along the way, starting with Swaffar, Arens, and Byrnes's first chapter of their volume *Reading for Meaning* (Swaffar, Arens & Byrnes, 1991), which sets forth the concept of the "new paradigm." Other readings include Oxford's (1990) *Language Learning Strategies,* which outlines the psycholinguistic aspects of language learning processes; Brown's (1989) *A Practical Guide to Language Learning,* written from the perspective of language learners themselves; Altman, Ewing, Pusack, Bohde, Otto, and Shoemaker's (1990) *PICS Videoguidelines* for the use of video material; Green and Grittner's (1990) *German for Communication* and Legutke's (1991) *German for the Learner-Centered Classroom* for practical suggestions from the frontline about conducting a proficiency-oriented German classroom; and Omaggio's (1986) *Teaching Foreign Languages in Context,* still one of the most comprehensive sources for insights and practical tips for the classroom of the 1990s. In addition, the two volumes of the AAUSC series previously published, Magnan's (1991) *Challenges in the 1990s for College Foreign Language Programs* and Teschner's (1991) *Assessing Foreign Language Proficiency of Undergraduates,* should also be included in a list of readings for new TAs, the first for its overview of the profession at the postsecondary level, the second for its insights into the use of evaluation strategies for TA-taught courses.

All of this assumes, of course, that TAs take a methods course in which they can discuss each of these works in some detail. Not all TAs, however, take methods courses, and most, being graduate students with a fixed program of study and often little time to complete it as scheduled anyway, will avoid another course if at all possible. For this reason, I have developed a kind of toolkit that has proven helpful in working with TAs within the "new paradigm" over the years, even though the paradigm has been called "new" only recently. Each of these "Tools" can be summarized in one or two pages for quick review and discussed at length as needed.

The Tools are: (1) the Integrated Brain, (2) the Triangle, (3) P/Review-Prime-Practice-Presentation, (4) the *Stundenthema*, and (5) Partner Work. The Integrated Brain (Tool 1) emphasizes the psycholinguistic dynamics within learners. The Triangle (Tool 2) emphasizes the relationships between learners, the language, and language classroom activities. P/Review-Prime-Practice-Presentation (Tool 3) underscores the sequence within classroom activities. The *Stundenthema* (Tool 4) outlines the relationships among classroom activities. Partner Work (Tool 5) guides the nature of interaction among learners within a classroom setting. The Triangle is my own creation, presented here in print for the first time. The Integrated Brain in its present form is adapted from materials developed by Carol Ann Pesola (personal communication, 1992). P/Review-Prime-Practice-Presentation is based on the Overview-Prime-Drill-Check model developed by Constance K. Knop (1982). *Stundenthema* is based upon materials developed by Jens-Peter Green (Green & Grittner, 1990), though presented in its current form here for the first time. Finally, Partner Work is more or less universal in language courses.

Tool 1: The Integrated Brain

Many new TAs have difficulties realizing, first, that their students are not necessarily like themselves and, second, that there are different kinds of learning. For this reason it is necessary to discuss with TAs what the profession knows — or thinks it knows — about the workings of the human brain.

Language does not exist in any one special place in the brain. Thanks to neurophysiological research, however, we have some idea how the brain divides certain kinds of language function. It appears that language input is processed (studied, analyzed, stored, and retrieved) in the left hemisphere of the brain, but that the motivation to learn and use language resides in the right hemisphere (Brown, 1989, p. 40). This reflects our natural inclination (observed in our own experiences in dealing with our native language) to absorb lots of "raw input" and, only later, to analyze it. Language classes tend to operate in the opposite direction, teaching "all the nuts and bolts at the beginning" and saving the "feel" for the language until later (Brown, 1989, p. 41). Understanding how humans function as integrated learning organisms is critical to becoming a good teacher, whether in the new paradigm or in any one of the old ones.

The Integrated Brain (see Tool 1, p. 144) attempts to illustrate how each of the brain hemispheres views the world. The left hemisphere views the world as an organized, paradigmatic, rule-governed system; it is orderly, as the Tool itself shows with its neat lines and left-to-right, top-to-bottom printing. The right hemisphere sees things as global, holistic, unique, experimental; it is chaotic, as the Tool itself demonstrates with ragged lines and goofy turns of phrase, some running down the right side of page, others with different kinds of type faces. The left brain seeks certainty, the right brain enjoys risk. The left approves orderliness, the right encourages innovation. However, little, especially language, can be learned unless the entire brain is engaged. While it may be necessary to memorize grammar rules and vocabulary lists (left), language still must be used in real-life situations (right). To emphasize the one without reference to the other is to deny long-term learning. In short, the left side of the brain may drive the car and read the map, but the right side tells us where to go and what to do when we get there.

Each of us has a brain that, in general, has a preference for operating on one side or the other. As a result, there are teachers and students who prefer to know the rules before proceeding with an activity. There are also teachers and students who prefer to try things out first before discussing the rules. Oxford, Ehrmann, and Lavine (1991, pp. 11–17) speak of Analytic (left-brain) Teachers and Global (right-brain) Teachers, whose teaching styles influence the classrooms they oversee. It is thus important for TAs to recognize their preferences and accept the reality of learning differences in their students.

Tool 2:   The Triangle

The language-learning Triangle (see Tool 2, p. 148) is an equilateral triangle, which from an engineering and architectural viewpoint is one of the most stable of geometric figures. In the middle are the learners (L) of the target language. Above them is the Topic (To), which is any real-life communicative situation. Topic can mean, for example, asking for and receiving directions to a hotel in Berlin; extending, accepting, and rejecting an invitation to a party in Barcelona; ordering a meal in a Thai restaurant; describing the contents of a high school locker in Sun Prairie, Wisconsin; telling students that Professor James will not be in class today and that they should listen to you for five minutes as you give them the assignment for tomorrow; and so on. The statement of a Topic answers for learners the question, Why should they be involved in the learning enterprise at all?

A caveat: Topic does not mean grammar! The *imparfait* in French is not a Topic, nor is the *Dativ* in German, nor is the *niph'al* in Hebrew, nor is the honorific *o*-prefix in Japanese. Where, then, is grammar in the Triangle? Text (Tx) is grammar, as well as vocabulary and idiomatic expressions, labels on bottles, captions under photographs, letters from friends, editorials in newspapers, stage plays on television, novels on audiotape, and poems written on posters. Text in the context of the Triangle answers the question, What "raw language" — the words and phrases and idioms that one may hear or read when confronted with actual users of the language — should be learned?

Task (Ts) means the same as in everyday English, that is, something to do with what you know. Historically, the primary task of learners has been to sit, to listen, and to fill in blanks, while the primary task of teachers (Tr) has been to stand, and to talk, and to provide the blanks to be filled in. The classroom in the 1990s looks quite different. Teachers give directions, walk around the room, distribute cue cards, and answer questions — in other words, use a variety of teaching techniques and strategies to present and guide learning (Tc). Learners look at pictures and write captions for them, talk to neighbors and summarize what they learn from them, write short descriptive paragraphs and read them aloud to the rest of the group. Do teachers still lecture? Yes, but not every day. Do students still fill in worksheets and hand them in? Yes, quite often, in fact, but again not every day nor as the sole activity for a given period of time.

Tool 3: P/Review-Prime-Practice-Presentation

P/Review-Prime-Practice-Presentation (see Tool 3, p. 148) is based on a set of handouts given to new TAs during orientation sessions adapted from Knop's Overview-Prime-Drill-Check sequence (Knop, 1982) at the University of Wisconsin–Madison. During orientation TAs prepare single-activity microteaching lessons to practice before their peers. Once in the classroom, however, lessons are expected to demonstrate the four stages presented in this model.

Although born during the 1970s, the sequence stands up well to scrutiny in the 1990s. In an attempt to update our understanding of teacher–learner behavior based upon Knop's model, I have renamed three of the four steps as follows, keeping Prime the same:

P/Review • Prime • Practice • Presentation

Before students begin work they must be reminded of what they already know (Review, the "R" in P/Review) and be told what they are about to work with (Preview, the "P" in P/Review). Then they must be shown a sample of what they are about to do (Prime) in the form of simple instructions or a picture about which a story is to be told, or a brief rehearsal of the material they are to use. Practice is the point where learners take what the teacher has shown them and try it out on their own, either individually or, better yet, with one or more partners. The final phase, Presentation, is perhaps the most critical of all, since this is the opportunity for learners to have their performance compared with the TA's and other learners' expectations.

In any event, when superimposed on the Triangle, P/Review states the Topic. The Text is more or less already given as the content of the lesson. The remaining three steps, Prime-Practice-Presentation, represent Task. When things start to go wrong during instruction, it is often because the instructor has left out one or more of these four steps.

Tool 4: *Stundenthema*

Parallel to the P/Review-Prime-Practice-Presentation sequence is *Stundenthema* (see Tool 4, p. 150), presented in its current form at a number of workshops between 1987 and 1990 by Jens-Peter Green. Literally "hour topic," the concept of *Stundenthema* is used in Germany as part of the training of language teachers for the secondary schools. It is a valuable concept for any teacher, since it focuses on what students should be doing in a given hour and what a teacher should be doing to help students do what they do. There may be more than one topic in a class hour, but if there is none, either explicitly stated (e.g., on the blackboard) or implicitly assumed (e.g., by the sequence of clearly interrelated activities), the hour can become quite "unparadigmatic," that is, with no clear pattern or focus.

Stundenthema has six major components: (1) objectives for the hour, (2) productive and receptive vocabulary collocation (i.e., use of words in phrases and sentences), (3) anticipated learner difficulties and potential learning aids, (4) possibilities for either shortening or lengthening the activity, (5) planned sequence of activities in instruction, and (6) material for presentation on the blackboard. Note that different instructional steps can be followed, starting with presentation or simple statement of the task, and ending with an assignment prepared at home and presented in class. Note too that there are different kinds of learner–teacher interaction, such as lecture or demonstration as well as partner work or individual response. The key words presented under the columns "I(nstructional) Step," "Planned T(eacher) Behavior," "Expected S(tudent) Behavior," and "Media" are by no means meant to be exhaustive. What is important are the four steps that precede the teaching sequence (step 5) for the particular hour (objectives for the hour in the various skill areas, vocabulary collocations, anticipated learning difficulties and learning aids, and possibilities for shortening or expanding the hour), plus the one step (step 6) after you prepare the sequence, namely, what you show students on the board or on the overhead. Recognition and implementation of these six parts of a typical class hour are essential to good teaching.

Tool 5: Partner Work

Partner Work (see Tool 5, p. 151) appears under a number of different terms, including small group activities (Omaggio, 1986, pp. 200–207) and peer tutoring (Scarcella & Oxford, 1992, p. 157). Whatever the term, if TAs learn to use only one tool from the new paradigm toolkit, this is the one. There are two reasons for its importance: (1) Partner Work is completely student-oriented, and (2) Partner Work operates extremely well in a classroom setting. There is also a third reason, namely, if you get it wrong, instruction turns into chaos, turning you and students off to partner work as a classroom technique. No textbook, no workbook, no worksheet, no quiz, no examination, no computer software, no videotape, no videodisc, no *501 German* (or *French* or *Spanish* or *Russian* or *Italian*) *Verbs* with all the trimmings can do what two people together can do with the language. Language is learned primarily through its interactions, not through its printed forms alone. Students can interact best in a target-language environment with others who are also learning to interact.

The main difficulty with Partner Work is that most people think it involves nothing more than giving students directions, allotting them a certain amount of time for the activity (10 minutes, perhaps), leaving the students alone, and then going on to something else entirely different once the time is used up. Many teachers see Partner Work as a kind of pedagogical babysitting, something to be assigned while the teacher does a silent mantra in hopes of receiving inspiration for the next fill-in-the-blank exercise. Thus, I have offered a one-page set of directions for setting up, conducting, and following through on Partner Work. The key is focus: focus on activity, focus on limits, focus on outcome. If the focus is clear, then Partner Work takes its proper place in the new paradigm, as an integral part of the arsenal of learning materials and teaching techniques, and especially as a way of personalizing language (Swaffar, Arens & Byrnes, 1991, p. 12).

Conclusion

According to *New Lexicon Webster's Dictionary of the English Language*, the term "paradigm" refers to "an example serving as a pattern," as well as to the traditional definition of "a conjugation or declension serving to demonstrate the inflection of a word" (1989, p. 727). The expression "new paradigm," as presented by Swaffar, Arens, and Byrnes (1991), might thus seem contradictory in the context of communicative language learning. Nothing is really "new" about what is presented in this chapter, except, perhaps, for our willingness to use it. Nothing is really "paradigmatic" about it either, especially if we use the term in the sense of the prescriptively formulaic.

Rather, the "new paradigm" refers to a set of guidelines for action to be taken when TAs interact with students in a language classroom as well as when students interact with the language itself. In a world of continually changing intellectual, professional, and economic needs, language teaching needs to become constantly "novelly paradigmatic." Teachers now believe, we hope, in the value of using authentic texts for oral and written work, connecting grammatical phenomena to the production of paragraph-length texts, asking students to work with grammar rules independently and then reporting back what they have learned and where they need assistance, spending class time doing simulations and partner work, and setting up activities that call for L2 contexts, all of which are recommended by Swaffar, Arens, and Byrnes (1991, p. 12). In the final analysis, then, if the expression "new paradigm," and the tools we develop to implement it, help us build a solid foundation under our language teaching, we can call it what we like.

Works Cited

Altman, Rick, Anny Ewing, James P. Pusack, Becky Bohde, Sue K. Otto & Patrick Shoemaker. *PICS Videoguidelines*. Iowa City: University of Iowa Press, 1990.

Brown, H. Douglas. *A Practical Guide to Language Learning. A Fifteen-Week Program of Strategies for Success*. New York: McGraw-Hill, 1989.

Green, Jens-Peter & Frank M. Grittner. *German for Communication: A Teacher's Guide*. Madison: Wisconsin Department of Public Instruction, 1990.

Knop, Constance K. "Overview, Prime, Drill, Check: An Approach to Guiding Student-Teachers in Lesson Planning." *Foreign Language Annals* 15 (1982): 91–94.

Legutke, Michael K. (Ed.). *German for the Learner-Centered Classroom*. Reports from Teachers for Teachers. Olympia, WA: Office of Superintendent of Public Instruction, 1991.

Magnan, Sally Sieloff (Ed.). *Challenges in the 1990s for College Foreign Language Programs*. AAUSC Issues in Language Program Direction 1990. Boston: Heinle & Heinle Publishers, 1991.

New Lexicon Webster's Dictionary of the English Language. New York: Lexicon Publications, 1989.

Omaggio, Alice C. *Teaching Foreign Languages in Context: Proficiency-Oriented Instruction*. Boston: Heinle & Heinle Publishers, 1986.

Oxford, Rebecca L. *Language Learning Strategies: What Every Teacher Should Know*. New York: Newbury House Publishers, 1990.

———, Madeline E. Ehrman & Robert Z. Lavine. "'Style Wars': Teacher–Student Style Conflicts in the Language Classroom." In Magnan, 1991: 1–26.

Scarcella, Robin C. & Rebecca L. Oxford. *The Tapestry of Language Learning. The Individual in the Communicative Classroom*. Boston: Heinle & Heinle Publishers, 1992.

Swaffar, Janet K., Katherine M. Arens & Heidi Byrnes. *Reading for Meaning: An Integrated Approach to Language Learning*. Englewood Cliffs, NJ: Prentice-Hall, 1991.

Teschner, Richard V. (Ed.). *Assessing Foreign Language Proficiency of Undergraduates*. AAUSC Issues in Language Program Direction 1991. Boston: Heinle & Heinle Publishers, 1991.

Appendix

The New Paradigm Toolkit

TOOL I

THE INTEGRATED BRAIN

The Integrated Brain...

- is a sophisticated PATTERN DETECTOR.
- processes stimuli MULTIMODALLY, SIMULTANEOUSLY.
- thrives on HIGH-VOLUME INPUT.
- requires COMMUNICATION to actualize its potential.
- needs REALITY-BASED FEEDBACK for optimal functioning.
- craves an atmosphere that encourages RISK.

Characteristically, the

LEFT BRAIN HEMISPHERE:

1. Is verbal.
2. Is logical.
3. Operates sequentially.
4. Reasons part to whole.
5. Exhibits strong time and schedule orientation.
6. Defends status quo, the familiar.
7. Resists change, risk-taking.
8. Finds faults, sees problems, reasons why an idea won't work.
9. Sets limits, acts as "gatekeeper."
10. Is defensive, may use sarcasm to ward off intruding ideas.

In contrast, the

RIGHT BRAIN HEMISPHERE

excels at

SPATIAL Relationships

COLOR!

music

HUMOR.

It is

nonsequential &

non | evaluative

and ⟹

deals in

το κινητικον, *the* visual, the auditory,

kinesthetic = haptic & is → open → to 👆 **NEW**

experiences and risks. It believes anything — but (*ANYTHING* — is possible! Time orientation is:

 sort of approximate

 kind of relative. →→→→ It is trusting.

It is creative.

∞∞∞∞∞∞∞∞∞∞∞∞∞∞∞∞∞∞∞∞∞∞∞∞

THE LEFT HEMISPHERE

▼ lectures on familiar material
▼ explains new material in terms of old
▼ commands the individual to conform
▼ rationalizes inconsistencies
▼ discusses rationales
▼ argues specifics
▼ debates principles
▼ reasons things through before acting
▼ calculates optimum approaches
▼ reduces phenomena to rules
▼ organizes everything.

Left-brained students have to fill in verb paradigm charts.

Left-brained teachers have to explain adjective endings.

Bir varmış, bir yokmuş.
Allahın kulu çokmuş...

Das Ewig-Weibliche

As for the right hemisphere...
• draws • shows
• plays games
• makes diagrams
• elicits activity •
gesticulates
pictures
well, she
demonstrates •
tells stories ⇒
• puts on skits •
• gives examples • illustrates •
takes foolish risks • experiments •
accepts error as a natural event • talks A LOT.

Ζωή μου, σᾶς αγαπῶ

❖
❖
❖ Right-brained students love to sing songs by Udo Lindenberg. ❧ ❧ ❧ Right-brained teachers love to read student rewrites of *Märchen*. ❧ ❀ ❀

Note: The above tool is based upon a handout used by Carol Ann Pesola of Concordia College (Minnesota) during presentations at the Central States Conference and elsewhere. It is reprinted here with her permission.

TOOL 2

THE TRIANGLE

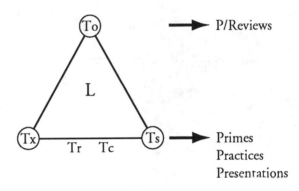

To = Topic, theme, interest — *Stundenthema* (WHY)

Tx = Text, words, visuals, etc., user "chunk" of language (WHAT)

Ts = Task, activity, learner "product" of language (HOW)

Tr = Teacher (WHO)

Tc = (Teaching) technique (HOW TO)

L   = Learner (FOR WHOM)

TOOL 3

P/REVIEW-PRIME-PRACTICE-PRESENTATION

(Based on Knop [1982])

1) P/Review (cf. "Overview")

   a) State the purpose or topic of the activity.

   b) Relate it to known material.

   c) State the outcome of the activity.

   Example: Teacher — "You have already learned to count from 1 to 10. Today you'll learn to count from 10 to 100. Then we'll do an inventory of the objects in the classroom."

2) Prime (cf. "Prime")

   a) Go through the material once. Use visuals to set the scene, role-play to show who is saying what, etc.

   b) Clarify procedures: are students to listen? repeat? imitate gestures? work with neighbor? work alone?

   c) Show how the activity is to be conducted. Give at least three examples of the kind of outcome you expect.

   Example: Teacher — "Listen to the numbers from 10 to 20 (30, 40,...). Now repeat each one after me." Student — "10, 11, 12, 13, 21, 22,...57, 58,...."

3) Practice (cf. "Drill")

   a) For each chunk of language, encourage students to use various techniques for developing their material, such as: (1) Gestures, (2) Objects, (3) Pictures, (4) Other members of the class, (5) Key words to frame the language to use, (6) Logical sequence, such as in a Gouin series.

   b) Give one or two examples.

   c) Set time limit.

Example: Teacher — "Here is a list of objects in the classroom. Go around the room and count the number of books, chairs, clocks,…that you see. You have three minutes." Student — (takes worksheet with list of items and goes around classroom to do inventory).

4) Presentation ("Check")

Call on individuals or groups of individuals to present their material.

Example: Teacher — "Tell us about various things in the classroom." Student — "Well, I count 32 chairs, 30 books, 20 pencils, and 16 jackets. And, of course, there are 22 students in the room!"

TOOL 4

STUNDENTHEMA

Step 1 → Objectives for the hour in
- Listening comprehension
- Reading comprehension
- Speaking
- Writing
- Culture

Step 2 → Productive/receptive vocabulary collocations

Step 3 → Anticipated difficulties/learning aids

Step 4 → Possibilities for shortening or expanding materials

Step 5 → Planned sequence of activities

Step 6 → Planned blackboard layout

I Step	Planned T Behavior	Expected S Behavior	Media

Lead-in*
Introduction*
Activation*
Statement of
  the topic*
Associogram
Transition
Presentation
Evaluation†
Reading
Fill-in
Homework†
  • giving
  • collecting
Spot check†
Calling on
  students†
	Lecture
	Demonstration
	Directions
		Individual
		  work
		Partner work
		Group work
			Blackboard
			Realia
			Film
			Slides
			Letters
			Cassettes
			Filmstrips
			Worksheets
			Other Students
			Photos
			Pictures
			Toys and other
			  props

[I = instruction   S = student   T = teacher]
* = "P/Review"
† = "Presentation"
Everything else is either "Prime" or "Practice."

TOOL 5

Partner Work

Before

1) Set Task: "You will tell your partner what you did last weekend.
Tell him or her at least three things you did, using at
least three different verbs."

2) Set Outcome: "You will report to the class what your partner told you.
You will then write up what you learned in 20 to
30 words for homework tomorrow."

3) Set Limits: "You have three minutes. Go!"

During

1) Move from group to group and *listen.*

2) Give guidance when requested, such as answering questions, suggesting
alternatives, encouraging use of dictionary, etc.

3) Announce final minute ("You have one more minute!"). Allow extra
time if students are still on task.

After (at least three groups report)

1) Listen — do not interrupt — while students report.

2) Have students repeat what they just said, even if — especially if — it is
already clear and distinct.

3) Encourage other students to react (correct, comment, ask questions,
and so forth).

"Poof! You're a Teacher!": Using Introspective Data in the Professional Development of Beginning TAs

Mary E. Wildner-Bassett
University of Arizona

When the fall semester starts, many beginning TAs in our language programs will be on the "other side of the desk" for the first time. They are not only beginning graduate students; many of them are absolute beginners in the role of teacher. While they have indeed chosen to pursue language and literature teaching as a profession, often they have not thought much more about teaching language classes than to see it as a means to an end, a method of earning enough money to support their graduate studies in order to go on to their first "real job" at another university. Our task as TA supervisors, or better, as "language teaching and culture specialists" (Rivers, 1992, p. 299) is to guide these bright and enthusiastic people into roles as professional teachers. We want to help them move, in the shortest possible time, from the perspective of a language student to that of a competent professional whose calling is the teaching of language. This formidable task can be accomplished so well at the University of Arizona that many of our advanced TAs are better, more flexible, and even more knowledgeable teachers for beginning and intermediate language classes than some of our more experienced colleagues.

The purpose of this chapter is to examine the process of leading beginning graduate students to the "other side of the desk" in a way that optimizes the time and opportunities we have to accomplish this task so that all our TAs have the tools to continue this development beyond the realm of our immediate supervision. My focus will be the professional development of beginning TAs through the use of learning logs to enhance awareness in four areas:

1) Professional development as an ongoing process

2) Teacher and learner roles and the change of roles in which they must become actively engaged

3) Teaching anxiety and ways to reduce it

4) Learning styles and strategies and ways that this knowledge can be utilized in the classroom.

All four of these topics are frequently discussed in the professional literature. The essential notion is that teaching is a research-based endeavor that can be constantly optimized by engaging in informal and formal, action-based, theory- or model-oriented research for oneself and for the profession. These ideas are the leitmotif of this contribution and of the professional development endeavors that it reports.

Opportunities for Professional Development

The professional development concepts discussed below take place in three stages of TA training in the Department of German at the University of Arizona: a 10-day presemester workshop required of all beginning TAs; a one-semester, three-credit graduate course on "Issues in Foreign Language Teaching" required of all beginning TAs, and one-to-one observation and supervision meetings held several times each semester. Further opportunities derive from participation in the annual Foreign Language Teachers' Symposium that takes place at the university with a nationally known keynote speaker in foreign language pedagogy and with language-specific sessions on different topics. Finally, perhaps one of the most fertile opportunities for development are the weekly, course-specific coordination meetings in which all aspects of teaching as a professional endeavor are "cussed and discussed."

TA Learning Logs as a Core for Professional Development

The best tool for all these aspects of professional development is the use of TA learning logs, a type of journal written by the beginning TAs as they engage in the opportunities described above. Using learning logs for TA professional development is one of the best ideas to have come along in many years. Porter, Goldstein, Leatherman, and Conrad (1990, pp. 227–40) outline the ideas upon which our program's use of learning logs for beginning TAs is based. The assignment is, in our version, a weekly entry of at least five hundred words for 12 weeks of the semester. But most TAs go far beyond the minimum assignment. The entries can be characterized as anything from brief, very formal papers to heart-rending and very personal pleas for help in personal and professional matters. TAs are very articulate about many of the key issues facing them as they engage in their professional development. The process of journal entry writing, along with thorough reading and commentary by the TA's supervisor, becomes a source of more intense and personalized exchange than could ever be accomplished in any classroom, group, or even one-on-one discussion. TAs learn to focus their own ideas and to respect their own experiences and thoughts by virtue of putting them on paper. Many also write about the process of writing the learning log itself. They realize that this form of introspective data represents a wealth of material that can help them in many ways. As this discussion proceeds, the value of this kind of data to all concerned will become evident. It will also become evident that the journal entries of the TAs best articulate the concepts under discussion. I will employ pertinent quotes from actual TA journals to illustrate the importance of this type of introspective data to language teaching and culture specialists. The citations include the initials of the TAs, all of whom have given their permission for the inclusion of their comments in this chapter, and the year of the journal entry.

The first example of the entries illustrates their value:

> Here as I write my last entry, I find that there is no rhyme or reason to my entries. I just grabbed on to something I thought I could talk about. But these entries showed me where my interests lie, made me organize my thoughts and ask why. In many ways it was therapeutic, and it has helped me not let most of the major concerns escape me until I've come to terms with them. [JH, 1991.]

Bailey (1990, pp. 223–24) points out that what she calls the "diary's awareness-raising function" is a very important one that cannot be replaced by any other mode of inquiry or, in the terms of this discussion, of professional development. While it is true that some TAs may not be comfortable with introspective writing, they do always have the option of discussing something they have read or of recording their thoughts about topics from graduate courses in pedagogy or the like. The learning-log process is invaluable for all of those who are involved. From the supervisor's perspective, it is an enormous source of insight, critical awareness, and sometimes flattering feedback about programmatic or supervisory issues, as well as about each TA's professional development. No term paper or other written assignment can accomplish the overriding goals of professional development for TAs as well as the learning log.

Teacher and Learner Roles: Easing the Transition

One of the primary concerns of TAs as they begin their teaching assignments is the reality of actually becoming teachers and the implications that this role has for them personally. As Wright (1987, p. 11) points out, language learning in the classroom is an extremely complex activity that consists of many factors, each of which can contribute to the specific roles that individuals adopt in the classroom. Before most TAs can even begin to become fully engaged in the professional development process, they have to struggle with the idea that they have actually become teachers and to wrestle with their own interpretation of this new role for themselves. One beginning TA describes in her journal a struggle with the role of teacher:

> It is difficult to explain, but I first need to get an overview of what I am actually doing, or a feeling for what is going on in the classroom, before I can be calm enough to organize my own teaching. I need to establish myself as a teacher and feel comfortable in this role in order to focus on my teaching. [BH, 1990.]

The way that each TA adjusts to the idea of becoming a teacher and "feeling comfortable in the role" depends very much on the individual's learning history and on what Wright (1987, p. 11) calls the "social and psychological 'baggage' that participants [in the group activity of a language classroom] bring with them." Culturally specific views of the status, rights, duties, and obligations of "the teacher" play a major role in these perceptions. Each TA's own assessments of his or her abilities in the language to be taught, of the "right" to be in graduate school or to be teaching others, and especially of the issues of the power relationships and the task of assigning grades and evaluating others, determine how smooth the transition into the role of teacher will be for the beginning TA. What makes professional development in this area particularly challenging is that the perceptions of the role of teacher are thoroughly bound to value judgments and to issues of self-esteem that go beyond the classroom. Many TAs have a very ambiguous relationship to the power structure of the university classroom and to finding themselves in a role that is traditionally more powerful and of a higher status (in the eyes of their students) than what they are used to. What is essential from a professional development point of view is that TAs become aware of the concepts of power and social distance and the ways that these issues are an essential part of the classroom structure. Our role as supervisors is, of course, not to dictate the level of social distance or to exaggerate issues of the power structure in the language classroom, but to make these ideas explicit in our discussions of the classroom and to guide TAs into establishing their own classroom roles.

Pennington (1990) suggests some excellent exercises to help guide beginning teachers toward uncovering attitudes about students and about teaching, and several of the suggestions in Wright (1987) are also pertinent. Pennington, for example, suggests exercises through which new teachers explore their own experiences as language learners or discuss the essential conditions for a class, the ideal student, or what constitutes effective teaching. Wright describes suggestions for in-service programs, including several stages where teachers identify beliefs and attitudes about language learning, discuss links between values and behavior in the role of a teacher, or observe and give feedback on actual classroom lessons that reflect on the role of the teacher and on systems of values and beliefs. Certainly these or similar exercises can be found in many professional development opportunities for TAs. The essence of these types of activities should be placed, whenever possible, on the issues of power and status and general values and attitudes as they relate to the role the TAs assume as teachers.

Another citation from the introspective data of TAs themselves serves to illustrate the importance of these activities. In this insightful entry the same TA cited above discusses her awareness, at the end of the first semester of teaching, of the power relationships in the classroom.

Being a teacher also implies having a certain amount of power. "Power" to me has a slightly negative connotation. It seems to imply injustice and rigidity. If the teacher chooses to, s/he can really make the students feel very uncomfortable and maybe even scared in class. S/he can simply pick on students, always letting them know how imperfect they are. There are these little ways of giving it back to those students who have been getting on your nerves all along. [BH, 1990.]

After this section of "true confessions" about the temptations of the power of the role of the teacher, this same TA goes on to write:

> [After a particularly good practice session], most of the students came up with [very good] sentences. I really like this, as I did not have to stand there as the figure of authority, giving them the rules of the game and sanctioning those who violated them....Of course I know that learning to take up responsibility for themselves is a process they have to go through. I cannot expect them to walk out of high school and into my classroom, and be able to stand on their own feet right away. I feel that I have only recently gone through these stages myself. Maybe we are never really done, as we constantly develop and learn new things. [BH, 1990.]

The exercises in Wright and Pennington cited above, and related ones adapted for our particular program, have been very successful in helping new TAs become aware of these basic concepts. They learn that classroom roles of teachers are reflections of values, beliefs, and attitudes that contribute greatly to expectations about behavior in the role relationships involved in the classroom. One TA sums up some of her own thoughts about these awareness-raising activities in the following journal entry:

> Our activities and discussions with the other TAs during the last [orientation] week about different attitudes of students and the roles of teachers have brought me to the conclusion that there are "German" and "American" views of these two positions....There are definite and essential differences in attitudes toward the teaching profession, in the practical orientation and in interests in the teachers as people. [AK, 1990, German native — translated from German.]

These perceptive comments by a TA just entering the classroom after a short but intensive orientation in which teacher and learner roles are central themes show the value of awareness raising. By virtue of the exercises and discussions outlined above, cultural conflicts can be avoided, or at least made much milder in their effects. Jorden (1992, p. 145) writes that when foreign language teachers are themselves native speakers of the language being taught, they bring to the classroom the target-culture mind-set. The degree of their experience with the learners' home culture certainly affects class-room interaction, but many continue "to follow their native pedagogical paradigm to the letter" (p. 145). She goes on to emphasize that the influence of acquired culture in the language classroom should be carefully examined, even in cases where the differences may be less extreme: "[I] magine cultures in which teachers are recognized as absolute authorities, are expected to transmit knowledge down to their students, are not to be questioned or challenged, and are certainly not subject to evaluation by the learners. What happens when such teachers face a class of American students?" If those teachers had the opportunity for awareness raising and peer discussions, role-plays, and reports from more experienced TAs from their home cultures, they would be more aware of the differences in the classroom situation, more able to assess them, and more prepared to establish their own new attitudes, new values, and a new teacher role that takes both their native culture and the American classroom culture into consideration.

One aspect of the roles of teachers and students that has, to my knowledge, received little direct attention, is the issue of the interaction of teacher and student roles with the cultural specificity of gender roles and attitudes toward gender. As Tannen (1990, p. 42) points out, women and men view and take part in conversational interactions in very different ways:

> If women speak and hear a language of connection and intimacy, while men speak and hear a language of status and independence, then communication between men and women can be like cross-cultural communication, prey to a clash of conversational styles. Instead of different dialects, it has been said they speak different genderlects.

Tannen (1990, p. 41) cites a study from the *Chronicle of Higher Education* in which male and female university professors were asked why they had chosen the teaching profession. All four men referred to independence as their main motive, while the two women emphasized the opportunity to influence students in a positive way. TAs are no less protected from cross-cultural genderlect differences than are the rest of us involved in the profession. What is important for them to know is that these differences do exist, and that by working with this knowledge they can understand some of the undercurrents in classroom interactions that may be related to gender differences, to cultural differences, or to both. Knowledge *is* power in this context, and by giving beginning TAs this knowledge, or self-awareness, many problems related to their assuming the role of teacher can be avoided.

To conclude this discussion about assuming the role of teacher and of the complexities that this process entails, I would like to cite two more instances of experiential support for these thoughts. The first is from a report by a language teaching and culture specialist colleague. She discusses the exponential difficulties that can arise from the combination of cross-cultural and gender differences in the case of a male Japanese TA who had a female professor as his supervisor. He was, by personality, culture, and gender, not able to accept this situation, would not cooperate with his supervisor, and was very ineffective in the classroom. The clash of sex roles and cultures was too much for him, and he failed to deal with them adequately so as to continue with his chosen profession. The second situation was described by a TA in the German program who found it very difficult to be taken seriously by her class — which was, by an accident of registration, mostly male. They engaged in a constant power struggle that became very trying for the TA. She described the situation in her journal as follows:

> I really wanted them to like me....The class turned into chaos. They never took me seriously any more. I had problems getting them to pay attention and to do their homework. They thought of me as a peer, rather than a teacher. I lost my respect as a figure of authority, and basically by the end of the semester they did what they wanted to do....Now, I think that students have more respect for a teacher and will like a teacher if there is order and fairness in the classroom. [CM, 1991.]

The two painful experiences cited here show that conflicts related to teacher–student roles, target versus instructional culture roles, and gender-specific roles are all serious issues in the classroom. Professional development for beginning TAs is necessary to raise awareness of these situations and to give the TAs some tools for understanding the role that relationships play in the classroom.

Language Teaching Anxiety

The next of the four areas of professional awareness reflected in the learning logs is the complex issue of teaching anxiety. For many beginning TAs, being *in front* of a class is the most terrifying thing they have ever had to do; indeed, the anxiety level seems to remain high for many language teachers.

In a summary form, the following will characterize and give examples of a programmatic approach to reducing language classroom anxiety by promoting coping strategies for both TAs and their students. These strategies are coupled with concrete activities for developing communication strategies for the speaking and listening skills during the first and second semesters.

Language learners and their TAs experience apprehension, worry, even dread during, before, or after their classes, exams, and oral interviews and activities. While there certainly may be other reasons for this behavior, the main one is anxiety. Horwitz, Horwitz, and Cope (1991, p. 29) report clinical experience at the University of Texas showing that anxiety centers on the two basic task requirements of foreign language learning: listening and speaking.

> Difficulty in or fear of speaking in class is probably the most frequently cited concern of the anxious foreign language learner....Anxious learners also complain of difficulties discriminating the sounds and structures of a target language message,...[or of] grasping the content of a target language message. Many [students] claim that they have little or no idea of what the teacher is saying in extended target language utterances.

Their TAs know that this is the case, yet they are at a loss as to what to do about the situation. The TAs are often so bound up by their own anxiety levels that they are blind to the truth that their students are suffering equal or worse anxiety. Teachers, supervisors, and curriculum developers generally have two options available to them when dealing with anxious individuals: they can help them learn to cope with the existing anxiety-laden situation *or* they can make the learning context less stressful.

In addition to general and specific awareness raising, a concrete way to reduce the performance and general language-use anxieties discussed above is to focus on the processes and strategies involved in both speaking and listening. These processes need to be broken down for TAs into a set of achievable goals, which then lead to cumulative language competence and strategic competence. We can thus give TAs the tools both for overcoming their own anxiety about engaging in foreign language interaction and for interacting successfully with their students. As with any activity, the more success TAs and students feel they can achieve, the lower their level of stress will be when they engage in the activity the next time around.

TAs are often anxious about their own ability to teach in the target language. For TAs who themselves are still polishing their skills in the target language, their anxieties are very similar to those of their students, if on a higher level of understanding. For TAs who are native speakers, their anxiety usually centers more around being able to "tone down" their own language to be understandable for their students, or to understand their own students' questions and comments in English or about the target language. Once again, a TA has expressed this anxiety and these difficulties very clearly in a journal entry:

> In the classroom…very soon it becomes obvious that it is hard to answer the things you always knew [about your own language]. I certainly have the competence but how do I bring my points across if I am not aware of it? This lack of awareness struck me suddenly this week when a student asked me about [a form of the genitive]….So in my opinion it is definitely not easier to teach your own language but it is rather very complicated. [AK, 1990.]

Another TA, a nonnative speaker, expresses his anxieties in a similar situation. The vocabulary he uses and his description of the situation reveal the ongoing anxiety involved in the situations encountered in the classroom, though he is also capable of a measure of self-irony in the end.

> Last night [a student] pointed out a mistake I made in front of the entire class….It was all because of a question that a student had asked me. After the [student] pointed out the error, I was not willing to accept any more questions and I simply continued on with the lesson as though nothing had phased [sic] me. This in the end may have been very bad because it might make the students more apprehensive in the future to ask me questions….On the one hand I want to encourage the students to ask a lot of questions, but on the other hand I am inclined to take control of the class in order to avoid being drilled by a student who might want to know something I do not know. Is this the fear of

every teacher? Is there a way to overcome this fear? Will I be fired for admitting that I'm not perfect? I'll wait and see. [DW, 1990.]

Oxford (1990, pp. 163–73) lists three general types of affective strategies that can be applied to speaking and listening situations in order to reduce the anxiety levels of the participants. One group of these strategies uses progressive relaxation, deep breathing, or even meditation. Another employs music. These ideas are familiar to most of us as among the basic ideas of suggestopedia. The third group of strategies consolidated by Oxford concerns self-encouragement. These techniques are used in our program in modified form and at the discretion of the instructors. In presemester training, TAs learn strategies for coping with their own anxiety. The results have been very beneficial. One main effect is that merely by addressing the issues of anxiety reactions, beginning TAs feel they can "come out of the closet" with this anxiety and discuss its various forms and causes. As we saw in the second excerpt from the TA journal, the fears themselves are not the only problem, but also the anxiety of "Am I the only one?" Simply opening the discussion about TA classroom anxiety leads to a reduction of anxiety levels. Oxford also suggests making positive statements privately to encourage beliefs that individuals can accomplish the tasks set for them, that they can be confident about their progress, that they will get their point across when teaching, and that they can learn from their mistakes. This suggestion is followed constantly throughout the duration of the relationships between TAs with each other and with their supervisor.

"Style Wars" Revisited: Learning and Teaching Styles and Strategies for TAs

The issues of learning and teaching style are extremely important ones. But it seems that TAs are not usually aware of these issues until the concepts are discussed and illustrated in their professional development opportunities. Once they have learned about these concepts, though, they become a major element in the learning log entries. In the first annual volume of the American Association of University Supervisors, Coordinators, and Directors of Language Programs, a contribution by Oxford, Ehrman, and Lavine (1991, pp. 1–25) entitled "Style Wars: Teacher–Student Conflicts in the Language Classroom" underlines the importance of awareness raising and education for both learners and their teachers in the diversity of learning styles and the concurrent and resulting diversity of teaching styles found in the language classroom. Oxford (1990) develops these ideas with both a theoretical foundation and practical suggestions for teacher and learner education about learning strategies in the foreign language classroom. I conducted an empirical study of TA learning styles in the Department of German at the University of Arizona, summarized in the appendix, to take a close look at learning style diversity in that context. Of most interest here are comments from the TA journals about the usefulness of awareness raising and professional development on the issues of learning styles and strategies.

Considerable time during professional development sessions in our program is devoted to the ideas of learning styles and strategies, assessment of TAs' own style preferences using standardized instruments, and workshop sessions on expanding TA repertoires of teaching styles and strategies to include those preferred by more of their students. The most recent results of assessments of 11 German TAs are included in the appendix.

As evidenced by reactions in their journal writings, TAs are usually very articulate about concepts related to learning styles and see them as immensely important for their continued professional development. Here are some excerpts:

> I liked seeing how my learning style compared with the learning styles of the students I am teaching. I appreciate you[r] having us make up lesson plans for our own style and then for the opposite style. I hadn't previously given this a lot of thought, and I found the whole process very helpful....You gave me an...understanding that I need to change my teaching style every day to accommodate all types of learners. I also knew that race and gender affected learning, but I didn't know exactly how to deal with this. [JH, 1991.]

Another TA was even more excited about the concepts of "Style Wars" and learning styles and strategies. She wrote a six-page, typed journal entry about her own style and what knowing about it in detail has meant to her. She also revealed some more facts about her assessed learning style as well as about gender specificity in her entry. Her discussion of the SF (Sensing-Feeling) type and learning style also overlaps with what Tannen (1990) claims to be typical traits of women in communication. (Incidentally, all of the TAs who were assessed as SF in our limited group were women.) An excerpt from her entry:

As far as the "SF" [scale from the Myers-Briggs Type Indicator] compares with my learning styles, most of the things listed do pertain to my style. For example, it is so true that I work best when emotionally involved....People that know me say that I tend to be over[ly] dramatic when it comes to feelings and emotions and such....I was talking to a woman at Stammtisch....It was really important to me to get to the heart of the matter of how she felt. This, of course, I find a lot easier to do with women than with men. I find that other women do have a tendency to open up about their feelings more. When it comes to teaching, I am truly an "SF." I like to see the students interacting with one another and getting along. [CM, 1991.]

This entry reveals much about the elements of awareness raising as professional development for TAs as related to cognitive/learning styles and their applications in the language classroom. The approach to awareness raising about learning styles and strategies gives TAs a chance to find similarities and differences with others and to practice expanding their teaching to accommodate students' styles that are perhaps at odds with their own from the outset.

Conclusion

The general goal of contributing to the ongoing discussion of language teaching as a research-based endeavor has been the focus of these comments. The elements of the discussion have highlighted recent, pertinent literature on teacher learning logs as an essential component of TA development, especially as they relate to teacher and learner roles and classroom behavior, language teaching anxiety, gender differences as relevant to teacher roles, and learning styles and strategies as a source of diversity in the classroom. This discussion has been augmented by introspective data in the form of quotes from TA learning log entries that illustrate the points made. These entries often give new and very insightful perspectives on that discussion. This method of exploring the issues of TA supervision is itself a microcosmic approach to the essentials of TA supervision and professional development, namely, that language teaching and culture specialists as supervisors and the TAs themselves have equally valuable contributions to make toward optimizing TA development.

Works Cited

Bailey, Kathleen M. "The Use of Diary Studies in Teacher Education Programs." In Richards & Nunan, 1990: 215-26.

Horwitz, Elaine K., Michael B. Horwitz & Jo Ann Cope. "Foreign Language Classroom Anxiety." *Language Anxiety: From Theory and Research to Classroom Implications.* Ed. Elaine K. Horwitz & Dolly J. Young. Englewood Cliffs, NJ: Prentice-Hall, 1991: 27-36.

Jorden, Eleanor H. "Broadening Our Traditional Boundaries: The Less Commonly Taught and the Truly Foreign Languages." *Teaching Languages in College: Curriculum and Content.* Ed. Wilga M. Rivers. Lincolnwood, IL: National Textbook Company, 1992: 141-56.

Keefe, James W. & John S. Monk. *Learning Style Profile.* Reston, VA: National Association of Secondary School Principals, 1989.

Myers, Isabel Briggs & Katharine C. Briggs. *Myers-Briggs Type Indicator.* Palo Alto, CA: Consulting Psychologists Press, 1990.

Oxford, Rebecca L. *Language Learning Strategies: What Every Teacher Should Know.* New York: Newbury House Publishers, 1990.

———, Madeline E. Ehrman & Roberta Z. Lavine. "Style Wars: Teacher–Student Style Conflicts in the Language Classroom." *Challenges in the 1990s for College Foreign Language Programs.* Ed. Sally Sieloff Magnan. AAUSC Issues in Language Program Direction 1990. Boston: Heinle & Heinle Publishers, 1991: 1-25.

Pennington, Martha. "A Professional Development Focus for the Language Teaching Practicum." In Richards & Nunan, 1990: 132-53.

Porter, Patricia A., Lynn M. Goldstein, Judith Leatherman & Susan Conrad. "An Ongoing Dialogue: Learning Logs for Teacher Preparation." In Richards & Nunan, 1990: 227-40.

Richards, Jack C. & David Nunan (Ed.). *Second Language Teacher Education.* Cambridge Language Teaching Library. Cambridge: Cambridge University Press, 1990.

Rivers, Wilga M. "The Program Director or Coordinator, the LTCS, and the Training of College Language Instructors." *Teaching Languages in College: Curriculum and Content.* Ed. Wilga M. Rivers. Lincolnwood, IL: National Textbook Company, 1992: 295-320.

Schaefer, Robert L. & Richard B. Anderson. *The Student Edition of Minitab.* Reading, MA: Addison-Wesley, 1989.

Tannen, Deborah. *You Just Don't Understand: Women and Men in Conversation.* New York: Ballantine, 1990.

Wright, Tony. *Roles of Teachers and Learners.* Language Teaching: A Scheme for Teacher Education. Oxford: Oxford University Press, 1987.

———. "Understanding Classroom Role Relationships." In Richards & Nunan, 1990: 82–96.

Appendix

An Empirical Study of TAs' Learning Styles

The Myers-Briggs Type Indicator (MBTI — Myers & Briggs, 1990), registered trademark of Consulting Psychologists Press, Inc., served to assess the learning styles of 11 TAs in the Department of German at the University of Arizona. The research by Katharine Briggs and Isabel Briggs Myers, drawing on the work of Carl Jung, demonstrates and delineates 16 personality types, each with its own way of looking at the world and each with its own advantages and disadvantages. The instrument is used in education to identify learning styles and to promote the use of teaching approaches that complement those styles. The scales reported below are as follows:

E	= Extrovert	T	= Thinking
I	= Introvert	F	= Feeling
S	= Sensing	J	= Judging
N	= Intuitive	P	= Perceiving

It is interesting to note, at least, that of the 16 possible learning styles assessed by the instrument, the 11 TAs showed 9 different combinations of the four scales. Diversity of learning styles is thus a major factor in our classrooms and, therefore, a major issue for the professional development of our TAs.

Sex	Nationality	Results of MBTI
F	A[1]	I N F P
F	G[2]	I S T P
F	G	E S T J
F	A	E N T J
M	A	I S T J
F	A	E S F P
F	A	I S F J
F	A	I N T P
F	A	I N F P
M	A	I N Y J
F	G	E S T J

[1] A = American
[2] G = German

Additional assessments were made using the National Association of Secondary School Principals' Learning Style Profile (Keefe & Monk, 1989). A correlation study among the variables resulting from the NASSP and Myers-Briggs assessments was completed using the *Minitab* (Schaefer & Anderson, 1989) statistical software package for the personal computer. Significant correlations were found between the following pairs of variables (a preliminary interpretation of the result is also included here):

◆ GENDER ‖ GROUPING ($r = -0.706$). Males do not find group membership a strong factor in their learning styles.

◆ COUNTRY ‖ GROUPING ($r = -0.725$). German TAs do not find group membership a strong factor in their learning styles.

◆ COUNTRY ‖ SIMULTANEOUS PROCESSING ($r = 0.704$). German TAs show simultaneous processing of information as a significant factor in their learning styles.

◆ VERBAL RISK-TAKING || T/F SCALE (MBTI) ($r = -0.868$). TAs who show the "thinking" scale on the MBTI to be a preferred learning style do not tend to take verbal risks, but to think more before they speak. This is a major factor concerning accuracy and acquisition in a natural setting for language learning and teaching.

◆ VISUAL LEARNING CHANNEL || MANIPULATORY LEARNING CHANNEL ($r = -0.734$). Those who prefer the visual learning channel do not tend to use the manipulatory or haptic learning channel. Individuals who prefer manipulatory or haptic learning prefer to touch and manipulate concrete objects while they learn and discover details about them. This finding indicates validity of the assessment instrument.

◆ SOUND || ANALYTIC ($r = 0.657$). Those TAs for whom sound (or silence) is a major factor for concentration are also analytic in their learning style.

◆ SOUND || T/F SCALE (MBTI) ($r = 0.631$). Those TAs for whom sound is a major factor for concentration tend to be assessed as "Thinking" types on the MBTI scale. This supports the finding of a significant positive correlation between sound and analytic style, but from a different perspective and using a different instrument.

These findings must, of course, be viewed as preliminary. Many of the significant correlations do indicate interesting tendencies. Much more research needs to be done regarding the absolute relationships between teaching style, learning style, gender, country of origin, and all the scales mentioned here. Nevertheless, a beginning has been made here and in similar studies, so that research and theoretical work can proceed.

Sensitizing Teaching Assistants to Native-Speaker Norms in the Communicative Classroom

Nadine O'Connor Di Vito
University of Chicago

Foreign Language Acquisition as the Acquisition of Norms of Communication

The idea that knowing a language not only involves knowing its grammatical rules but also knowing how to use those rules appropriately in communication is certainly not a new one in ethnolinguistic and sociolinguistic research (Gumperz, 1968; Hymes, 1971; Labov, 1972; Sankoff, 1980 — among many others).[1] However, its growing acceptance as a fundamental principle in foreign and second language acquisition research has recently produced a rather dramatic change in attitude toward foreign and second language acquisition both as processes and as products (Bachman & Savignon, 1986; Jakabovits & Gordon, 1974; Moirand, 1990; Roulet, 1974; Swaffar, 1989; Valdman, 1982a).

While few would deny the importance of teaching grammar, many language researchers now believe that the process of language acquisition is primarily stimulated by exercises that engage the language learner in meaningful communication and allow for some possibility of self-expression, and that language acquisition implies the acquisition of both target language structures and their use in communication (Breen & Candlin, 1980; Clarke, 1991; Ellis, 1984; Kramsch, 1986; Prabhu, 1987; Rivers, 1986).

This increased emphasis on the communicative aspects of foreign language teaching and learning has resulted in a call for a reduction in the quantity of grammar covered in language classes, the inclusion of more extensive and more interesting readings, and the development of more exercises that focus on the target language as a means of communicating information, ideas, feelings, and values in particular social contexts (Kennedy, 1987; Prabhu, 1987; Rivers, 1986; Robinson, 1988; Rutherford, 1980; Terrell, 1986; Valdman, 1982b; Valdman & Warriner-Burke, 1980; van Dijk, 1981; Walz, 1989; Warriner, 1978).

Numerous textbook authors have responded to these research developments by either creating new, or revising existing, materials to include a wide variety of contextualized exercises and personalized activities that emphasize various functions or situational uses of target language structures.

The question is, of course, to what extent do these "communicative" exercises promote — or are they even potentially useful in — the acquisition of communicative skills (i.e., the means of expressing oneself in various settings) and nativelike communicative competence (i.e., the means of expressing oneself in various communicative settings according to socially acceptable native-speaker norms)? In order for our teaching assistants (TAs) to guide students most effectively in acquiring the ability to communicate according to socially acceptable norms, they must understand the relationship between "communicative" textbook exercises and native speaker norms, and know how to use their textbook rules and exercises in ways that potentially lead not only to the development of communicative skills, but also to the development of communicative competence in a foreign language.

The Value of Sociolinguistic Research in Understanding the Nature of Textbook Grammar

Despite the growing belief in the importance of contextualized exercises and communicative activities in the foreign language classroom, recent examination of language textbooks indicates that the grammar rules found in textbook exercises are still more or less the same rules presented in the textbooks of years past (Finnemann, 1987) and that present-day textbook exercises and activities still function primarily to help the language learner work through a comprehensive grammatical syllabus (Schulz, 1991). Investigation of current foreign language textbook exercises has also shown that not all "contextualized" exercises are communicative (Walz, 1989), and a growing body of research indicates that textbook exercises — even those specifically designed to promote communicative interaction — sometimes fail to reflect either spoken or written educated native-speaker norms (Bland, 1988; Calvé, 1983; Di Vito, 1991a, 1991b, 1992; Herschensohn, 1988; Holmes, 1988; Joseph, 1988; Noyau & Véronique, 1986; Scotton & Bernsten, 1988; Walz, 1986, 1989).[2] In other words, while it is probably safe to assume that textbook rules and exercises present forms that exist *somewhere* in the target language, it is less safe to assume that these rules and exercises will help the learner understand the linguistic and social contexts in which those forms are typically used.[3]

Numerous studies have cited the differences between the language emphasized in textbook exercises and the language used by native speakers in both spoken and written contexts. Although the examples discussed here will be taken from studies conducted by myself and other researchers of French native-speaker grammar, similar research exists for languages other than French (in ESL research, for example, see Bland, 1988; Holmes, 1988; Scotton & Bernsten, 1988). The three examples of such differences are as follows:

1) INTERROGATIVE SYNTAX. Research overwhelmingly indicates that subject–verb inversion in spoken French questions is restricted to a very limited number of expressions in informal contexts and is even relatively infrequent in the spoken discourse of highly educated speakers in formal contexts (Désirat & Hordé, 1988; Di Vito, 1991a; Gadet, 1989; Terry, 1970; Valdman, 1965; Walz, 1986). While this trend away from subject–verb inversion can also be seen in the evolution of written French (Di Vito, 1991c), inversion is still clearly the preferred interrogative structure in contemporary written French. Despite these findings, most French textbooks have exercises that oblige students to produce not only written questions but also spoken questions using inversion in linguistic and discourse contexts where one would be hard-pressed to find a native speaker using inversion. Of course, one might claim that inversion should be emphasized because of its higher frequency in written French and its possible (albeit infrequent) use in spoken French. However, in

exercises intended to promote the acquisition of spoken communicative competence and aural comprehension skills, emphasizing syntactic structures that are in the clear minority in any description of spoken French can only be seen as counterproductive.

2) RELATIVE PRONOUNS. Although many textbooks still present the entire range of relative pronouns in French or, at the very least, *(ce) qui, (ce) que,* and *(ce) dont,* research shows that the frequency of *(ce) dont* and all of the *lequel* variations is extremely low in both spoken and written French (Blanche-Benveniste & Jeanjean, 1987; Di Vito, 1991a; François, 1974; Gadet, 1989; Walz, 1981). Thus, while one could certainly claim that all relative pronouns are possible in the language, and therefore should be taught to language learners, it is clear that frequency of occurrence across a wide range of written genres and spoken contexts supports a selective rather than a comprehensive introduction of relative pronouns in beginning- and even intermediate-level French language classes.

3) OBJECT PRONOUNS. Again, research has shown that certain types of object pronouns are much more common than others in both spoken and written French and that double object pronouns are infrequent in written French and virtually nonexistent in French spoken by university-educated native speakers in both formal and informal contexts (Di Vito, 1991a). Nevertheless, French language textbooks continue to place equal emphasis on the different object pronoun series and often include spoken and written double object placement exercises. Again, it is true that French sentences with double object pronouns are possible and do occur; however, their extremely low frequency in both the spoken and written language makes one question the utility of emphasizing such structures in communicative textbook exercises.

These examples of research in the spoken and written uses of French language structures and the existence of similar research into other languages suggests that foreign language textbooks, in general, may inaccurately or incompletely reflect native-speaker norms, both spoken and written.

Given the comprehensive view of grammar still prevalent in current textbooks, TAs should be made aware of the continually growing number of studies describing and explaining various aspects of native-speaker language use in communication (found in journals such as *Applied Linguistics, Foreign Language Annals, French Review* [and other AAT journals],

Modern Language Journal, Language Learning, and *Studies in Second Language Acquisition*). Such research can be extremely helpful to TAs in clarifying relationships between language structures and their use in communication that are not represented in textbook exercises.

The Value of "Looking Behind" Textbook Exercises

Even without a sophisticated background in sociolinguistic and applied linguistic research, TAs can and must be trained to understand the communicative potential of the various exercises in their textbooks. To do this, they must first recognize whether a textbook exercise requires the learner to focus on: (1) grammatical or lexical structures, (2) communicative skills, or (3) native-speaker norms of communication.

As a preliminary step in such training, TAs should first look to the textbook authors to understand their reasons for pairing specific linguistic structures with particular communicative uses. If one compares current editions of various foreign language textbooks, one finds that almost all textbook authors assure the teacher that the language contained was chosen to promote the acquisition of "communicative competence." How do the authors explain or justify these claims? In reading through the prefaces of their textbooks, TAs can use the following questions as guidelines in such an inquiry:

- Do the authors state why they emphasized particular aspects of the target language *grammar* over others (e.g., general frequency in the spoken or written language, or association with a particular speech function or situational use)?

- Do the authors justify the choice of the *vocabulary* with which to present and practice the grammar rule (e.g., association of such vocabulary items with that particular grammar rule, speech function, or situational use)?

- Do the authors justify their pairing of particular linguistic structures or rules (lexical and grammatical) with particular *speech functions* or *situational uses* in their exercises (e.g., citing supportive sociolinguistic research, appealing to learners' communicative needs)?

It would be wonderful if textbook authors consistently indicated the relationship between the linguistic structures and rules they chose to present and their discourse value. Unfortunately, except for generally vague references to communicative usefulness, textbook authors rarely (if ever) state exactly why particular grammatical rules and usage rules were chosen for emphasis in a given chapter. In the absence of explicit justification for the selection and presentation of grammar rules, the TA may be tempted to judge the appropriateness of a textbook exercise by the degree to which it allows personalized, purposeful, interactive communication to occur. However, even in exercises clearly emphasizing communication skills, the question remains whether the grammar point is presented as it functions in native speech.

What we now commonly find in French language textbooks are pseudofunctional chapter titles, such as: "Giving Orders: The Imperative." Rather than presenting the various ways in which orders may be given in French (e.g., by using the present, the immediate future, and the simple future, as well as the imperative) or various functions or situational uses of the imperative, these textbooks instead provide a thin communicative "cloaking" of a primarily grammatical objective: teaching the imperative by giving orders.

With more and more researchers and teachers stressing the need for communicative activities in language textbooks, we now find "communicative" exercises requiring students to use the imperative to give orders to all sorts of people in all sorts of situations, including imaginary waiters and various public servants, classmates, and even their professor! Although meaningful communication can often be claimed in these situations, one might certainly question how many native French students would give such orders by using the imperative and in contexts where they would typically show some degree of respect or deference to the other person.

Of course, not all textbook exercises force communication to conform to grammatical objectives. Some textbook exercises do, in fact, clearly guide the language learner to observe and understand native-speaker norms. Such exercises can be found in the intermediate-level textbook *Interaction* (St. Onge, St. Onge, Kulick & King, 1991). In each workbook chapter one finds an aural comprehension section that consists of a taped excerpt from an authentic (unscripted) conversation among French native speakers and written questions that guide students in listening for certain types of information contained in the conversation. These excerpts of native speech were carefully chosen and incorporated into the workbook exercise to provide students with comprehensible native speech related to each lesson's linguistic and communicative objectives.

These examples of nativelike and nonnativelike communicative activities found in French language textbooks illustrate the need for TAs to be aware of which textbook exercises clearly reflect language used according to native-speaker norms and which exercises do not. With respect to the written language, the TA may be relatively confident that an exercise reflects native-speaker norms if it requires students either to analyze or model their own written work on a literary text, article, or example of popular written culture (menus, travel guides, announcements, advertisements, recipes, and so on). With respect to the spoken language, TAs will find that comprehension and production exercises involving unrehearsed video clips, TV broadcasts, and tape recordings of native speakers also expose students to various native communicative norms.

Of course, most textbooks contain a combination of authentic native-speaker texts and "made-to-seem-authentic" texts, video clips, and recordings. Common examples of such invented language include: scripted videos and tapes, adapted or modified texts, and many types of texts and tapes created by the textbook authors to simulate native speech, including letters, stories, menus, and dialogues. While there are numerous reasons for including scripted, adapted, and other such "artificial" language in a textbook, it is important to recognize that such language *is created* for the textbook and is, therefore, more likely to misrepresent native-speaker norms.

It is clear that great attention must be paid to the issue of "authenticity" with respect to pedagogical materials and exercises. Many teachers are reluctant to use unscripted native discourse or unmodified native texts (i.e., authentic language) in the classroom, either because they view them as too complex (lexically, grammatically, or culturally) or too tangentially related to the limited objectives of the lesson. Finally, one must decide what constitutes an "authentic" text appropriate for classroom use.[4] On the other hand, some studies have indicated potential dangers in the simplification or modification of native texts. First, research has shown that efforts to "simplify" texts grammatically may, in fact, result in making them more complex to comprehend in other ways (Wood, 1982). Second, it has not been proven that the ability to understand texts that have been modified will eventually lead to the ability to understand unmodified native texts (van Els,

Bongaerts, Extra, van Os & Janssen-van Dieten, 1984). Also, issues such as stylistic authenticity and discourse cohesion cannot be lightly dismissed in advocating the modification of native speech for foreign language teaching purposes.

Rather than deal with the problems of incorporating authentic or modified native speaker texts into an exercise, many textbook authors include as target language "models" various written texts and spoken discourse that are not directly transcribed from native speech or reproduced from native texts but that, the authors claim, are "patterned after" native spoken and written discourse. Nothing is "wrong" with such "nativelike" texts, as long as they are truly patterned after native speech and not according to one or a few opinions of what a native might say. Unless reference is made to particular native-speaker models after which this language is patterned, however, one must assume that these "models" are actually intuitive and not based on empirical observation or research. Of course, the problem with basing model texts on intuitions is that studies of language have shown that people's intuitions about their own language use are not always consistent (Carroll, Bever & Pollack, 1981) and frequently differ from an objective study of their actual language use (Roulet, 1974).

The inaccuracy of people's intuitions about their own speech was illustrated rather humorously in a conversation I had not so long ago with a colleague. After presenting a paper in which I had talked about native-speaker use of the present tense, even after a conjunction such as *quand,* a well educated, native French professor came up to me and respectfully yet firmly denied that any native speaker would use anything but the simple future after the conjunction *quand.* Neither of us could continue the debate there; therefore, we agreed to talk further at a later date and turned to the topic of when we would see each other next. Since I was due to take a trip shortly, the native speaker asked in a normal, conversational tone, *"Alors, quand est-ce que tu pars?"* (loosely translated, "So, when are you going to leave?"), using the present tense after the conjunction *quand.* Even then, however, the speaker did not realize what she had said. Only after I had repeated the question, emphasizing the present tense of the verb, did she blush, laugh, and admit that maybe native speakers did produce such sentences from time to time.

Incorporating Native Speech into Textbook Exercises

Of course, one might question whether we should be teaching what native speakers actually say, what native speakers think they say, or what native speakers think is appropriate for nonnative speakers to say. This issue is extremely complex and involves such questions as native-speaker evaluation of nonnative speakers and nonnative speech and the social acceptability and appropriateness of various linguistic forms in different communicative contexts. These questions, in turn, involve such factors as the age, sex, education, and social status of the speaker, the medium of communication, and register. Given the fact that sociolinguistic research has not yet established any extensive grammar of native-speaker language use that is "teachable" in a foreign language classroom as well as the numerous issues involved in choosing any one native-speaker text as a representative "target language model" for classroom use, some may argue that it is much easier to devise a text that includes acceptable native-speaker "features" and that reflects appropriate target language use. But, as I see it, the problem is still not resolved. How does one decide which features are "acceptable" and which uses are "appropriate"?

While these are issues of which TAs should certainly be made aware, I would not recommend that TAs themselves be encouraged to rule on the sociolinguistic appropriateness or acceptability of either authentic or made-to-seem-authentic texts. Nevertheless, if the classroom experience is supposed to facilitate the acquisition of language as a system of communicative norms, then TAs must understand the communicative "backbone" of their textbook rules and exercises. In other words, TAs must be trained to recognize the extent to which the language in textbook exercises focusing on communication reflects native-speaker norms, and they should be encouraged to sensitize students to such norms.

One way to understand the relationship between one's textbook exercises and native speech patterns is to compare the communicative uses of textbook grammar with native samples. Of course, some caution must be given to the choice of the native speech sample. Depending on the particular focus of the textbook exercise (e.g., to promote aural comprehension skills or oral production skills), as well as the particular nature of the language-learner population (e.g., a university, high school, or grade-school population), certain speech samples will be more appropriate than others. The important point is, of course, that these samples must reflect socially acceptable language in communicative contexts relevant to the language learner. In order to ensure the selection of appropriate and relevant native samples, TAs should consider the speech functions and situational uses of language emphasized in their textbook exercises as "communicative" guidelines and library and language laboratory resources as their native-speaker corpus.

For example, "talking about the weather" is a situational use of language generally found in beginning-level French textbooks when only the present tense has been introduced. One often finds the topic of weather and the present tense in everyday conversation. Of course, we normally learn about weather conditions through radio, TV, or newspaper forecasts. Thus, these spoken and written contexts are also appropriate ones to examine when presenting how one talks about the weather in French in various contexts.

If one actually checks written weather forecasts in French newspapers and spoken weather forecasts in radio broadcasts, one sees the consistent use of the future tense (rather than the present tense or the immediate future), even for the current day's weather prediction (Di Vito, 1991b). While admitting the necessity for uniformity in multisection courses, native-speaker use of the future tense predominantly in both spoken and written weather forecasts suggests that TAs should be encouraged to "revisit" either the future tense or weather vocabulary (depending on the organization of their textbook) in order to help students see relationships between spoken and written target language forms and their situationally specific uses in communication.

Incorporation of spoken and written weather forecasts into the classroom also provides an opportunity to look at both typical and situationally specific weather vocabulary, including verbs (*se produire, alterner, être en baisse, dépasser*), nouns (*éclaircie, orage, vent, nuage, brume, averse*), and adjectives (*nuageux, orageux, brumeux, lourd, frais, faible, fort*). Examination of such vocabulary with one's students provides, in turn, an opportunity to introduce, review, or expand various grammatical formation rules (e.g., ADJECTIVES: (m.) *nuageux* → (f.) *nuageuse*; VERBS: future tense formation of several verb categories). In short, TAs must be trained to treat their textbook's organization of discourse topics, speech functions, and situational uses of grammatical rules as means of expanding their students' knowledge of various native-speaker communicative norms. In other words, in order for TAs to become competent language teachers, they must have some background in discourse analysis, pragmatics, sociolinguistics, and applied linguistics.

A second situational use of language commonly found in textbooks is the giving of street directions. Like the giving of orders, this activity is typically used to practice the imperative in spoken French. However, examination of empirical data indicates that native speakers often use the present tense, the immediate future, and the simple future (rather than the imperative) to give both directions and orders, especially in more formal contexts (Bryant, 1984; Di Vito, 1992). Thus, while practicing the imperative in such discourse contexts may help students to develop communicative skills (i.e., ways to express their ideas, needs, and so forth), TAs must realize that these exercises will do little to promote the acquisition of communicative competence. In fact, they may instead lead students to develop inaccurate expectations about target language norms and encourage them to internalize norms that could be viewed by native speakers as impolite or rude.

A third and final example of comparing textbook communicative exercises with comparable native speech is drawn from personal narratives. Spoken and written narrative is generally practiced in chapters that emphasize use of the *passé composé* and *imparfait* in French; spoken and written narratives in French, however, reflect not only use of the *passé composé* and the *imparfait*, but also a relatively frequent appearance of the narrative or historical present to introduce quoted speech (especially with verbs such as *dire* and *faire*) and to recount the most dramatic portion of the narrative (Di Vito, 1992). Thus, textbook presentation of the *passé composé* and the *imparfait* to recount narratives is justified if one examines native French speech. However, presentation of the *narrative present* (at least for recognition) also appears warranted.

TAs could incorporate the *narrative present* into classroom lessons in a variety of ways: as a way of reviewing present-tense formation and expanding its functions, as a way of examining how spoken narratives are constructed and what gives them dramatic intensity, or as a listening comprehension exercise of native speech. If the student does not yet have the ability to understand and produce the various tenses found in typical French native-speaker narratives, then perhaps the language coordinator should direct TAs to emphasize specific aural comprehension skills or the intellectual understanding of narrative structure, reserving the production of spoken narratives as a targeted function for a higher language level.

Of course, in comparing textbook communicative exercises and communicative norms in native speech, one can certainly take a grammatical element (rather than a language function or situational use) as one's starting point. In other words, in order to understand the degree to which the textbook's presentation of the future tense allows the learner to see and acquire various communicative uses of the future tense, one can look through native written and spoken texts for examples of the future tense. However, while many may feel that building a lesson around a grammar point is more "solid" than building a lesson around a language function or situational use, I seriously question the pedagogical usefulness of this technique. First, it is somewhat like looking for a needle in a haystack and requires the close examination of an enormous amount of data. Second, this technique encourages TAs to organize lessons around grammatical structures rather than view a grammatical structure as one of several interrelated pieces contributing to an effective communicative act.

TAs should also be discouraged from taking the grammatical structures of a lesson and, guided by their own intuitions and hypotheses about the target language, examining their use by native speakers in different communicative contexts. Again, by constructing a communicative lesson around grammar, TAs run the risk of overlooking the relationships between the targeted grammar points and other aspects of contextualized spoken and written discourse. Also, as I argued earlier, this intuitive technique for relating grammar and communicative use yields results that may be severely biased. Since one is looking only where one expects to find the future tense, any communicative uses falling outside of one's expectations may be ignored.

Some may argue that finding native speech samples and using them as "guides" for presenting, practicing, and expanding the communicative value of textbook exercises is too time-consuming and too difficult. However, language laboratories have TV broadcasts, video clips, and tape recordings of unrehearsed speech or can acquire them, and, for the written language, most school libraries contain newspapers and a wide variety of popular and literary texts in the target language. Since such language materials are typically organized (or catalogued) by either topic or situational use, finding particular types of native speech can be much easier than one might think.

Another possible objection to supplementing textbook exercises with native speech samples is that the lesson will become too complicated for the student. However, if the native speech sample faithfully reflects the situational use or speech function highlighted in the textbook exercise, one could argue that any difference in complexity should not be hidden but, rather, treated as an important issue to be handled in the classroom. From knowledge of general patterns of language forms and their use in communication comes the ability to recognize and acquire variations in these patterns. It is this ability to use language according to socially acceptable variable patterns that one calls "communicative competence."

Recommendations for the Training of TAs

Given the preceding discussion, it is clear that TAs must be trained to look at their textbooks as but one of many tools to use in guiding students toward the acquisition of a foreign language. Although an abundance of "communicative" exercises can be found in most current textbook editions, many of these exercises have questionable communicative potential or questionable utility in guiding language learners to acquire the target language according to native-speaker communicative norms.

I have proposed several specific recommendations throughout this chapter for training TAs to use textbook exercises to help language learners understand how particular target language forms are used for communicative purposes in particular contexts. These recommendations can be grouped into three main categories:

1) TAs should be encouraged to keep abreast of relevant sociolinguistic and applied linguistic studies;

2) TAs should be encouraged to "look behind" the communicative gloss of textbook exercises in order to understand the communicative purpose for which the exercises were designed and the extent to which that purpose is rooted in native-speaker norms;

3) TAs should be encouraged to examine samples of native speech that illustrate the speech functions or situational uses of the language presented in textbook exercises in order to use these exercises more effectively to promote the development of communicative skills and communicative competence.

The preceding discussion has focused primarily on the need to sensitize TAs to some of the issues involved in using textbook exercises to promote the development of communicative skills and communicative competence.

The focus of the discussion was primarily on helping TAs to understand the degree to which the language content and the communicative contextualization of textbook exercises may or may not reflect native-speaker norms and on suggesting ways to incorporate aspects of native-speaker norms into these exercises. Of course, the responsibility of incorporating these norms into classroom exercises should not fall solely on the TA; ideally, this responsibility should be a major concern of all involved in language curriculum and materials development, including language coordinators, textbook authors, and editors.

Language coordinators can help promote the incorporation of native-speaker norms into the foreign language classroom experience in at least three ways. First, one of the criteria used in the selection of language textbooks can be the degree to which the authors justify the grammar selected and its pairing with particular communicative uses, not merely by the existence of functional or pseudofunctional section titles, but by research support cited and by the quantity and quality of native speech samples provided (or, at least, referred to) in the body of the textbook. Second, since proficiency goals are set at the curricular level, language coordinators can provide TAs with a general outline of the speech functions and situational uses of language to be emphasized in each textbook/language level and the grammatical structures identified in research studies as used by native speakers in such contexts (especially in language programs where TAs have little sociolinguistic or applied linguistic background and might have difficulty understanding such research). Coordinators could also require that evaluation measures for each language level reflect the students' knowledge and mastery of both formation and usage rules of target language structures.

Third, textbook authors and editors must also be encouraged to rethink their selection and presentation of target language structures. In the preface of most current language textbooks, one reads claims of authentic, nativelike speech. Textbook reviewers and publishers must hold textbook authors accountable for such claims by requiring them to justify their selection and presentation of grammatical structures with the support of both research findings and native-speaker texts. Contextualized exercises and engaging and personalized activities are not sufficient. In order for language learners to attain nativelike competence in a foreign language, those exercises and activities must lead the learner to understand and produce the target language according to native-speaker norms.

Notes

1. I am grateful to Dorothy Betz, Joel Walz, and two anonymous reviewers for their helpful comments on earlier versions of this chapter.

2. Given the many issues involved in defining language use as "standard" or "popular" (Valdman, 1982a), the expression "native-speaker norms" is to be understood here without any evaluative connotations. Throughout this chapter, "native-speaker norms" will simply refer to speech used by university-educated native speakers of the target language or the speech used by native speakers of undetermined educational backgrounds with whom language learners might have contact in the target country (waiters, merchants, and so forth). It should also be noted that the focus of studies of French native-speaker norms referred to throughout this chapter is predominantly on the French spoken in France or written by authors from France. Of course, when incorporating "native-speaker norms" into the classroom, students should know what types of natives are speaking (e.g., from France, Canada, or Senegal? children, teenagers, or adults? merchants, university students, or government officials?) and what type of language use is being examined (e.g., spoken or written? formal or informal? in which contexts?).

3. Although outside the topic area of this study, differences between what is taught and how native speakers use the language are not restricted to grammar, but extend to other domains, including orthographic style (Pons-Ridler, 1987) and vocabulary (Rivenc, 1979).

4. Some have argued, for example, that the use of authentic material does not automatically ensure an "authentic" lesson. See Breen (1985) and Nostrand (1989) for enlightening discussions on the meaning of authenticity in the foreign and second language classroom.

Works Cited

Bachman, Lyle F. & Sandra J. Savignon. "The Evaluation of Communicative Language Proficiency: A Critique of the ACTFL Oral Interview." *Modern Language Journal* 70 (1986): 380–90.

Blanche-Benveniste, Claire & Colette Jeanjean. *Le français parlé.* Paris: Didier Erudition, 1987.

Bland, Susan K. "The Present Progressive in Discourse: Grammar versus Usage Revisited." *TESOL Quarterly* 22 (1988): 53–68.

Breen, Michael. "Authenticity in the Language Classroom." *Applied Linguistics* 6 (1985): 60–70.

———— & Christopher N. Candlin. "The Essentials of a Communicative Curriculum in Language Teaching." *Applied Linguistics* 1 (1980): 89–112.

Bryant, William H. "Demythifying French Grammar." *French Review* 58 (1984): 19–31.

Calvé, Pierre. "Un trait de français parlé authentique: La dislocation." *Canadian Modern Language Review* 39 (1983): 779–93.

Carroll, J.M., T.G. Bever & C.R. Pollack. "The Nonuniqueness of Linguistic Intuitions." *Language* 57 (1981): 368–82.

Clarke, David F. "The Negotiated Syllabus: What Is It and How Is It Likely to Work?" *Applied Linguistics* 12 (1991): 13–28.

Désirat, Claude & Tristan Hordé. *La langue française au 20ᵉ siècle.* Paris: BORDAS, 1988.

Di Vito, Nadine O. "Incorporating Native Speaker Norms in Second Language Materials." *Applied Linguistics* 12 (1991a): 383–96.

————. "Looking at and towards the Future in French Textbooks." *Georgetown University Round Table on Languages and Linguistics 1991. Linguistics and Language Pedagogy: The State of the Art.* Ed. James E. Alatis. Washington: Georgetown University Press, 1991b: 250–59.

————. "Toward SV Question Word Order: A French Evolution." Paper presented at the Georgetown University Round Table on Languages and Linguistics, April 1–4, 1991c.

————. "'Present' Concerns about French Language Teaching." *Modern Language Journal* 76 (1992): 50–57.

Ellis, Rod. "Can Syntax Be Taught?" *Applied Linguistics* 5 (1984): 138–55.

Finnemann, Michael. "Liberating the Foreign Language Syllabus." *Modern Language Journal* 71 (1987): 36–43.

François, Denise. *Français parlé: Tomes I and II.* Paris: S.E.L.A.F., 1974.

Gadet, Françoise. *Le français ordinaire.* Paris: Armand Colin, 1989.

Gumperz, John. "The Speech Community." *International Encyclopedia of the Social Sciences.* New York: Macmillan, 1968: 381–86. Reprinted in *Language and Social Context.* Ed. Paolo Giglioli. New York: Penguin Books, 1972: 219–31.

Herschensohn, Julia. "Linguistic Accuracy of Textbook Grammar." *Modern Language Journal* 72 (1988): 409–13.

Holmes, Janet. "Doubt and Certainty in ESL Textbooks." *Applied Linguistics* 9 (1988): 21–44.

Hymes, Dell. "Excerpts from 'On Communicative Competence.'" Philadelphia: University of Pennsylvania Press, 1971. Reprinted in *Sociolinguistics.* Ed. Janet B. Pride & Janet Holmes. New York: Penguin Books, 1972: 269–93.

Jakobovits, Leon A. & Barbara Gordon. *The Context of Foreign Language Teaching.* Rowley, MA: Newbury House Publishers, 1974.

Joseph, John E. "New French: A Pedagogical Crisis in the Making." *Modern Language Journal* 72 (1988): 31–36.

Kennedy, Graeme. "Quantification and the Use of English: A Case Study of One Aspect of the Learner's Task." *Applied Linguistics* 8 (1987): 264–86.

Kramsch, Claire. "From Language Proficiency to Interactional Competence." *Modern Language Journal* 70 (1986): 366–72.

Labov, William. *Sociolinguistic Patterns.* Philadelphia: University of Pennsylvania Press, 1972.

Moirand, Sophie. *Enseigner à communiquer en langue étrangère.* Paris: Hachette, 1990.

Nostrand, Howard Lee. "Authentic Texts and Cultural Authenticity: An Editorial." *Modern Language Journal* 73 (1989): 49–52.

Noyau, Colette & Daniel Véronique. "Survey Article." *Studies in Second Language Acquisition* 8 (1986): 245–63.

Pons-Ridler, Suzanne. "Orthographe: Pourquoi être plus royaliste que le roi!" *French Review* 61 (1987): 229–38.

Prabhu, N.S. *Second Language Pedagogy.* Oxford: Oxford University Press, 1987.

Rivenc, Paul. "Le français fondamental vingt-cinq ans après." *Le Français dans le Monde* 148 (1979): 15–22.

Rivers, Wilga M. "Comprehension and Production in Interactive Language Teaching." *Modern Language Journal* 70 (1986): 1–7.

Robinson, Gail L. Nemetz. *Crosscultural Understanding.* New York: Prentice-Hall, 1988.

Roulet, E. "Vers une caractérisation linguistique des normes dans l'enseignement des langues." *Linguistic Insights in Applied Linguistics.* Ed. S. Pit Corder & E. Roulet. Paris: Didier, 1974: 143–56.

Rutherford, William. "Aspects of Pedagogical Grammar." *Applied Linguistics* 1 (1980): 60–73.

St. Onge, Susan, Ronald St. Onge, Katherine Kulick & David King. *Interaction.* 3d. ed. Boston: Heinle & Heinle Publishers, 1991.

Sankoff, Gillian. *The Social Life of Language.* Philadelphia: University of Pennsylvania Press, 1980.

Schulz, Renate A. "Bridging the Gap between Teaching and Learning: A Critical Look at Foreign Language Textbooks." *Challenges in the 1990s for College Language Programs.* Ed. Sally Sieloff Magnan. AAUSC Issues in Language Program Direction 1990. Boston: Heinle & Heinle Publishers, 1991: 167–82.

Scotton, Carol Myers & Janice Bernsten. "Natural Conversations as a Model for Textbook Dialogue." *Applied Linguistics* 9 (1988): 372–84.

Swaffar, Janet. "Competing Paradigms." *Modern Language Journal* 73 (1989): 301–14.

Terrell, Tracy D. "Acquisition in the Natural Approach." *Modern Language Journal* 70 (1986): 213–27.

Terry, Robert M. *Contemporary French Interrogative Structures.* Montreal: Cosmos, 1970.

Valdman, Albert. "Norme pédagogique: Les structures interrogatives du français." *International Review of Applied Linguistics in Language Teaching* 1 (1965): 3–10.

_____. "Français standard et français populaire." *French Review* 56 (1982a): 218–27.

_____. "Toward a Modified Structural Syllabus." *Studies in Second Language Acquisition* 5 (1982b): 34–50.

_____ & Helen Warriner-Burke. "Major Surgery Due: Redesigning the Syllabus and Texts." *Foreign Language Annals* 13 (1980): 261–70.

van Dijk, Teun A. "Discourse Studies and Education." *Applied Linguistics* 2 (1981): 1–26.

van Els, Theo, Theo Bongaerts, Guus Extra, Charles van Os, & Anne-Mieke Janssen-van Dieten. *Applied Linguistics and the Learning and Teaching of Foreign Languages.* London: Edward Arnold, 1984.

Walz, Joel. "The Relative Pronouns in French, 1: Empirical Research." *French Review* 54 (1981): 643–54.

_____. "Is Oral Proficiency Possible with Today's French Textbooks?" *Modern Language Journal* 70 (1986): 13–19.

_____. "Context and Contextualized Language Practice in Foreign Language Teaching." *Modern Language Journal* 73 (1989): 160–69.

Warriner, Helen P. "High School Foreign Language Texts: Too Much between the Covers to Cover." *Foreign Language Annals* 11 (1978): 551–57.

Wood, A.S. "An Examination of the Rhetorical Structures of Authentic Chemistry Texts." *Applied Linguistics* 3 (1982): 121–43.

Toward a Revised Model of TA Training

Cynthia A. Fox
State University of New York at Albany

A review of the literature on foreign language teaching assistant (TA) training over the past 30 years reveals the emergence of a widely accepted model consisting of a preservice workshop followed by an in-service methods course.[1] The ostensible goal of this model is to provide first-year TAs with classroom techniques considered the most practical for teaching elementary language courses. These courses emphasize developing communicative language skills, and as a result recommended practices tend to include activities that encourage contextualized speaking practice or Total Physical Response activities to develop listening comprehension (Asher, 1977).

Since the theoretical assumptions about language and language learning that are the presumed source of these practices are only implied, the model must make one of three suppositions about TAs: (1) that they already possess the requisite assumptions; (2) that they do not need to share or understand the assumptions behind the recommended practices in order to teach in a manner that is consistent with those assumptions; or (3) that they do not possess the assumptions but can derive them from recommended practices and from other teaching resources available to them.

My experience over the last six years while supervising some 80 TAs in French suggests that each of these suppositions is false. In the case of the first

191

supposition, it is clear that despite considerable proficiency in using French, TAs hold many beliefs about language in general and French in particular that are unsupportable from a linguistic point of view. Moreover, these beliefs are also frequently incompatible with theories of language that provide the theoretical bases of communicative language teaching as outlined, for example, in Canale and Swain (1980).[2]

Regarding the second supposition, my visits to TA classrooms indicate that a given theory of language influences classroom practice only to the extent that the theory corresponds to the teacher's own mental model of language. For instance, a TA who believes that French is a set of prescriptive grammar rules will devote an extraordinary amount of time to, say, past participle agreement in transitive verbs, even though most native speakers ignore those rules.

In the case of the third supposition, an examination of the resources upon which TAs routinely draw, such as their own experiences as language learners, teaching gimmicks, and, most importantly, their textbook, reveals that typically all are inadequate sources of information about both language in general and French in particular. Although all the examples given here are drawn from my personal experiences working with TAs in French, I think I can safely assume that the problems I identify are neither program- nor language-specific.

It is my thesis that effective language teaching depends on the teacher's possession of a conceptual understanding of language that is grounded in linguistic theory. However, since practical and political constraints make it unlikely that TA supervisors will be able to add required coursework in general and applied linguistics or in second language acquisition to their programs, other solutions must be found. By examining more closely the development of the current model of TA training and the resources that TAs use to organize their teaching, I will suggest a practical way in which TA training might be improved.

Two Models of TA Training

TA training in foreign languages is a relatively recent phenomenon in American universities. Less than 30 years ago an MLA/U.S. Department of Education survey of graduate schools granting Ph.D.'s in foreign languages revealed that 60% of the 51 responding departments provided absolutely no training for TAs (MacAllister, 1966). While subsequent surveys, such as one discussed by Schulz (1980), have reported decreases in this shocking baseline figure, TA training is still by no means either universal or particularly rigorous (Devens, 1986; Elling, 1988; Weimer, Svinicki & Bauer, 1989). Indeed, it appears that at least some individual members of foreign language departments still believe that TA training is totally unnecessary. For instance, Koop (1991) reports the results of a survey of 76 professors of French culture and civilization from 63 American institutions in which 16% of the respondents did not agree that Ph.D. candidates should be required to take at least one course in the pedagogy of French, and in which 24% of respondents also opposed requiring at least one course in the pedagogy of the candidate's speciality.

With the increase in TA training programs over the last 30 years, a small body of literature has developed on what ought to be included in such programs. This literature tends to fall into two categories. The first and older category places TA training within the framework of a general preparation to enter the academy. For example, MacAllister (1966) reports the conclusions of a panel of experienced language scholars and teachers in response to the MLA/U.S. Department of Education survey cited previously. Their recommendation was that graduate schools require work not only in the principles of language teaching, but also in the principles of linguistic analysis, cultural analysis, and the presentation of literature to undergraduates. Similar concerns are expressed by Ryder (1976), Hagiwara (1976, 1977), Showalter (1984), Elling (1988), Azevedo (1990), and Murphy (1991).

The more recent trend identifies TA training almost exclusively with pedagogical issues and focuses on preparing TAs in their first year of graduate studies to teach elementary-level language courses. The model of training most often proposed involves a workshop that takes place shortly before the teaching assignment is to begin, followed by a quarter- or semester-length methods course in the first or second semester of teaching. Representative of this school are Di Donato (1983), Ervin and Muyskens (1982), Freed (1975), Knop and Herron (1982), Lee (1989), Nerenz, Herron, and Knop (1979), Rava (1987), Rogers (1987), and Schulz (1980).

Scholars in this second category have a tendency to use the TAs' own perceptions of their needs as an argument for organizing the programs described or recommended. For example, Ervin and Muyskens (1982) report on a survey in which 303 subjects from four universities were asked to rank 29 previously identified "interests and concerns regarding…teaching duties." Items given top priority by the respondents were (1) "learning practical techniques and methods," (2) "teaching the four skills," (3) "teaching conversation/getting the students to speak," and (4) "making the class interesting." Other items were of an equally practical nature and included "motivating students" (seventh) and "gaining experience, self-confidence" (thirteenth).

Only one item on the survey, "improving my command of the target language; improving my knowledge of subject matter," mentions content, but this item seems to conflate what I consider to be two separate issues, language proficiency (command of target language) and linguistic knowledge (command of subject matter). This last concern was only ranked seventeenth, however, which is presumably what lead Ervin and Muyskens to make no recommendation that TA trainers concern themselves with what TAs do or do not know about the language they teach.

In a similar vein, Lee (1989, p. 26) describes practically oriented workshops on "Grading Written Work" and "Assessing Oral Performance," which were added to his program in "a direct response to the specific needs of the TA's teaching in our particular language program."

Weimer, Svinicki, and Bauer's (1989, p. 63) findings, which summarize attitudes and trends across departments, indicate that even when "content" is identified as a problem area, it is viewed in quantitative rather than qualitative terms:

> Basically, new college instructors need help in two areas: content and method. With respect to content, departments need to ensure consistency across different sections. Sometimes TAs need help learning content. More often, it is a matter of teaching pace and organization and ensuring uniformity of evaluative practices.

The extent to which this second, more narrow school of thought has gained acceptance can perhaps be seen in the fact that arguments for advanced methods courses, for example, Lalande (1991a), are beginning to appear in print.

It seems reasonable to suppose that at least two factors explain why an essentially streamlined model of TA training has become so widely accepted. On the one hand, the kind of comprehensive training suggested by MacAllister (1966) is impractical. Such a program would mean increasing faculty while reducing the number of courses students could take within their own discipline. At the same time, advocates of TA training are up against a system that, ironically enough, does not always assign teaching a high priority. In fact, it is no secret that TA supervisors and language program coordinators have often been regarded as second-class citizens in foreign language departments (Dvorak, 1986; Lee & VanPatten, 1991). As Lalande (1991b) has pointed out, a current trend toward moving supervisor/coordinator positions out of the professor series and into the lecturer series is evidence that these negative attitudes persist. Thus, the narrow scope of the current model probably has to do with the difficulty of establishing and maintaining support for training programs, not with any philosophical objection to a more comprehensive approach.

Practical considerations may also help explain why methodology and not some other likely candidate, such as applied linguistics or second language acquisition, has been the focus of TA training. On the one hand, knowledge of linguistics and its subdisciplines is commonly thought to require more specialized training than does knowledge of methodology. If the emphasis of TA training is on methodology, that training does not have to be the exclusive domain of the linguist. For some departments, then, training does not require special hiring, but can be carried out by virtually any member of the department.

On the other hand, the imposition of rigid time constraints on the training process makes it crucial that trainers provide TAs with what they need to fulfill their basic mission. Under these circumstances it is natural to turn to TAs themselves for input. Since most inexperienced TAs are unaware of the usefulness of training in various linguistic fields, it is not surprising that their responses should focus on classroom practice.

In all probability, however, the reasons for the emphasis on methodology merely dovetail with other, more compelling, ones. Indeed, such emphasis seems to follow naturally from three important developments in foreign language education: (1) the increased prominence of oral proficiency as a primary goal of instruction; (2) the shift from a structural to a functional view of language; and (3) research in second language acquisition that suggests that a language is not learned through conscious analysis of rules, but is naturally assimilated through use (Krashen, 1981). While no general consensus exists that explicit teaching of language through structural analysis and practice has no place in the communicative classroom, few would now disagree that these activities should be minimized in favor of what Freed (1975, pp. 12-13) describes as "contextual, challenging and useful practice in the language." Emphasis on methodology in TA training, then, encourages TAs to learn how to provide as many contexts for natural acquisition as possible by taking the focus off talking *about* the language and placing it on talking *in* the language.

Inadequate TA Resources

One way of arguing the case that TA trainers need to be concerned about TAs' beliefs about language is to look at what TAs must otherwise rely on to help them organize their classes and to answer student questions. My experience suggests that the information they impart to students comes from one of three sources: memories about how they themselves were taught; teaching gimmicks shared by other, often equally inexperienced TAs; and the textbook. Whether it is because they do not think they need other help, because they are unable to predict what they will need to know in front of the class, or simply because making an appeal to authority is to risk presenting themselves as incompetent, it is very rare for TAs to seek help of this sort from their supervisor.

Problems of changing perspectives on the goals and methods of language teaching, if not with memory itself, make the first source, "memories about how they themselves were taught," one of doubtful utility. For instance, TAs who learned French by explicit learning of grammar rules will naturally turn to those rules to answer student questions, often using terminology that, to the student, may be arcane. Likewise, TAs who as students were made to respond in complete sentences or to sound out passages intended for reading comprehension will call on their own students to do the same even though these activities may not be consistent with the goals of communicative language teaching. Frustration with materials that are very different from what they used when learning the language may also lead them to refer to those same materials, and consequently to fall back on outdated pedagogy.[3]

The second source, teaching gimmicks that TAs share with one another, are frequently mnemonic devices such as the acronym BAGS (Beauty, Age, Goodness, Size) — the letters of which help students remember the semantic categories of adjectives that precede nouns — or the *maison d'être* for remembering which verbs take *être* as the auxiliary. Sometimes, however, the gimmicks are intended to provide insight into the language by explaining or clarifying the conceptual difficulties that students may have with constructions like causative *faire* or the partitive determiner. These explanations involve making claims about how native speakers interpret sentences that are ungrammatical and also tend to present speakers as conscious agents in the creation of forms that fill what would appear to be gaps in their language, particularly when it is compared with English.[4]

TAs would not be so vulnerable to these pitfalls if the third source of information upon which they draw to organize their courses, the textbook, were a reliable source of descriptive information about the language. Unfortunately, the literature suggesting that textbooks are actually contributing to the problem appears to be growing.

In a study of 22 elementary-level college French textbooks published in the United States, Walz (1986) found that while all the books include speaking as a major goal, many base their presentations of the grammar on written forms and most fail to provide clear and consistent information about oral forms that would promote proficiency in speaking. Similarly, Herschensohn (1988) studied the linguistic accuracy and clarity of presentation of the French determiner system in 11 representative college textbooks according to six linguistically based criteria and was unable to find even one that included an accurate descriptive account of the forms. Her discussion of how the partitive is presented is particularly enlightening. If, she argues, the article system is described in terms of assertion (indefinite articles) and presupposition (definite articles), and these terms are used consistently, then the partitive, a designation of "indefinite mass," should not cause undue difficulty. However, she found that only two of the textbooks classified these articles as indefinites and made the count/mass distinction, while the rest presented it as a complex syntactic and semantic structure.

Finally, Di Vito (1991) studied the distribution and productivity of French negation, object pronouns, relative clauses, and question formation in four different text types and compared her results with the treatment these structures receive in three representative college textbooks. She found, for example, that no textbook mentioned that the preverbal negative particle *ne* is characteristically absent in informal conversations of educated native speakers and may even be absent in formal speech. Conversely, all three textbooks treated the placement of two preverbal object pronouns together in a clause, although the data revealed that this syntactic configuration is virtually nonexistent across text types. Her conclusion (1991, p. 393), that "striking differences in frequency and function are typically ignored, and examples of grammatical structures can often be found which are completely unsupported by native speaker use," casts serious doubt on the usefulness of the textbook as a guidepost in pointing TAs toward an understanding of language that is grounded in linguistic theory. Indeed, since recognizing inaccuracies and inconsistencies in the textbook requires a high level of analytic and sociolinguistic sophistication, fanciful notions about language may even be spawned and perpetuated.

The problem, however, is not just that textbooks need to be better informed about the linguistic, pragmatic, and sociolinguistic features of the language described. They also need to be better grounded in current theories of linguistics and language acquisition. Schulz (1991) cites evidence from several studies to argue convincingly that despite considerable upheaval in foreign language teaching methods in the last 20 years, little about the textbook has changed since the heyday of audiolingualism. In spite of a surface veneer of communicative-language teaching jargon, textbooks present language as a series of discrete grammatical points that are learned mainly through habit formation:

> Without question, the prefaces of textbooks read differently than those of yesteryear. They use all the right "buzzwords" such as "proficiency-oriented," "real language use," "functional–notional organization," "authentic language," "real-life contexts," "communicative focus," "communicative tasks," "personalized activities," etc. A careful examination of the actual instructional sequences reveals, however, that we have a long way to go to translate current theories of second/foreign language acquisition and communicative language learning and teaching into practice. (Schulz, 1991, p. 168.)

Among what she terms the "emerging insights, or commonly agreed upon tenets, based either on second language acquisition theory or empirical research which inform how languages might be learned" (p. 171), she cites Acculturation/Pidginization Theory, Linguistic Universal Theory, Interlanguage Theory, Discourse Theory, and Krashen's Monitor Model. It should be added that the notion of "text" is expanding quite rapidly to include video materials. If, as Cummins (1989, p. 412) says, "an important use of the AV [audiovideo] model is to show interaction between native speakers, and teachers can point out features of kinesics, such as distance between speakers or how gestures correlate with words and meaning," then textbooks must also be informed about kinesic theory and include pedagogically sound techniques for teaching students appropriate nonverbal behavior.

Toward an Integrative Model

Much of my argument that TAs need more linguistic training is based on anecdotal evidence, and is thus suspect until it is tested by more systematic means.[5] Moreover, the question of how much beginning graduate students really know about the language they teach is only part of the problem that needs to be examined. First, it has been assumed throughout this chapter that knowledge about the language is a prerequisite for effective teaching. This truth seems intuitively obvious, but it leaves open the problem of exactly what constitutes sufficient knowledge. Second, the case has been made that TAs carry with them certain implicit assumptions about what languages are and how they are learned, and that these assumptions are not only unscientific but also incompatible with current theories of language and language acquisition and with the goals of communicative language teaching. Third, it has been argued that the current trend to do nothing systematic to develop both specific and general knowledge about language in our TAs leaves them seriously underprepared to teach despite their participation in what otherwise may be rigorous training programs. This last argument raises the question of what kinds of intervention in TA training would be most effective. It does not wholly exclude the possibility that the experience of teaching may be such that knowledge about language will develop on its own.

One way of investigating the relationship between linguistic knowledge and teaching performance is through longitudinal studies that examine TAs' knowledge and beliefs about language as they enter graduate school and ask how that knowledge and those beliefs change over time. Assuming that, for the time being, even those programs with the most support from their departments cannot or will not require more coursework directly related to TA training, these studies should also include experimental groups of TAs who receive various types of explicit linguistic training during their apprenticeship. These types could then be compared regarding their effectiveness.

The problem of what to include in linguistic training sends us back to the question raised earlier concerning what constitutes sufficient knowledge about the language. One possible source of answers is the standards put forth by the Committee on Applied Linguistics of the Commission on Professional Standards of the American Association of Teachers of French (Murphy & Goepper, 1989, pp. 19-20). These standards use two general categories of knowledge — aspects of the French language and research in applied linguistics — to define a "basic" and a "superior" level of teacher competence. The descriptions could easily be adapted as guidelines for teacher competence in other languages.

As defined by the committee, teachers with a basic level of competence should know features of articulatory phonetics, phonemic versus phonetic contrasts in the language, sound–symbol correspondences, rules of word formation, the basic dictionaries of French and how to use them, basic word order, the major levels of style (including differences between spoken and written language), and culture-specific features of spoken and written French beyond the sentence level. Their knowledge of research in applied linguistics should include contrastive analysis, error analysis, the acquisition/learning distinction, cognitive style, discourse analysis, and the relationships among theories of linguistic analysis, the psychology of learning, and teaching methodologies. Teachers with a superior level of competence should know more about the phonological system of French (including phonological variation, the theory of distribution, and morphophonological generalizations), levels of style, topic construction, organization of ideas in spoken and written French, and important aspects of at least one regional variety of standardized French. They should also know the research fields mentioned above in more depth than teachers at the basic level.

The program is obviously ambitious, and in discussing its implications for TA training, Murphy (1991, p. 137) states:

> This imperative would…seem to require conscious coordination of academic work in learning theory, linguistics (general and applied), and language teaching methodology. More precisely, it would seem desirable for the graduate program to include a minimum of one course in language acquisition theory, one in applied linguistics, and one linguistically oriented methods course.

For schools that cannot afford this trio of experience, he goes on, it might be possible to develop a one-term practicum consisting of outside readings in linguistics and meetings that focus on the linguistic content of lesson plans and exams. For many schools, however, even the addition of a practicum would be problematic. Thus, creative ways must be found to incorporate this knowledge into existing structures.

Some guidance in developing appropriate training techniques may be available in a small but growing literature in ESL that draws its inspiration from the British educational reform known as "language awareness."

Proponents of language awareness argue that language is central to human learning, whatever the subject matter, because it is the medium of instruction across the curriculum. As described by Donmall (1985, p. 97),

> [W]ork in the field of Language Awareness is directed towards the development of the conscious perception of and sensitivity to language allied in explicit terms to skill and performance....The pupil already has high performance skills in and intuitions about language. These are the spring-board for pupil-based investigations during which the unconscious and intuitive becomes conscious and explicit.

Some typical examples of language awareness activities can be found in Thomas (1988). In one case, a worksheet containing sentences that participants in a teacher development workshop must complete by choosing between "some" or "any" provides the basis for a discussion of how these quantifiers may change the meaning of an utterance and, in turn, influence behavior. For TAs in French, this type of exercise could be profitably adapted to a discussion of, for example, the relationship between the periphrastic future (*je vais partir* 'I am going to leave') and the simple future (*je partirai* 'I will leave'). These forms, which are often taken to be interchangeable, actually differ in determinacy: the periphrastic form signals a future whose outcome is settled, whereas the simple form signals a future whose outcome is not settled (Blanche-Benveniste, 1984).[6]

One contrasting pair is *je vais avoir/j'aurai un enfant* ('I'm going to have/I will have a child'), a context where the choice of form indicates whether the speaker is actually pregnant or merely intends to have a child. The next example could be a pair such as *Les enfants seront?/vont toujours être les enfants* ('Kids will be?/are going to be kids'), where the statement refers to a general, indeterminate future and the speaker does not have a choice of form: only the simple future is possible. Sentence-level pairs where the difference in meaning between the two forms is not obvious, such as the above-mentioned *je partirai/je vais partir*, can then be introduced and serve as a springboard to a discussion of the role of context and the adequacy of the decontextualized sentence as the basic unit of either linguistic analysis or a pedagogically oriented grammatical explanation.

Another exercise described by Thomas that can also be easily adapted to other languages asks participants to come up with four ways of offering someone assistance and to grade each sentence for politeness. After explaining their choices, they must imagine themselves in situations (for example,

"You are in a hurry, but feel obliged to offer help" and "You are surprised your help is not needed") and explain why they would use one construction in preference to another. For French, contrasts between, say, *Ça va?* ('Everything ok?'); *Je peux vous donner un coup de main?* ('Can I give you a hand?'); *Voulez-vous que je vous aide?* ('Do you want me to help you?'); and *Permettez-moi de vous assister!* ('Allow me to help you!') can serve as starting points to a discussion of how word choice, address forms, and syntactic structure interact in expressing politeness. As a follow-up, TAs can also consider the role that sociolinguistic appropriateness plays or should play in determining the type of language they emphasize in their teaching.

These types of activity offer at least four advantages to the TA trainer. First, as the AATF Committee (Murphy & Goepper, 1989, p. 20) pointed out, "a knowledge of all aspects of linguistics as applied to the teaching of French takes many years to acquire." However, since these activities do not require any knowledge of linguistic theory or even much technical vocabulary, they can be introduced very early in the training program. Second, language awareness activities are simple in design and thus relatively easy to create and administer.

A third advantage to using language awareness activities is that they can be keyed to specific points in the textbook TAs use in the classes they teach. As in the examples I have given, the discussion of activities that seem at first glance to involve problems of grammatical analysis can be sequenced in such a way as to address the issue of how the decontextualized grammar explanations that drive the syllabi of current textbooks fail to take into account important generalizations about language functions and language use. TAs are thus encouraged to use their intuitions about language in evaluating textbook presentations.

Finally, and most importantly, while the knowledge gained from language awareness activities obviously cannot replace the knowledge gained from the systematic, scientific study of language that linguistics offers, these activities nevertheless encourage a way of thinking about language that approximates the way a linguist thinks about language. By looking at well-chosen contrasts, competing forms, or alternate ways of expressing the same idea, and by placing emphasis on the observation of how native speakers actually *use* the language rather than on how textbooks tell us the language *ought to be used,* we can help our TAs to become more flexible in their approach to the subject. These activities may also set them on the path toward more systematic study of linguistics and its subdisciplines.

Murray (1990), who has undertaken research to discover how the language awareness of ESL teacher trainees changes during their training course, reports preliminary findings that buttress the arguments I have been making here. Through semistructured interviews as well as examples of written work from diaries to language analysis assignments and two video-taped experiments concerning awareness of student errors, she has traced the development of 11 teacher trainees over a seven-month period. Her preliminary results indicate fairly clear changes in language awareness. For instance, she cites the case of one trainee who acquired what she terms the superordinate concept "difference between speaking and writing." Despite this change, however, the same trainee held on to the beliefs that "(a) spoken language can by nature sound 'rather muddled' and 'sort of nervous sounding...but isn't really' and (b) written language is 'clearer' and 'better'" (p. 27). How, asks Murray, will this trainee, now a teacher, approach teaching the spoken language if she holds these two beliefs? Shouldn't the training model be changed to help the trainee come to terms with the spoken language?

Conclusion

It would be tempting to conclude that what TAs need is simply more required coursework in linguistic analysis and to call for the type of comprehensive TA training first advocated by MacAllister (1966). It is possible that some departments, reluctant to give academic credence or credit to methods courses, might be more open to work they felt had content of a more "academic" nature. It is probably more likely, though, that requests for increased coursework that is specifically linked to training would not be greeted with much enthusiasm.

One alternative would be to replace the current model of TA training based on work in foreign language methodology with a new model based on linguistic training. Such a drastic move is unwarranted, however, since there is much that is positive about current practices. The other alternative is to modify existing programs to include linguistic training. This solution, though imposed by necessity, is not unattractive since it looks toward developing a model that integrates knowledge and beliefs about language with language teaching practices. It is time, then, for TA trainers to take a critical look at the assumptions behind communicative language teaching, the knowledge and beliefs about language that TAs bring with them into the classroom, and the kinds of training current models of preservice workshops and in-service methods courses provide. Then we should go about finding ways to modify our programs to assure a better fit between theories of language and actual classroom practice.

Notes

1. Many of the ideas discussed here were first presented in a paper entitled "Rethinking the Foundations of TA Training," which I read at the American Council on the Teaching of Foreign Languages Annual Meeting, held in Nashville in November 1990. I am grateful to Deborah Piston-Hatlen for her helpful comments and to the editor and three anonymous reviewers for their remarks on earlier drafts.

2. Yaguello (1988) contrasts the linguist's objective approach to language analysis with the nonlinguist's subjective approach. What she terms explicative, appreciative, and normative attitudes lead members of the latter group to seek rational explanations for phenomena such as grammatical gender, to attribute to languages aesthetic or moral characteristics such as beauty or clarity, and to discredit all forms in a language that do not conform to prescribed usage.

3. A major component of the orientation described in Lee (1989) is meant to provide TAs in Spanish with the experience of learning a new language from a communicative approach. His reasons echo the remarks made in this chapter:

> Many of the TA's who have come through the Department have learned Spanish through the audiolingual method....Their learning experience would serve them well as instructors if they were going to teach with those methods. Communicative language teaching involves a different methodology, however, so they *need* an orientation to communicative language teaching. (p. 27.)

4. Explanations for the need for the verb *faire* 'to make, to cause' in sentences like *je fais cuire le bifiek* 'I'm cooking the steak' (literally, 'I'm making the steak cook') often suggest that to use the grammatically odd, but parallel with English *je cuis le bifiek* (literally, 'I'm cooking the steak') means that the speaker is claiming to be an oven or to be in the oven (with or without the steak). In reality, *cuire* falls into a class of intransitive verbs denoting processes that take place without reference to an agent and that require auxiliary to make agentivity explicit. An example from English that illustrates how these verbs function and would help the TA who thinks of grammar as a system based on rational principles is "laugh": "I laugh," "*John laughs me," "John makes me laugh."

A common explanation for the need for the partitive determiner *de la* in sentences such as *je vais prendre de la soupe* 'I'm going to have some soup' begins by contrasting its use with that of the definite determiner *la* in sentences such as *je vais prendre la soupe* 'I'm going to have the soup.' It is then asserted that the speaker of the second sentence would be claiming to be having all of the soup in the world. This claim depends on the confusion of the notion of mass noun with that of generic or nonreferential use. In actual discourse it is unlikely that coconversationalists hearing the second sentence in a context where the first was appropriate would think the speaker was making this extraordinary claim. Rather, they would wonder to which soup the speaker was referring.

5. This type of argument has often been made in the broader context of preparation of foreign language teachers, however. For instance, the AATF Subcommittee on Applied Linguistics of the Committee on Professional Standards (Murphy & Goepper, 1989, p. 19) stated, "It is not sufficient to know a language; good teachers must know *about* the language. They must be able to explain, to the extent it is possible and desirable, why a language works as it does." See also Hammerly (1982) and Thomas (1988).

6. I am now conducting a study of 147 first-year TAs in French at 20 graduate schools throughout the United States. The preliminary results reveal that this contrast is not at all obvious to them. When asked to imagine how they would answer a typical beginning student question about the contrast between *je vais partir/je partirai demain* ('I'm going to leave/will leave tomorrow'), 36 respondents said the sentences contrasted in terms of definiteness and indefiniteness, but 12 of these assigned indefiniteness to the periphrastic form. Otherwise, in descending order, 23 TAs claimed a stylistic difference (either an informal/formal or a spoken/written distinction, with one claiming that the periphrastic future is "incorrect"), 22 TAs claimed no difference between the forms, and 20 mentioned a contrast between a "near future" and a "distant future" time frame. In addition, 17 respondents described the contrast as the same as the English pair "I am leaving/I will leave" without explaining what that contrast is, 9 talked of how the constructions differ in formal terms, 10 left the item blank, 3 said they were not sure, and 4 gave explanations that do not fall into any category ("the speaker decided to go/was made to go," "one focuses on the action of leaving, the other on the person leaving," "one focuses on the action, the other on tomorrow," and "they apply to different contextual situations." The number of responses adds up to more than 147 because some respondents gave multiple answers.

Works Cited

Asher, James J. *Learning Another Language through Actions: The Complete Teacher's Guidebook.* Los Gatos, CA: Sky Oaks Productions, 1977.

Azevedo, Milton M. "Professional Development of Teaching Assistants: Training versus Education." *ADFL Bulletin* 22, 1 (1990): 24–28.

Blanche-Benveniste, Claire. *"Connaissance 'naturelle' et connaissance 'secondaire' de la grammaire."* Paper presented at the American Council on the Teaching of Foreign Languages, Chicago, 1984.

Canale, Michael & Merrill Swain. "Theoretical Bases of Communicative Approaches to Second Language Teaching and Testing." *Applied Linguistics* 1 (1980): 1–47.

Cummins, Patricia W. "Video and the French Teacher." *French Review* 62 (1989): 411–25.

Devens, Monica S. "Graduate Education in Foreign Languages and Literatures: A View from Five Universities." *ADFL Bulletin* 17, 3 (1986): 14–18.

Di Donato, Robert. "TA Training and Supervision: A Checklist for an Effective Program." *ADFL Bulletin* 15, 1 (1983): 34–36.

Di Vito, Nadine O'Connor. "Incorporating Native Speaker Norms in Second Language Materials." *Applied Linguistics* 12 (1991): 383–96.

Donmall, Gillian. "Some Implications of Language Awareness Work for Teacher Training (Pre-service and In-service)." *Language Awareness.* Ed. B.G. Donmall. London: CILT, 1985: 97–106.

Dvorak, Trisha R. "The Ivory Ghetto: The Place of the Language Program Coordinator in a Research Institution." *Hispania* 69 (1986): 217–22.

Elling, Barbara. "National Trends: Implications for Graduate Student Training and Career Placement." *ADFL Bulletin* 19, 2 (1988): 45–48.

Ervin, Gerard & Judith A. Muyskens. "On Training TAs: Do We Know What They Want and Need?" *Foreign Language Annals* 15 (1982): 335–44.

Freed, Barbara F. "Why Train Teaching Assistants? — Foreign Language and Communication at the University Level." *ADFL Bulletin* 7, 2 (1975): 9–14.

Hagiwara, Michio P. "The Training of Graduate Assistants: Past, Present, and Future." *ADFL Bulletin* 7, 3 (1976): 7–12.

———. "The T.A. System: Two Wrongs Do Not Make a Right." *ADFL Bulletin* 8, 3 (1977): 26–28.

Hammerly, Hector. *Synthesis in Language Teaching. An Introduction to Languistics.* Blaine, WA: Second Language Publications, 1982.

Herschensohn, Julia. "Linguistic Accuracy of Textbook Grammar." *Modern Language Journal* 72 (1988): 409–14.

Knop, Constance K. & Carol A. Herron. "An Empirical Approach to Redesigning a T.A. Methods Course." *French Review* 55 (1982): 329–39.

Koop, Marie-Christine Weidmann. "Survey on the Teaching of Contemporary French Culture in American Colleges and Universities, Part 1: The Professor's Perspective." *French Review* 64 (1991): 463–75.

Krashen, Stephen D. *Second Language Acquisition and Second Language Learning.* Oxford: Pergamon, 1981.

Lalande, John F., II. "Advancing the Case for the Advanced Methods Course." In Magnan, 1991: 151-66.

———. "Redefinition of the TA Supervisor–Language Program Coordinator Position into the Lecturer Series: A Sensible Idea?" *ADFL Bulletin* 22, 2 (1991b): 15–18.

Lee, James F. *A Manual and Practical Guide to Directing Foreign Language Programs and Training Graduate Teaching Assistants.* New York: Random House, 1989.

——— & Bill VanPatten. "The Question of Language Program Direction is **Academic**." In Magnan, 1991: 113–28.

MacAllister, Archibald. "The Preparation of College Teachers of Modern Foreign Languages." *Modern Language Journal* 50 (1966): 400–15.

Magnan, Sally Sieloff (Ed.). *Challenges in the 1990s for College Foreign Language Programs.* AAUSC Issues in Language Program Direction 1990. Boston: Heinle & Heinle Publishers, 1991.

Murphy, Joseph A. "The Graduate Teaching Assistant in an Age of Standards." In Magnan, 1991: 129–50.

——— & Jane Black Goepper (Ed.). *The Teaching of French: A Syllabus of Competence.* The Report of the Commission on Professional Standards, the American Association of Teachers of French. *AATF National Bulletin* 14 (October 1989). (Special issue.)

Murray, Heather. "Tracing the Development of Language Awareness in EFL Teacher Trainees." *Actes des Journées suisses de linguistique appliquée II Neuchâtel, 17–19 mars 1989. Bulletin CILA* 51 (1990): 21–28.

Nerenz, Anne G., Carol A. Herron & Constance K. Knop. "The Training of Graduate Teaching Assistants in Foreign Languages: A Review of Literature and Description of Contemporary Programs." *French Review* 52 (1979): 873–88.

Thinking Culturally: Self-Awareness and Respect for Diversity in the Foreign Language Classroom

Madeleine Cottenet-Hage, John E. Joseph, and
Pierre M. Verdaguer
The University of Maryland

The word *culture* derives etymologically from *colo,* the Latin verb for tilling soil, and has gone through numerous metaphorical transfers before arriving at its present range of meanings. But within nearly all those meanings one can still detect the trace of two underlying agricultural facts: first, that farmed land is more productive than unfarmed land; second, that there is no single "right" way of farming, but rather a variety of local customs that presumably reflect local topographical and climatic conditions. A farmer of flat bottom land who emigrates to a country of rocky hillsides will be well advised to learn something of the local "culture" (in the etymological sense); if he stubbornly insists on doing things as they were done back home, he risks starving himself and his family.

There is a moral here for foreign language students and teachers alike. *Cultures* in the modern sense develop in significant part in response to local conditions. That part of language that is culturally determined often appears to reflect these conditions, though never obligatorily or completely. Nevertheless, the knowledge of a language one might gain in the absence of cultural knowledge would be highly incomplete — a meager thing indeed. To take a very simple example, an American student who learns that the French words *pain* and *vin* correspond to "bread" and "wine" has learned part but by no means all of their meaning (on *vin*, see Barthes, 1957, pp. 74–77). The word *pain* has a totally different value to most French speakers than "bread" has to most Americans because of its place within the broader framework of culture. Here, "bread" is one member among many others of the starch food group, and is often eaten less for its own sake than for its convenience in holding sandwich fillings; it often is not served with meals in American restaurants, and one may be charged extra for it. In France and many francophone cultures, on the other hand, *pain* remains the staff of life, the one food that should never be omitted from any meal. It is the sustenance of both body and soul — with inevitable resonances of the Catholic doctrine of transubstantiation, even for non-Catholics — and provides a sort of communion among all people, of whatever social class. Its unique status is reflected in the special set of strict standards and price controls placed upon it by the French government; special price controls on bread in the United States are unimaginable. The sort of cultural "meaning" we see in the case of *pain* could be documented throughout the language, including at the level of grammar — where an obvious example would be polite and informal second-person address, discussed later in this chapter.

Gaining cultural knowledge has an additional value beyond supplementing knowledge of the language: it is the most direct route to *self-knowledge*. People have always wondered which aspects of human experience are attributable to nature (heredity) and which to convention (environment). In learning what is not universal in our culture, we learn what is not constrained by nature. We then become like the farmer who, now conscious of two different ways of plowing, can for the first time evaluate the advantages and disadvantages of each.

Because culture is basic to meaning and because the study of culture contributes substantially to self-knowledge, teaching culture must be an important part of our curriculum. We must prepare TAs so that they can teach culture with as much guidance, thought, and creativity as they put into teaching grammar and vocabulary. Such preparation will be one of the main focuses of this chapter. The other main focus has to do with an additional fact about language classrooms: they are often the location of cultural clash, particularly when foreign TAs confront their first classes of American students. We shall argue that such clashes should be anticipated, prepared for, and in fact *exploited* for their very real value in bringing contrasting facets of the two cultures out into the open.

Although most of the examples we cite pertain directly to the teaching of French, we have tried to formulate our methods and conclusions in such a way that they should be applicable, *mutatis mutandis,* to teachers of all languages. Furthermore, because considerably more attention has already been given to incorporating francophone material into the teaching of French, we will focus our remarks on the treatment of diversity *within* France. It might be objected that the teaching of culture in a "world language" like French, Spanish, or English is very different from the case of a language that appears to be more culturally unified, such as Japanese, Italian, or Swedish; we would argue, however, that this is to overlook the very real diversity that exists within any society large enough to constitute a nation. One can always find separate cultures distinguished by some combination of social and economic status, race, religion, geography, politics, age, and sex. Nevertheless, we agree strongly that any French or Spanish course must cover a wide range of francophone and hispanophone countries.

Our chapter has three primary goals. The first is to describe the method we call "thinking culturally" and to provide an illustration of a lesson using this method. The second is to explore the reasons we believe an "anthropological" approach to culture to be superior to the didactic approach to Culture that continues to characterize most language textbooks and classrooms. Finally, the third goal is to show how the language classroom can function as a laboratory for the discovery and celebration of cultural diversity and how TAs can be guided toward this end.

Teaching TAs to Think Culturally

The expression "near-native" has become a watchword of the teaching profession. All instructors are expected to be as near-native as possible with respect to the oral and written mastery of the language they teach. However, there is no equivalent expectation in the area of culture, since no one is ever requested to be culturally near-native. It is nonetheless generally understood that effective language instruction, which relies essentially on so-called near-native language skills, is not possible if the instructor does not have a good understanding of one or more of the major cultures within which a given language is spoken natively.

As we noted above, the syntactic, lexical, and cultural dimensions of a language are sufficiently interconnected that it is artificial to separate these components. In this we disagree completely with Brewer's (1983, p. 150) assertion that, at least for purposes of lower-level instruction, "language structure is a discrete and practically culture-free entity." The awareness of how much of the cultural dimension inherent in any text is inevitably lost in the translation process has contributed to the rejection of translation as the cornerstone of contemporary language-teaching methodology. The earlier predilection for translation was in part a manifestation of the Western ideological context within which the languages were taught. Translation is first and foremost an exercise whereby cultural differences are vastly lessened, if not nullified, because when a text is translated, the cultural dimension inherent in this text is "naturalized," in the legal sense of the term: to turn something alien into something domestic, and therefore culturally acceptable. If we consider this context of officially accepted national superiority — cultural, ideological, racial, or otherwise — it is clear that it was difficult if not impossible to acknowledge fully the right to cultural "otherness." We would define such a context today as essentially ethnocentric and inimical to cultural diversity.

When we try to identify our priorities for lower-level courses taught by TAs, it seems that we should first determine which cultural "elements" should be "taught" alongside the language and which should not, or at least what kind of activities designed to promote cultural awareness should supplement language teaching in the classroom. We may also want to ask ourselves whether the notion of "teaching," when it comes to culture, is relevant. Do we actually "teach" when we rely on strategies meant to develop a greater sensitivity to a foreign culture? Ideally, we would like TAs to focus in class on activities promoting greater awareness of similarities and differences between the target culture and the students' own culture — for example, by first observing typical everyday situations (receiving compliments, table manners, dating, hygiene) and attitudes (toward education, sex, food, work, leisure), and then drawing conclusions from these observations. Depending on the level of the class, a variety of documents can be used to that end: posters, slides, videotaped materials showing physical surroundings or allowing observers to see how people interact on specific occasions, scenes from films, and so forth. This approach, anthropological in nature, is encouraged by researchers such as Carroll (1987). Its obvious advantage is that it fosters a spirit of neutrality on the part of the observer, since it is not concerned with value judgments and purports to avoid them. Through a mirror effect, it should also allow for the enhanced understanding of one's own culture.

The TA is the primary cultural consultant in the classroom, providing students with a source of information on differences in clothing, gestures, greetings and leave-taking, proxemics, giving and receiving compliments, and the like. But most TAs will have direct knowledge of at most just one culture's practices within the great diversity of cultures that speak any language; hence native-speaking TAs are not at so great an advantage over nonnatives as might initially appear to be the case. Even a native TA will need to turn to other sources of information in order to explore the multiplicity of cultural issues that could arise in connection with the course content at any given time. Authentic videos, television series, and films are invaluable; so are such inexpensive materials as slides, photographs, and magazine ads, which all offer possibilities for cultural decoding.

In a recent article, Madeleine Cottenet-Hage (1992) describes how a 1990 poster displayed on walls in Paris was used to lead students into a discussion of the changing relationship between French citizens and their local governments. The poster shows a winter scene in an urban neighborhood. People, young and old, obviously from diverse economic backgrounds, are outside shoveling snow from the sidewalk, while city employees are busy clearing the street. The poster reads:

S'IL NEIGE

NETTOYONS

VOUS   NOUS

LE TROTTOIR   LA CHAUSEE

(If it snows, let's clean it up — you do the sidewalk, we'll do the street). A step-by-step process of questioning focuses the students' attention:

1) The use of the pronouns *vous* 'you' and *nous* 'we' — what are their referents?

2) The position of these pronouns on the poster — on the same line, hence receiving equal attention, and not establishing a priority or hierarchy.

3) The use of *nettoyons*, a first-person imperative form. To whom does it refer? The answer is obviously *nous* and *vous*, hence the appeal to collaboration and cooperation. The students are asked to compare this usage with other injunctions formerly common in France such as

Défense de marcher sur les pelouses (Keep off the grass) or *Prière de jeter les papiers dans la corbeille* (Please don't litter). They are also asked to substitute *nettoyez* 'clean up' for *nettoyons* 'let's clean up' and to evaluate how significant the difference would be.

4) Finally the class focuses on the means by which the message — cooperation and solidarity, rather than authority and rule enforcement — is conveyed. Students discuss the mixture of social classes in the picture, as indicated by clothing, suggesting an integrated neighborhood and harmonious class relations. They comment on the use of soft, pleasant colors and the cartoonlike drawing style, designed to create a utopian, therefore seductive image. The use of an American icon, a Santa Claus figure with a reindeer, rather than a traditional French Père Noël, is a puzzling and more ambiguous pointer in this visual text, one for which students are encouraged to explore alternative explanations.

Thus, through a directed decoding, which can be as short as 15 minutes or as long as an entire period, and can be conducted in French as early as the second semester of instruction, students are made aware of changes taking place in French society regarding the relations between citizens and the "administration," traditionally thought of as "them" or "it," that is, some coercive entity separated from and dominating the private lives of French individuals. Building a new sense of *collective* responsibility can thus be seen as an interesting and necessary development in a country that is about to embark upon a new "joint venture," cooperation with a united Europe. Neither the novelty of this campaign, nor the somewhat naive social didacticism of the poster, may strike American students unless the instructor can, in leading the discussion, bring in the historical context in a few words. Again, this can be done simply and rapidly — and increasingly so as students become used to such exercises in "thinking culturally." (Along similar lines, see Scanlan, 1980.)

Can *culture* and *Culture* Ever Be Reconciled?

Within this anthropological approach, which favors the analysis of the cultural context, it has become commonplace to reinforce the difference between *culture* and *Culture* (see Hofstede, 1980; Morain, 1983). This differentiation, though clearly practical, is nonetheless potentially harmful. Briefly, we could say that we "teach" *Culture*, in so-called civilization courses, for example, which usually focus on artistic trends as well as historical, social, and political developments. In such courses the notion of Culture is closely linked to that of History (the emphasis being on the *emergence* of major trends, including again artistic, sociological, and political phenomena). What matters is that the outlook is primarily diachronic and that it reveals the complexity and richness of the Cultural background of a nation. Activities encouraging cultural awareness in the classroom, on the other hand, revolve around the notion of *c*ulture, meaning whatever composes our daily environment. From this point of view, it is interesting that in her introduction, Carroll (1987) indicates that the form of *c*ultural/ anthropological analysis that she has chosen — and which is probably the dominant one today — must not involve ecological, geographical, economic, religious, or historical considerations. It is therefore the opposite of the diachronic approach described above. We can naturally infer from this division that Culture entails the acquisition of knowledge (one learns about artistic trends, for example, which implies some form of memorization); *c*ulture, on the other hand, is understood as whatever composes our everyday environment, and simply requires a process of observation and interpretation on the part of students who can, for example, learn how to analyze behavioral patterns. It can also be added that the process by which Cultural knowledge is transmitted within the classroom is mostly didactic, whereas the *c*ultural approach is not.

This division emphasizes a type of hierarchy between the two cultures. In spite of the fact that observing and interpreting *c*ultural situations requires more acute analytical skills than the "study" of Culture, Culture is globally perceived by the academic community — often including TAs — as more worthwhile than *c*ulture. The reason is clear: this division coincides with the traditional rift between literature and language. Literature and Culture are regarded as pertaining to a sphere of higher pursuits, whereas the process by which *c*ulture is analyzed tends to be perceived as a more frivolous endeavor. So even though language and *c*ulture may be seen as complementary, they still considered to be a somewhat inferior subject matter.

The preparation of TAs, therefore, should address not only the type of culture to be "taught" in the language class and the methods for implementing such forms of "teaching," but also the various implications inherent in this two-tier hierarchy. It is essential to understand why it is so difficult to escape negative or positive categorization.

One can expect graduate students who have been studying a foreign literature to have to some extent internalized the sense of hierarchy that is reflected in this categorization. If we consider the European context, it should first be pointed out that the use of the word "*culture*" is relatively new and not as widespread as one might imagine, even today. France is an interesting case in point. It is a country where democratic education has, since the end of the nineteenth century (the beginning of the Third Republic), focused on the acquisition of Culture, which is perceived as the road to social success. In today's France upward mobility is still largely determined by criteria of a Cultural nature. In other words, the French educational system — much more so than its American counterpart — still largely favors the most "Cultured" individuals and thus perpetuates the idea of a Cultural *élite* that is deemed essential for the good of the nation. This educational system, of which the French are by and large still very proud, is seen as democratic because it aims at identifying those individuals, regardless of origin (at least theoretically), who will eventually become part of the national *élite*.

Within such a context there is relatively little room for the acceptance of the concept of *culture*. The latter is mostly perceived as a cheapened form of Culture. One may recall that the Cultural centers known in France as "Maisons de la culture," instituted by André Malraux in the 1960s, had the ambition of democratizing "Culture" by making it available to every citizen. It probably would not have occurred to Malraux, who was the minister of culture and therefore the guardian of French Cultural integrity, that there was another way of defining the concept of culture. It was as a reaction to this national policy that in the late 1960s a very famous French comedian, Jean Yann, started his daily radio program with the slogan: *Quand j'entends le mot «culture» je sors mon transistor!,* which roughly translates as: "When I hear the word 'culture,' I get out my radio!" The "*cultural*" implications behind the slogan are mostly lost in the translation; a *cultural* equivalent might be: "When I hear the words 'classical music,' I think of the Beatles!" The point is that associating "radio" with "culture" is not incongruous in the United States, where the anthropological acceptation of the latter word is widely used — unlike in France, where radio and television are generally seen as the prime instruments of Cultural debasement.

Making sure that TAs understand the bias against *culture* is essential, particularly if their courses of study have focused mainly on literature, one of the fundamental pillars of Culture. Without such understanding, it is doubtful that they can achieve the distance necessary to promote an atmosphere conducive to cross-cultural analyses in their classrooms. What is more, attitudes regarding culture and Culture can themselves serve as components of the larger investigation of cultural difference.

The Politics of Culture

Any discourse on culture, including that which takes place in the foreign language classroom, is fraught with potential political dangers. These should, we believe, be pointed out directly to both American and foreign TAs as part of their initial preparation. If possible, they should not simply be laid down in the form of axiomatic rules, but instead should be discussed at some length in order to tease out the specific cultural content underlying them. After all, the very fact that these are "political dangers" is part of American culture of the late twentieth century — yet there is no guarantee that either American or foreign TAs will recognize this truth.

First, any discussion of "national" culture presents obvious dangers of overgeneralization and stereotyping. It also leads quite naturally into statements that perpetuate a long-discredited romantic idealism, and that at the very worst can border on racism. This is true regardless of whether the culture in question is being praised or denigrated. As we shall discuss further on, the observations that it is valuable for an instructor to make are those related directly to his or her own immediate milieu and experience. Culture, like language, is a social phenomenon that is nevertheless embodied in individuals, despite our idiosyncrasies. The point is not for the TA to become an amateur anthropologist, but rather the equivalent of an anthropological "consultant" (what used to be called an "informant"). It is the students who will be cast in something more akin to the anthropologist's role.

Second, despite the preceding observation, *not* to discuss culture is even more dangerous; for it will result in students trying to impose their own cultural framework onto the language they are learning. Needless to say, it can only be an imperfect fit, leaving students with the perception that the target language and the people who speak it are inferior. (It is hard to see how, under such circumstances, anyone could *fail* to reach this conclusion.)

Third, our insistence on a relativistic treatment of cultures means that one must not automatically impose a moral judgment when confronted with a cultural difference. On the other hand, we cannot ignore the reality that moral judgments do exist and are a powerful force; neither should we exempt ourselves from making and expressing our own moral judgments, provided they are buttressed with accurate information and substantial reflection. We are thinking in particular of cultures in which human rights are conceived in a fundamentally different way than in modern Western societies — cultures where, for instance, slavery or genocide are being practiced. To treat slavery or genocide in a relativistic, value-neutral way is amoral, regardless of whether one's observations may make no immediate difference. The same could be said of personal or political repression based upon race, sex, sexual orientation, religion, or ideology; yet here already the matter of what constitutes "repression" leans toward the realm of personal opinion, and probably no culture, however "civilized," could escape criticism for some kind of oppression of this sort.

A balance must be sought, such that the language classroom does not serve as the instructor's political soapbox or "bully pulpit," but neither does the instructor appear to condone the most heinous violations of human rights by passing them over in silence. Since the latter case will be the exception rather than the rule, our emphasis in this chapter will be on making the teaching of culture less judgmental, and more anthropological. Even in the case of slavery, our model should be the anthropological study of a slave-holding society in which, after making clear her loathsome aversion of slavery, the scholar goes on to give as dispassionate an account as possible of her field observations.

Working with the Cultural Material in Language Textbooks

Most first-year language textbooks include cultural information in the form of "cultural notes" appended to each chapter. TAs, especially nonnative speakers of the language being taught, rarely know what to *do* with this material, especially when it is not concerned with Culture. Examining the cultural notes found in one widely used French textbook — one that we find admirable in many ways — we discover a range of topics that, on the surface, simply aim at providing students with necessary background knowledge on certain aspects of the society to which they are being introduced. It should be pointed out that similar cultural notes, with similar shortcomings, are to be found in all the most widely used language textbooks. Surveys of them may be found in Arizpe and Aguirre (1987), Joiner (1974), Levno and Pfister (1980), and Moreau and Pfister (1978). All these surveys cite numerous examples of textbooks containing stereotyped, idealized, prejudiced, and just-plain-wrong information; and we have little reason to believe that the situation has since improved significantly.

The first major shortcoming of the notes is precisely that they are didactic in nature. They are first and foremost aimed at "teaching" culture and virtually preclude any interpretative process. So even though they provide information that is not Cultural, the didactic process by which such information is provided is typical of the very traditional educational approach that, since it aims at promoting Culture, is closed to cross-cultural interpretation.

Well into the 1940s a reader entitled *Le Tour de la France par deux enfants* (Bruno, 1976) was universally used in French schools. In many ways it can be regarded as one of the sources revealing the spirit that still pervades cultural notes today. This textbook is organized around a story line, the trip of two children from Alsace-Lorraine to Marseille. Aside from its patriotic and moral aspects, what is striking is its extraordinary didactic dimension: information is provided on every possible occasion during the trip. The cultural notes of our textbooks are very much the products of this tradition, emphasizing the importance of "learning" what is seen as being specifically national. Within the French educational context this tradition has always been perceived as the preliminary foundation students should gain to have access to Culture, and therefore be successful in life. In spite of appearances, cultural notes are thus directly linked to the acquisition of Culture.

This in turn explains why those notes are so often irrelevant. Since they are not written from a cross-cultural perspective but from an essentially ethnocentric one, American students frequently cannot relate to the information they contain, unless of course this information is first properly "explained," presumably in English, since cultural notes touch upon concepts that could not be tackled in the target language at the lower levels. Let us briefly consider some specific examples in our sample textbook.

Most notes are designed to provide the kind of didactic information that one might find in guidebooks. They touch upon geographical and climatic characteristics, the relationship between continental France and its overseas territories, francophone areas and countries, travel, and so on. Offering an overview of a particular aspect of the target society (or societies) is innocuous enough except for an obvious shortcoming: this approach lends itself to reductive and somewhat simplistic interpretations. One of these cultural vignettes, for example, aims at defining national traits, no less. The French are thus inevitably described as individualistic, sociable, private, respectful of tradition, and so on — traits that can be ascribed equally well (or poorly) to all Europeans, and, for that matter, to Americans. The problem, however, is that such notions are not necessarily understood in the same way in all cultures. It should also be noted that the *Culture/culture* distinction is manifested nowhere so much as in the coverage of *France* relative to the rest of the *francophone* world.

Overall, the central characteristic of many of these notes remains their marked cultural specificity. The notes entitled *"La classe ouvrière"* (the working class), *"Paris et le reste de la France"* (Paris and the rest of France), *"Les agents de police"* (the police), to take just a few, reflect unmistakably a fundamentally French outlook. This outlook is revealed as much by the choice of the topic itself as by the manner in which it is presented. There can be an underlying and not readily identifiable perspective inherent in the note "How do the French relate to their police?" How do they perceive the Cultural and political status of their capital (which implies understanding the notion of centralization)? How do they understand the function of a town center?

Similarly, the concept of the "working class" and its multiple and complex connotations is mostly unknown to American students, who are used to dealing with rather different class determinants. Inevitably, the ideological slant and the brevity of the cultural notes are such that the contention that they can be used successfully as a basis for classroom discussion cannot be taken seriously. Indeed, it is extraordinary that "cultural notes" should still constitute the backbone of the "teaching" of culture at the lower levels. In many ways, relying on them is thus counter-productive. As long as they remain omnipresent, TAs have to be aware of their insidious dimension. Unless they can learn to critique the slant of these notes, it would be best for TAs not to use them at all.

The root of the problem, therefore, lies to a great extent in the differentiation between *culture* and *Culture*, which is largely an artificial distinction. After all, in order to understand *culture* one has to become familiar sooner or later with notions of a *Cultural* nature, since even the physical objects that compose our immediate environment have historical resonances, some with profound emotional overtones — the word *pain,* discussed earlier, is a case in point. We could say, in other words, that

Culture fits into a broader concept known as culture. This does not mean that everyone within the target cultural context is necessarily aware of this interrelationship. However, TAs, like all other language instructors, should be. From the perspective of their training, therefore, what should be advocated more than the standard distinction between culture and Culture is the link between the two and the constant overlapping of Cultural elements of a historical, literary, or artistic nature with the global cultural background against which a language is spoken. Strictly speaking, there is *no* opposition between the two. It is therefore essential that the preparation of TAs focus on the need to reassess the complementarity between culture and Culture.

The Need for Critical Self-Awareness

Many foreign language departments employ foreign TAs in their lower-level foreign language courses. While their presence might well be perceived as an asset on account not only of their language skills but also of their knowledge of the foreign culture, we shall use their case to highlight some of the difficulties attached to the teaching of culture in the classroom. This will help us make recommendations regarding the preparation of both foreign and American TAs to be better cultural informants and interpreters.

Unquestionably, native-speaking TAs bring to the classroom a wealth of firsthand knowledge of *one* native day-to-day culture that few nonnatives can ever possess. As for Culture, native TAs do not necessarily come equipped with a broad and accurate knowledge of the vast interdisciplinary body of Culture as defined by the history, the literary and artistic productions, the institutions and laws, and so on, of their nation. In this respect, nonnatives may be just as knowledgeable, since there is nothing to Culture that cannot be acquired from studying and reading, and indeed nonnatives may profit from the objective "outsider's" understanding and perspective they bring to bear upon that knowledge. We will therefore concern ourselves solely with the question of culture.

What TAs, native or nonnative, usually lack is a critical perspective on their own experience. As a result, they tend to assume that what is true of themselves and their own group — family, peers, friends, region, class — is true of the nation at large. They will therefore present a limited and subjective experience as general truths. Consequently, they will need to be shown how to look at their own experience critically, and to become aware of the autobiographical, sociological, economic, and geographic determinants that have shaped their own lives. Unless they can assign specific boundaries to the information shared with their students, such as "a small town in the south of France," "a middle-class Protestant family," "the generation born after 1960," that information runs the risk of being inaccurate if not grossly misleading. In this case, TAs will merely compound the problem that plagues the teaching of a foreign culture and repeat the mistakes often made by experienced teachers of a language and by most textbooks, by insisting on the reality of *Difference* and ignoring the reality of *Diversity*.

A specific language-related case is the use of polite and informal address (*tu* vs. *vous*), for example, within families. Here is a cultural feature that varies widely according to social class, region, age, and sex — so much as to defy any attempt at generalization. Yet the average native TA, lacking exposure to milieus other than that to which he or she was born, is unlikely to be aware of the full extent of this variation, and may present the patterns of his or her own family as being universally valid. Students may be taught, then, that in French families *tu* is used reciprocally among all members, when in fact some families (particularly of the upper middle class) still place a strong value on the use of *vous* to members of the parents' and especially the grandparents' generation. This is a particularly salient example because of the unique power of both *tu* and *vous* to give offense when used inappropriately, which is to say against the rules of the specific "subculture" at hand.

An uncritical acceptance of their own cultural practices and norms by native TAs will frequently translate in the classroom into value-laden assertions, judgments privileging the home culture as "good," while the American culture is seen as "lacking." Students may perceive this in a general way as a "superior attitude" and are almost certain to resent it (and justifiably so). Even a simple item such as coffee may become an occasion to celebrate loudly the aroma and body of the Latin American "cafe" served in small cups to the appreciative native, and to dismiss the American beverage served in large mugs as weak and flavorless.

Needless to say, this is counterproductive, since our objective is to promote not just the knowledge of Difference but a nonjudgmental acceptance of Otherness and Diversity. In this respect, American TAs often do a better job, provided they themselves do not hold a somewhat romanticized or, conversely, jaundiced view of the foreign culture, in which case the objectives outlined above will not be met either.

It is undoubtedly very difficult, if not impossible, to teach anyone — including oneself — not to pass hasty judgments on the unfamiliar and not to hold what is familiar as what is good. But awareness is the first step toward more tolerance and understanding. The very difficulty inherent to the development of cultural understanding should therefore become a matter for renewed discussions in TA training sessions specially designed to encourage TAs to think culturally. In these sessions TAs could be asked to present short autobiographical sketches, stressing their education, social background, and so forth. Doing this will make them aware of how their views and interpretations of the cultural reality are framed by who they are and where they come from. The group could then enter into a discussion of how their differences might be reflected in their classroom teaching (style, content, attitudes, and so on). TAs should also be required to confront interpretations of specific social situations (hypothetical or real). Several objectives can be pursued in these sessions. One is methodological: how to lead a successful investigation into cultural items. The other is educational: at this point, the session leader must be able to bring in available ethnographic information — or, alternatively, refer students to available sources, and, better still, bring in a specialist — to allow the TAs to check the validity of their conclusions and cast them in a more theoretical perspective.

Some additional activities for promoting cultural awareness can be found in Morain (1976).

The Classroom as Cultural Lab

Not infrequently, as much cultural information is embodied in *how* TAs teach as in *what* they teach. As the cultural beacon in the classroom, they may contribute to the development of positive or negative attitudes toward the target culture. In order to generate attitudes that are realistic and not counterproductive, foreign TAs must become not only interpreters of their own culture, but enlightened mediators between the two cultures, theirs and their students'.

Such a task requires them to know and understand the American culture as it functions at the microlevel of the classroom. This is often not the case — even with American TAs — hence the many misunderstandings that arise, to the detriment of both language learning and the development of cross-cultural communication. In the following discussion we shall examine a few of the ways in which ignorance of some basic American values (see Kohls, n.d.) — shared by *most* American students and reflected in classroom behavior — may prevent the establishment of a positive classroom climate.

We have all heard foreign TAs comment, usually with implied if not explicit criticism, on the fact that some of their American students chew gum, bring drinks to class, slouch in their seats, and hand back assignments scribbled in pencil on pieces of paper torn from notebooks. Foreign TAs are quick to interpret such behavior as signs of insufficient interest in the course and disrespect for the instructor. While it is true that not all students behave this way, nor would all American teachers accept such practices, it is nevertheless important that foreign TAs understand to what extent they are seeing signs of a key American cultural value, *informality*. Informal dress, informal greetings, and informal speech patterns when addressing an instructor during or after class are all manifestations of this same tendency to attach less importance to form than in most of the societies from which foreign TAs come, whether they are African, South American, Asian, or European. Indeed, there is a positive value to informality in American culture, as an icon of friendship and solidarity.

We have all observed newly arrived foreign TAs make critical remarks to a student in public or comment on an individual assignment in front of the whole class (whether to praise or condemn it). We have all cringed, together with the class. The TA has just violated a whole set of American norms that are hard to separate from one another. One of them is the right to *privacy* — the very term defies translation into French and many other languages besides. One does not publicly reveal personal information about private individuals without their consent, particularly when the information is potentially damaging to their image and ego. (Note that the fundamental distinction between private citizens and public figures made in libel cases is uniquely American, distinguishing our legal system even from the British common law to which it is most closely related.) The other norm involved is *egalitarianism*. The instructor has upset the fundamental assumption that all individuals in the class are equal by establishing a hierarchy based upon success and failure. This touches upon another fundamental assumption on which the performance of the class is based: that success is within the reach of any individual and that innate differences in ability and intelligence count less than sheer effort. In an American classroom the teacher is careful to praise a student's effort even though the fruit of that effort might not, objectively speaking, be praiseworthy. But for the foreign TA, not only is the result the tangible evidence of work, but commenting on it in public is his or her right and duty as teacher — as the *authority* in charge. This brings us back to the concept of egalitarianism, which is suddenly brought into conflict with the foreigner's assumption — and experience — that *position* gives you rights over another in a lesser position.

Of course, not all foreign TAs will act in like manner. Many show sensitivity, if only because they are so close to their students in age that they tend to adopt an informal rather than a formal and authoritarian style. Some will even "go native" and become more informal than their American counterparts (who may themselves go native in the opposite direction). Nevertheless, the deep-seated cultural patterns of their own countries may resurface, particularly when a conflict or a stressful situation arises. Deference, rank, acceptance of a superior's right to negative evaluation — all of which are rather foreign to American culture — are intrinsic to many other cultures, and all are effective defenses against the kind of insecurities that beginning TAs are bound to feel from time to time.

Does this mean that foreign TAs need to conform silently to American norms? This is where, we believe, their presence in the classroom becomes invaluable. They may choose to conform, but rather than do so silently they might want to seize the opportunity to *discuss* how and why they experience discomfort, how and why they are tempted to set different class rules, and so on. In lower-level classes, such discussions would have to be conducted in English, but they could remain circumscribed and to the point. The danger, of course, is allowing English discussions to use up precious time for language instruction. For this reason, carefully prepared questions will prevent improvisation and meandering. In more advanced classes (and in some cases as early as the second semester) discussions in the target language provide a marvelous opportunity for language practice with a content that is more appealing and more relevant to students because it calls upon their input, reactions, and interpretations, and makes connections with their own lives. But again, TAs can only lead students into an enlightening discussion if they themselves have been taught to reflect upon both their own experience and the American context, if they themselves have received in the course of their preparation an acceptable theoretical framework that will help them interpret and make sense of the differences that they encounter.

Conclusion

We have argued for increased preparation of TAs in the area of culture and presented a number of points to include in that preparation. The problems faced by American and foreign TAs, despite superficial differences, are fundamentally the same: native-speaking TAs are likely to have an insufficient understanding of the extent to which they can generalize their own experience and of those aspects of American culture that differ from their own. American TAs typically lack enough exposure to the target culture (if not the Culture) to supplement the textbook in significant ways. Both face the same political dimension in the teaching of culture, and both are equally likely to need guidance in developing an understanding of the relative importance of culture and Culture, as well as in developing an appropriately nonjudgmental outlook on cultural diversity. The actual cultural conflicts that arise in the foreign language classroom setting provide an ideal opportunity for the exploration of cultural differences in a way that is maximally relevant to the TA's own experience.

Works Cited

Arizpe, Victor & Benigno E. Aguirre. "Mexican, Puerto Rican, and Cuban Ethnic Groups in First-Year College-Level Spanish Textbooks." *Modern Language Journal* 71 (1987): 125–37.

Barthes, Roland. *Mythologies.* Paris: Seuil, 1957. English translation: *Mythologies.* Tr. Annette Lavers. New York: Hill and Wang, 1972.

Brewer, William B. "The Truisms, Clichés, and Shibboleths of Foreign-Language Requirements." *Modern Language Journal* 67 (1983): 149–51.

Bruno, G. [pseudonym of Madame Alfred Fouillée]. *Le Tour de la France par deux enfants.* Réédition. Paris: Belin, 1976.

Carroll, Raymonde. *Evidences invisibles: Américains et Français au quotidien.* Paris: Seuil, 1987. English translation: *Cultural Misunderstandings: The French–American Experience.* Tr. Carol Volk. Chicago: University of Chicago Press, 1988.

Cottenet-Hage, Madeleine. "Enseigner la culture." *Le Français dans le Monde* 250 (juillet, 1992): 66–69.

Hofstede, Geert. *Culture's Consequences: Institutional Differences in Work-Related Values.* Beverly Hills, CA: Sage Publications, 1980.

Joiner, Elizabeth G. "Evaluating the Cultural Content of Foreign Language Texts." *Modern Language Journal* 58 (1974): 242–44.

Kohls, L. Robert. "The Values Americans Live By." Mimeograph distributed by Meridian House International, Washington, DC (n.d.).

Levno, Arley W. & Guenter G. Pfister. "An Analysis of Surface Culture and Its Manner of Presentation in First-Year College French Textbooks from 1972 to 1978." *Foreign Language Annals* 13 (1980): 47–52.

Morain, Genelle. "The Cultural Component of the Methods Course." *Designs for Foreign Language Teacher Education.* Ed. Alan Garfinkel & Stanley Hamilton. Rowley, MA: Newbury House Publishers, 1976: 25–46.

_____. "Commitment to the Teaching of Foreign Cultures." *Modern Language Journal* 67 (1983): 403–12.

Moreau, Paul H. & Guenter G. Pfister. "An Analysis of the Deep Cultural Aspects of Second-Year College French Texts from 1972 to 1974." *Foreign Language Annals* 11 (1978): 165–71.

Scanlan, Timothy M. "Another Foreign Language Skill: Analyzing Photographs." *Foreign Language Annals* 13 (1980): 209–13.

Improving Inter-rater Reliability in Scoring Tests in Multisection Courses

Robert M. Terry
University of Richmond

At many colleges and universities lower-level foreign language courses are most frequently offered in multiple sections. Typical multisection courses have the following elements in common: course goals and objectives, syllabus, textbooks, tests (including final examinations), and a teaching corps often composed primarily of untrained graduate teaching assistants (TAs). Normally, the course goals and objectives, syllabus, and textbooks are determined either by a consensus of the teaching staff or by the coordinators of the course. Course tests and examinations may come from or be based on the test packet that accompanies the textbook, or they may be newly developed each semester or quarter by the instructional staff involved or by the course coordinators. A problem exists, however, with tests administered to all sections. Whether multisection courses are taught by TAs, part-time or adjunct faculty, or full-time faculty, and whether the tests from all sections are combined and graded by all instructors or individual instructors grade their own tests, the fundamental problem that arises is ensuring consistency among the instructional staff in scoring the tests.

This consistency in scoring is called *inter-rater reliability,* the "correlation between different raters' ratings of the same objects or performance"

(Henning, 1987, p. 193). While inter-rater reliability normally refers to scores on a given test that are independent assessments by two or more judges or raters, the term refers here to the correlation of scores on common tests among course sections, with each test being scored either by the TA of that section or randomly by one of the total group of TAs. High inter-rater reliability is important in order to ensure that course goals are being met and that student knowledge and performance are measured with a common yardstick.

Testing and Proficiency-Oriented Instruction

A major trend in current foreign language instruction is the shift in emphasis along the achievement/proficiency continuum. We have moved away from focusing on the knowledge of discrete grammar points and structures toward encouraging a more comprehensive, functional ability to carry out spontaneous, autonomous communicative tasks and exchanges in the target language in the four skill areas of reading, writing, listening, and speaking. Tests administered in those courses that claim to have such a communicative focus, however, regardless of their surface appearance, are often achievement tests that measure specific features of the language from a finite corpus of specific teaching materials. True proficiency tests, on the other hand, are performance-oriented and require the application of acquired knowledge to carry out communicative tasks. As Larson and Jones (1984, p. 116) note, "They are based on functional language ability and are not limited by a closed set of course materials nor constrained by instructional variables." Although many tests today include proficiency-oriented items that are contextualized and more comprehensive, that is, global, in scope, TAs may use them essentially for measuring student achievement. This is not contradictory, however, as Medley (1985, p. 35) so aptly points out:

> The fact that a curriculum is proficiency-oriented does *not* mean that there is no need for achievement testing. Quite the contrary, since achievement testing will be the primary means at the teacher's disposal for day-to-day assessment of student progress and instructional effectiveness. Tests will be designed to measure the specific features of the language the students are learning, and how well they are learning them. As a result, achievement will remain the principal determining factor in the measurement of progress and the assignment of grades.

Sections of a test containing items that are presented in a relatively traditional format, for example, fill-in-the-blank, multiple choice, sentence rewriting, cloze, and so on, contain essentially convergent items. Convergent items may be either discrete-point (focused) or in an integrative format scored by discrete points. This traditional format is most often used in evaluating the receptive skills (reading and listening), vocabulary, and basic knowledge of grammar. Those items or sections of the test that measure and evaluate the productive skills of speaking and writing are often more open-ended, global comprehension items that call for divergent answers (Omaggio, 1986, p. 315). Discrete-point scoring is objective, while the scoring of items with divergent answers tends to be subjective.

It is this latter category of subjective scoring that causes the most concern in ensuring high inter-rater reliability, since subjective scoring may be impressionistic, based on subjective reactions to responses to test items. Reactions can be positive toward the work of the student who shows strong communicative skills, who proves to be very creative, or who is very accurate. They can be negative toward the work of the student who, though he or she communicates well, possibly demonstrating a high degree of creativity, exhibits serious grammatical errors. As Magnan (1985, p. 130) cautions, "[W]e need to guard against judging all aspects of [a student's performance] in terms of only one dimension of it.... In grading, as in giving feedback, we should not let attention to errors in mechanics overshadow more communicative aspects."

The primary problem is, therefore, how to reduce subjectivity in evaluating student performance on divergent items without narrowing evaluation to a form of discrete-point scoring in which grammatical, lexical, and stylistic errors often overshadow other aspects of performance.

Errors of any sort and severity should not go unnoticed, since measuring and evaluating student performance should measure *all* aspects of the communicative act, whether communication takes place through writing or through speaking. Language is, after all, comprehensive; it is predicated on the appropriate combination and use of grammatical, lexical, stylistic, and sociolinguistic elements in order to convey intended meanings. A communicative act, even one marked by errors, is effective when, in fact, it communicates meaning. Nonetheless, we cannot let errors go unnoticed. Richards (1974, p. 49) wisely cautions: "If grammatically deviant speech still serves to communicate the speaker's intent, why should we pay further attention to it? Simply because speech is linked to attitudes and social structure. Deviancy from grammatical and phonological norms of a speech community elicits evaluational reactions that may classify a person unfavorably." The same principle clearly exists for writing.

Scoring Techniques and Guidelines

Since the basic problem addressed in this chapter is how to ensure consistency among TAs in evaluating student performance on common tests, especially on divergent items, I will present many grading models for both writing and speaking. More important, however, than the model selected is the manner in which it is used in the multisection course.

The following imperative is offered: establish clear guidelines for assessing and scoring such tests. Supervisors and TAs should draw up these guidelines *before* administering tests. The guidelines should contain clearly written descriptions that specify the variety of types of performance that TAs can expect according to the level of the course, the material that has been covered, the students' level of linguistic sophistication and knowledge, and what the students are expected to know at this particular stage of language learning. It is only logical to assume that the descriptions will be based on experience with students at a given level of study. Such a set of guidelines will establish a priori the common yardstick against which all students will be measured.

TAs must be trained in using the guidelines since, in reality, no one student's test will match letter for letter the descriptions of any one level of performance. TAs must realize that each test will exhibit certain key traits that are indicative of performance for each level. For this reason, the guideline descriptions must be specific enough to discriminate between levels of performance, identifying the key traits that are manifested at each level, without being so specific that every mistake that could be made is enumerated. They should also be general enough to include all anticipated varieties of typical student performance.

The operative word in the preceding paragraph is *trained.* The problem of ensuring inter-rater reliability is exacerbated when the instructional personnel in core multisection courses are made up of novice TAs "whose appointment rests primarily upon the survival needs of an understaffed system of higher education" (Murphy, 1991, p. 130). While TAs must fulfill the requirements to earn their graduate degree, they must also be trained in foreign language pedagogy, which adds yet another course to their already overcrowded program of study. Such methods courses are crucial for instilling a high degree of professional competence in tomorrow's group of foreign language teachers. As Murphy (1991, p. 141) points out, "The new TA suffers from a flawed educational system in which he/she enters graduate school deprived of requisite background knowledge. The problem is two-dimensional: (1) undergraduate programs in the liberal arts are often inadequate for personal development needs and (2) professional or specialist training in the rudiments of teaching is missing."

The AATF (Murphy & Goepper, 1989), AATSP ("AATSP," 1990), and ACTFL ("ACTFL," 1988) have identified general competencies for foreign language teachers, among which are found:

- The teacher who possesses the Basic level of competence will "know how to prepare *instruments with which to diagnose and evaluate the skill areas* of speaking, listening, reading, and writing as well as a knowledge of culture" (Murphy & Goepper, 1989, p. 21; my italics).

- Indicators of program consistency with the goal of instruction include: "coursework and experience in devising *appropriate testing techniques*" ("ACTFL," 1988, p. 77; my italics).

The AATF's "Teaching of French: A Syllabus of Competence" (Murphy & Goepper, 1989) recommends both a preservice and an advanced methods course. For TAs especially, the preservice course should offer these prospective teachers "some theoretical concerns and a variety of techniques with which to enter the profession and develop a routine" (Murphy & Goepper, 1989, p. 21). The variety of techniques must include practice in the evaluation and grading of student performance, since evaluation techniques must be clearly understood before the first test is actually administered and graded. Through such intensive training the common yardstick can be introduced, practiced, and understood, thereby ensuring consistency in scoring throughout multisection courses.

Solution 1: Holistic Scoring

The essential purpose of all testing is to determine levels of student performance (knowledge) based on the comparison of performance against the standards established for a course. One type of guideline that can be drawn up for assessing student performance is a global scale in which comprehensive, descriptive criteria are written for each of the expected levels of performance. A holistic (global) scale is based on an overall, total *impression* of student work, since certain components in free, creative responses cannot be quantified as discrete-point items because there can be no clear-cut anticipated response. In evaluating student performance on highly creative test items and activities, there is no substitute for the judgment of the evaluator in determining the overall impression of the response, that is, the balance that students have achieved between grammatical accuracy and meaningful communication. In spite of this necessity, such judgment is still subjective. Holistic criteria help reduce the subjective nature of scoring by providing clear descriptions of levels of performance against which student performance can be determined. The descriptive criteria should be written for each different divergent test item as well as for each test since student abilities are expected to increase and improve over time. Even if the same test is used in subsequent years, the criteria should undergo periodic revision and refinement, resulting in a more precise reflection of the various levels of performance expected in the program, and the development of scales that are clearer and easier to use by the TAs, "enabling them to assign a grade with as little arbitrariness as is humanly possible" (Johnson, 1983, p. 17).

Holistic scoring is used in scoring the Advanced Placement (AP) Examinations of the College Board. We must realize, however, that AP tests are administered to high school students who are at an advanced level. The expectations of performance and the resultant scoring scales advocated by the College Board far surpass the pragmatic reality of beginning- and intermediate-level college and university courses in which students are only starting to reach the level of typical AP students. Nonetheless, these scoring scales are worth examining, since they can be adapted for use at a level commensurate with the expectations of performance for lower-level students.

Standards for each question on the AP examination have an associated grading scale that is designed to allow readers to make distinctions among answers. "The scales — usually from 0 to 9 or 0 to 15 — avoid the problem, on the one hand, of too few points which allow only coarse distinctions and, on the other hand, of too many points which require overly refined, often meaningless, discriminations. The grading standards guarantee that no matter when a candidate's answer is read or by whom, it will, in all probability, receive the same grade" (Johnson, 1983, p. 3). *This* is inter-rater reliability.

The standardization of scoring is carried out by having a supervisory group of readers score sample answers individually, then compare their scores. After discussing the sample answers, they reach a consensus on the grade that the sample answers should receive. Significant examples are chosen for each grade level, that is, level of performance, defining the exact standards by which all examinations are to be graded, providing examples of the application of these standards, and ensuring that there is a common understanding of how the standards are to be applied (Johnson, 1983, p. 17).

The sample answers selected by the supervisory group are then scored, analyzed, and discussed with the group of scorers. Much attention is paid to those borderline cases that fall just to one side or the other of the critical line dividing an acceptable performance from one that does not suggest achievement acceptable at the AP level. Then, a group of preselected essays is distributed and individually scored. The process of constantly comparing scores and discussing reasons for assigning a given score leads to a clear understanding of the gradations of the scale by the scorers. Once this understanding is achieved, formal scoring can begin. This same type of training program is used for scoring student-taped oral performance on the speaking section of the examination.

As I noted above, similar training programs should exist for TAs who teach multisection courses, whether they are experienced teachers or neophytes. In the case of TAs, it is crucial that training in evaluation go hand in hand with teacher training. Many TAs have no prior teaching experience and rely solely on impressions or recollections of how they themselves were taught and tested. Optimally the evaluation training period for TAs should take place before instruction in the course actually begins. The training program should familiarize the TAs with the goals and objectives of each course and give them practice in scoring tests, thereby ensuring a clear understanding of the application of the scoring system.

Writing

The scoring standards for the essay-writing section of the AP French examination are found in Table 1. "The score that is given to any particular exam is determined largely by the student's use of language as measured against the scale given" (Johnson, 1983, p. 18).

Table 1

Advanced Placement Scoring Standards: Writing

Demonstrates Superiority	9	*Strong* control of the language: proficiency and variety in grammatical usage with few significant errors; broad command of vocabulary and of idiomatic French.
Demonstrates Competence	8 7	*Good* general control of grammatical structures despite some errors and/or some awkwardness of style. Good use of idioms and vocabulary. Reads smoothly overall.
Suggests Competence	6 5	*Fair* ability to express ideas in French: correct use of simple grammatical structures or use of more complex structures without numerous serious errors. Some apt vocabulary and idioms. Occasional signs of fluency and sense of style.
Suggests Incompetence	4 3	*Weak* use of language with little control of grammatical structures. Limited vocabulary. Frequent use of anglicisms which force interpretations on the part of the reader. Occasional redeeming features.
Demonstrates Incompetence	2 1	*Clearly unacceptable* from most points of view. Almost total lack of vocabulary resources, little or no sense of idiom and/or style. Essentially gallicized English or *charabia*.
Floating Point		A one-point bonus should be awarded for a coherent and well organized essay or for a particularly inventive one.

From Johnson, 1983, p. 18.

Reschke (1990, p. 101) points out that there are two aspects to global assessment of *any* linguistic performance, regardless of modality, that are important in assessing writing (as well as speaking) skills: (1) the shift in the focus of the evaluation from the usual preoccupation with student errors to what the student does *well* and *correctly;* and (2) the degree to which the student *succeeds* in expressing and communicating his or her ideas. Reschke has modified the College Board's nine-point AP scale slightly to make it applicable for use by foreign language teachers. He provides two different scales: a basic, intuitive scale that serves both as an initial and as a final check in the evaluation process (see Table 2), and a complementary articulated scale (see Table 3) with more complete descriptions of each of the five proficiency levels it identifies.

Table 2

**Reschke's Holistic Essay Grading Scale: Basic Scale —
Range and Minimal Description**

Upper Half

9	Demonstrates superior writing skills
8	
7	Demonstrates strong writing skills
6	
5	Demonstrates competent writing skills
4	

Lower Half

3	Suggests incompetent writing skills
2	
1	Demonstrates incompetent writing skills

From Reschke, 1990, p. 102.

Table 3

Reschke's Holistic Essay Grading Scale: Articulated Scale

Upper-Half Responses

9 to 8   Demonstrates superiority through outstanding control of the language with regard to syntax, grammar, idiomatic usage, and vocabulary. The student makes few significant errors and demonstrates a broad command of the language and obvious fluency. The difference between an 8 and a 9 is one of degree.

7 to 6   Demonstrates strong command of the target language with, however, some grammatical inaccuracies and errors and some awkwardness of expression. Shows good, although not always accurate, use of vocabulary and idioms. Errors do *not* detract from the generally clear demonstration of competence. The difference between a 6 and a 7 is one of degree (quality, fluency).

5 to 4   Demonstrates good to acceptable use of the language and suggests that the candidate is basically competent. The student makes occasional serious grammatical and syntactic errors and has a less impressive range of vocabulary and idioms than a student in the category above. There are occasional signs of fluency in the written work. Recurring doubt about the competence of a student lowers the score to a 4.

Lower-Half Responses

3 to 2   Weak use of the language suggests incompetence. The composition displays numerous errors and frequently uses anglicisms and/or English syntax and thought patterns. The composition contains sentences that paraphrase or essentially repeat what has been stated earlier, lists activities and places or things in series without giving reasons, and/or forces interpretation on the part of the reader. The lack of an occasional redeeming feature, such as the correct use of advanced grammatical constructions and vocabulary, tends to lower the score to a 2. (Getting a simple sentence grammatically correct now and then is *not* a sufficiently redeeming feature.)

1   Clear demonstration of incompetence. The student has little or no sense of syntax and has very few vocabulary resources. The content of the student's written work is essentially incomprehensible Germanized English.

Additional Comments:

a.   One point is *subtracted* if the essay or composition does not address the assigned topic.

b.   One point is *subtracted* if the essay or composition is poorly organized *or* is substantially shorter than called for (i.e., less than 90% of the assigned length).

c.   One point is *added* if the essay or composition is especially well organized *and* well written.

d.   No more than two points are deducted from any essay or composition.

e.   In case of doubt about what score to assign to an essay or composition (a high 6/low 7 or a strong 7/weak 8), the spelling is carefully looked at. If it is obviously phonetic and poor (many errors), the lower score is assigned.

From Reschke, 1990, p. 103.

For our purposes, both the rationale and the principles that are the bases for creating such scales are what is important, not the specific wording as illustrated in the tables. It is clear that students in lower-level classes are not asked to write compositions or essays that involve high-level stylistic features. Often the TA cannot assess the value of the content given the autobiographical nature of many topics. Nonetheless, the student is demonstrating a developing writing skill along with a knowledge of the rudiments and formal aspects of the target language, and the impact of the entire writing sample must be considered in evaluation.

The principles of such scales as those illustrated in Tables 1, 2, and 3 can be readily adapted to suit the content and linguistic levels of the students, even students in the second semester of a beginning-level language class. It should be obvious that the wider the scale (the more ratings there are within each level), the more subjective the scoring becomes. With a range of 1–9, it is relatively easy to decide between a 5 or a 4, or even across levels between a 7 and an 8. However, if the scores were to range from 1 to 20, with five possible scores in each level, it would be extremely subjective to decide whether a composition should receive a 16 or a 17. The narrower the scale, the more effect the floating bonus or penalty points would have, since a bonus/penalty of 1 point could move a composition from a 6 to a 7 on the AP scale (7 to 8 on the Reschke scale), thereby recognizing and rewarding those elements that contribute to the overall positive impression of the composition. Conversely, penalty points could lower a 4 to a 3 (Reschke scale) and thus affect the score of the student who wrote a grammatically accurate composition that exhibited poor organization, did not address the topic, was shorter than called for, or demonstrated other problems.

For beginning-level students, the holistic scale can be reduced even more, if the evaluation is to indicate a general impression and not detailed scoring of writing performance. Such a limited scale is found in the Virginia Standards of Learning, Cumulative Assessments, French II, Writing (Virginia Department of Education Standards of Learning: French, Spanish, German, and Latin, 1988, p. 4). (See Table 4.)

It is extremely important to react to *what* the student has said, not only to *how* it was said. Such reactions prove that the message is as important as the means of expressing it, in other words, that appropriate communication has taken place between a writer and his or her audience. Simply because student performance has been evaluated on a test and a grade has been assigned is no reason to think that the test is an end in itself. When samples of student writing have been evaluated, it is not unrealistic to ask students to revise their work. The subsequent revisions can be counted as homework, quizzes, or extra credit. Through encouraging rewriting and revising, TAs underline the necessity for clear communication and indicate that the writing *process* is as important as the written *product*.

The choice of the particular scale to be used is best determined by weighing several factors:

1) The level of the students
2) The amount of training in writing they have received
3) Expectations of performance
4) The weighting of the written section of the test with respect to the remainder of the test
5) The degree of refinement needed in order to assess student performance accurately.

Table 4

Limited Holistic Scale (General Impressions)
Virginia Standards of Learning: Cumulative Assessment,
French II, Writing

---

4   Can communicate a message in declarative, negative, and interrogative sentences. Errors in vocabulary, syntax, and mechanics are not consistent and do not interfere with intelligibility. They are able to recombine vocabulary and structures from the prompt. Most verbs may appear in the present tense. Past and future time may be expressed. Where sample is a letter, the appropriate date, salutation, greeting, and closing are included.

3   Can communicate most of the message intelligibly, but some errors in grammar, syntax, and mechanics interfere with the meaning. Where sample is a letter, date, salutation, greeting, and closing are included.

2   Can communicate some of the message, with minimum intelligibility. The message is greatly confused due to frequent and consistent errors in syntax, vocabulary, and mechanics.

1   Can communicate virtually none of the message intelligibly.

Virginia Department of Education, Cumulative Assessment,
French II, Writing, 1988, p. 4.

We can expect more from students as their abilities increase with continued study of the language. With training in the development of writing skills and the elements and principles that make up "good writing," we can expect students to demonstrate a broader range of knowledge. Students, in turn, should expect the evaluation of their written work to be more detailed, following the more refined (maybe even more demanding) scoring guidelines that will be commensurate with their level of training and abilities.

Speaking

It is significantly more difficult to evaluate oral than written performance, since speaking is much more transitory than writing, unless it is captured on tape. With writing, the evaluator can read and reread. With speaking, the evaluator can hear the message only once. Taping can help to solve this problem, but introduces others: wearing earphones and listening to many different students over and over again is fatiguing, and the tapes themselves are often of poor technical quality. All of this makes evaluation extremely difficult and tedious.

Nonetheless, tape-recorded speaking test sections are administered on the AP examination. In one section, students hear questions or directions that establish a situation and must then respond to each situation with an appropriate answer. Each response is scored using a 4-point scale (see Table 5).

Even in scoring this relatively short section of the test, however, there are hazards: sometimes it is difficult to determine whether the student has really understood the question; sometimes the difference between a "major" and a "minor" error is unclear.

In the other section of the AP speaking test, students see a sequence of pictures illustrating a story that they are then asked to tell or interpret within a given time. This lengthier section is scored using a scale similar to the 9-point scale used for scoring the essay portion of the examination (see Table 6).

Table 5

Holistic Scoring for Questions and Directions
Advanced Placement — Speaking

4 points: 1)   A correct answer to the question, delivered with excellent to good pronunciation, correct grammar, and considerable fluency.

2)   A longer, more elaborate answer to the question, but with a minor error or two in grammar, pronunciation, or usage.

3 points: 1)   A correct answer to the question with fair pronunciation and intonation, perhaps a minor grammatical error or two, and some awkwardness in usage or delivery.

2)   A longer, more elaborate answer, with not more than *one* major grammatical error.

2 points: A correct answer to the question, with less than fair pronunciation and intonation, delivered haltingly and/or with one or two major flaws in grammar or usage.

1 point: 1)   An answer given in very faulty French, with little control of either grammar or pronunciation. The student is unable to express his thought with any competence.

2)   A comprehensible answer that shows that the students did not entirely understand the question.

3)   A response in which a major part of the answer is missing or not complete (two-part question, for example).

0 points: 1)   An answer indicating total failure to understand the question.

2)   An answer so fragmented as to be incomprehensible.

3)   An answer such as "Je ne sais pas," "Je ne comprends pas," or any similar effort to evade the problem posed.

4)   No answer.

Johnson, 1983, p. 24.

Table 6

Holistic Scoring: 9-point Scale
Advanced Placement — Speaking

Demonstrates Superiority	9	*Strong* control of the language: excellent grammatical and idiomatic usage; broad command of vocabulary, and obvious ease of expression. No significant grammar or pronunciation errors.
Demonstrates Competence	8 7	*Good* control of the language, with some grammatical accuracies or some awkwardness of expression. Good intonation and use of idiom and vocabulary. Few glaring errors of grammar or pronunciation.
Suggests Competence	6 5	*Fair* use of language without numerous serious grammatical errors but with a less impressive range of vocabulary and idiom and less good pronunciation and intonation. Occasional signs of fluency.
Suggests Incompetence	4 3	*Weak* use of language with serious errors. Restricted vocabulary and knowledge of idioms and/or frequent use of anglicisms or sentences which force interpretations on the part of the reader. Some redeeming features.
Demonstrates Incompetence	2 1	*Unacceptable:* few vocabulary resources, little or no sense of idiom or French style, glaring weakness in pronunciation and grammar.

Johnson, 1983, p. 24.

The College Board recognizes the difficulty of using their holistic scoring scale and recommends an analytic scoring scale to double-check the grade given. (Analytic scoring is discussed later in this chapter.)

Because of the nature of the AP examination, such scoring criteria may prove to be too detailed for use with lower-level students. A very simple 4-point scale (see Table 7), similar to one used for writing, has been created for speaking in the Virginia Standards of Learning, Cumulative Assessment,

French II, Speaking (Virginia Department of Education Standards of Learning: French, Spanish, German, and Latin, 1988, p. 4).

Table 7
Simplified 4-Point Scale
Virginia Standards of Learning: Cumulative Assessment,
French II, Speaking

---

4   Can communicate a message intelligibly. Answers are in complete sentences, including simple interrogative and negative structures. Common and regular verbs are used in the present tense with some degree of accuracy. Some errors may occur, but these do not interfere with the message.

3   Can communicate most of the message intelligibly, but errors may cause some misunderstanding. Most answers are in complete sentences, including simple interrogative and negative structures. Common and regular verbs are used in the present tense, but some are misconjugated. Vocabulary limitations, grammatical errors, and weak pronunciation may cause some difficulty in communication, but do not interfere with the basic message.

2   Can communicate some of the message with minimal intelligibility, but errors cause frequent misunderstandings. Simple declarative, negative, and interrogative sentences are attempted, but most structures have fractured syntax. Verbs are used in the present tense, but most forms are misconjugated. Problems in vocabulary, grammar, or pronunciation sometimes interfere seriously with the basic message.

1   Communicates very little of the message intelligibly. Every sentence is marked by long pauses and serious errors, garbled syntax, or lapses into English.

Virginia Department of Education, Cumulative Assessment,
French II, Speaking, 1988, p. 4.

It should be obvious that holistic scoring of speaking ability, even with scoring scales and tape recording, is still impressionistic. Nothing can be formally marked for correction or feedback. Errors and comments can only be noted as the mistakes are made, which interferes with listening, or after the fact, when specific errors are more difficult to remember.

Scoring scales do, however, provide less subjective guidelines for evaluating oral performance. Here, as with writing, the vital role of evaluation training sessions can be seen. Concentrated practice in evaluating sample tapes will help ensure that scorers understand the scoring system and its application. Thus, TAs will have guidance in determining what to listen for when rating the students' level of performance and in determining their grade.

Although the Oral Proficiency Interview (OPI) also calls for holistic scoring, it was never intended to be used in an academic setting as a means of evaluating student performance in speaking, since its very purpose is to determine a *proficiency* level, not *achievement*. There are several logistical problems encountered in administering the OPI in a classroom setting:

1) It should not be administered by someone who knows the person being interviewed.

2) It should be administered in a one-on-one situation.

3) It should last from 15 to 25 minutes.

Proficiency ratings *must not* be used to determine achievement or a grade. These aspects of formal proficiency interviews preclude their use in a typical classroom testing situation.

Solution 2: Analytic Scoring

According to Perkins (1983), cited in Omaggio (1986, p. 265), analytic scoring "involves the separation of the various features of a composition into components for scoring purposes." Analytic scoring offers more objectivity than holistic scoring in assessing student performance because it is more focused: the categories of language use to be evaluated are spelled out, and descriptions of performance levels within each category are provided.

In order to ensure standardization and consistency in scoring, each of the categories of language use must be clearly defined. It can be assumed that TAs understand terms such as "grammar," "vocabulary," "content," "fluency," "organization," "mechanics," "pronunciation," and so forth. Yet, to ensure that the focus of each of the categories is clearly understood, each term should be defined, since the categories represent the components of student performance that are to be evaluated. Each category, furthermore, should be weighted in reference to the degree of importance that it carries in the test items being evaluated.

Writing

Table 8 illustrates a complete analytic scoring scale for writing in a beginning-level French class. (I wrote this analytic scale myself for evaluating a test item that involved answering a letter from an imaginary pen pal. Since the letter was seeded to elicit particular grammatical forms and structures that had been studied in the course, the grammar category is more specific than the other categories.)

As Table 8 suggests, one of the most attractive features of such a scoring scale is the grid that is used in indicating performance in each of the five categories. Students should receive a copy of the analytic scoring criteria in advance. They will then know what is expected of them and how to interpret the evaluation of their written work. They can readily see where their strengths and weaknesses lie and can, over time, visualize their progress with subsequent evaluated samples of their writing.

It is a simple matter to convert the total of the scores in the various categories by converting them to a scale of 100. If a 100-point scale is routinely used for grading in class, TAs simply multiply the total earned in the five categories of the writing sample by 4. The score can also be weighted as to its relative importance on the entire test if the writing sample is only one section of a longer test.

It must be pointed out again that the specific categories, definitions, and descriptions of levels of performance should be spelled out before grading student papers. Furthermore, the same analytic scale should not be used throughout the course, since both the categories and descriptions should change with the widening scope of course content. There is nothing sacred about having five categories as in Table 8; the number and types of categories should be determined by the particular emphasis put on the development of writing skills in the course. Similarly, the descriptions should become more refined as course content increases.

Table 8

Analytic Scoring

	5	4	3	2	1
Grammar					
Vocabulary					
Mechanics					
Fluency					
Relevance					

COMMENTS: _____

_____

GRAMMAR: Use of grammatical elements, i.e., various parts of speech: correct pronouns (subject, object, reflexive, stressed), verb persons and tenses, adjective agreement, appropriate use of articles, correct genders, appropriate negative elements, etc.

5   Excellent use of grammatical elements; very limited errors in gender and adjective agreement; correct pronoun substitutions (both subject and object); correct use of articles (definite, indefinite, partitive); widely varied use and correctness of verb tenses; errors are relatively insignificant and do not hinder comprehension.

4   Very good use of grammatical elements; few errors in gender and adjective agreement; verb tenses are limited, primarily in the present, but some effort at using other tenses; errors in verb forms but not serious enough to hinder comprehension; correct but limited use of pronoun substitutes.

3   Satisfactory use of grammatical elements; some significant errors but overall impression of text is affected by errors; noticeable errors in pronoun usage, genders, verb forms and tenses, adjective agreement and position, and article usage.

2   Unsatisfactory use of grammatical elements; too many serious errors hinder comprehension; significant amount of anglicized French in constructions; extremely limited pronoun substitutes

with incorrect forms or position; verb tenses limited to present with little or no effort at using other tenses; genders are often incorrect; adjectives show limited or no agreement; many errors in article usage.

1   Totally unsatisfactory use of grammatical elements; the severity of the errors obstructs comprehension of most of the text; strictly limited to present tense, and even then with serious errors; no grasp of genders and adjective agreement; articles are used haphazardly.

VOCABULARY: Appropriate lexical items, variety of types of lexical items.

5   Exceptional range of vocabulary; subtleties and idiomatic expressions are used appropriately, giving a sense of strong control of lexicon. Vocabulary elements go far beyond routine elements suggested by the task/stimulus.

4   Good range of vocabulary; awareness of subtleties is demonstrated although with some errors; some extraordinary vocabulary elements included not expected to be found in task/stimulus and used appropriately.

3   Limited range of vocabulary; predominantly copies vocabulary from stimulus or uses very routine vocabulary, at times inappropriately; significant errors in choice of certain items.

2   Extremely limited vocabulary; even items expected to be found in task or provided in stimulus are inappropriate with incorrect spelling or use.

1   Shows no grasp of appropriate vocabulary; serious errors in word choice; serious misspellings.

MECHANICS: Appropriate use of pronoun substitutes, varied sentence structures (including simple, compound, and complex structures), logically sequenced writing, appropriate use of cohesive elements (adverbs of time, conjunctions, pronouns).

5   Excellent control of a variety of structures: a variety of sentence types; excellent use of cohesive elements, including appropriate pronoun substitutions for both subjects and objects; writing is appropriately sequenced, illustrated with the use of time elements and other connective elements.

4   Strong control of structures: good sentence variety, not limited to simple, affirmative, active, declarative, sentences (SAAD); appropriate but limited use of pronoun substitutes; limited use of cohesive elements and time words.

3   Adequate control of structures; most sentences are SAADs with one or two attempts at compound/complex structures; limited use of pronoun substitutes, some inappropriate or incorrect; very limited use of sequencing elements.

2   Poor control of structures; text is limited to SAADs with much repetition of words rather than appropriate pronoun substitutes; even short simple sentences are often incorrect.

1   Demonstrates virtually no control of mechanics, including appropriately structured simple sentences; no evidence of cohesion and coherence in text.

FLUENCY: The amount of information provided, i.e., does the student go beyond what is called for in the task/stimulus and contribute further information or comments? How inventive and/or creative is the writing sample? What is the degree of risk-taking seen in the writing sample?

5   Student goes far beyond the task/stimulus and contributes additional information; creativity is evident and is in general appropriate. Student clearly demonstrates risk-taking in going beyond what was called for; text reads very smoothly.

4   Above average work; student goes beyond the task/stimulus but is hesitant in taking many risks; some additional comments and reactions expressed, most of which are acceptable and logical; evidence of creativity in responding and some inventiveness; text reads smoothly but with some awkwardness; writing sample is complete, i.e., adequately responds to the task/stimulus.

3   Limited fluency demonstrated; student basically responds to stimulus or performs on task without going beyond giving what is called for; some evidence of creativity, but errors impede comprehension when student attempts to go beyond the task; relatively limited amount of content, but what is there is appropriate; text is generally awkward and jerky.

2   Very limited evidence of creativity or inventiveness; student simply copies cues from the stimulus, often inappropriately; writing sample

is extremely short and incomplete; text is very awkward, jerky, and disconnected.

1 No evidence of creativity; text is totally uncreative; many stimulus questions and comments are left unanswered; stimulus text is simply copied and poorly at that; writing sample is entirely too brief and incomplete; text is virtually unreadable.

RELEVANCE: Student responses and reactions are relevant to the stimulus questions or comments.

5 Student responses and comments are totally appropriate and relevant; additional comments are consistent with the context of the task/ stimulus; all of the writing sample is on task.

4 Student responses are in general appropriate and relevant but some extraneous, irrelevant information is given; most of writing sample is on task.

3 Student responses are often inappropriate due to misreading or lack of comprehension of task/stimulus.

2 Most student responses are irrelevant and incomplete, based on serious misinterpretation of task/stimulus cues.

1 Student shows no grasp of relevance due to strong lack of comprehension of task/stimulus text. Responses and comments are essentially "off the wall" with little meaning (such responses and comments are not creative in nature, but due to faulty comprehension).

Speaking

Analytic scoring again provides a less subjective manner of evaluating student oral performance. The categories to be evaluated are spelled out with a rating scale for the levels of performance for each category. TAs can use several different types of analytic scales, each of which can be adapted to fit a specific learning, teaching, or testing situation.

Bruschke (1989, p. 18) provides three different scales, two of which are based on the proficiency functional trisection of accuracy, content/context, and function (see Table 9 and Table 10). In her third scale (see Table 11) we find more specific categories and a more detailed description of each. What is particularly interesting in the scoring chart in Table 11 is the relative importance of each of the seven categories and the weight assigned to each: vocabulary, functions, and accuracy receive the highest weight of 5, fluency and pronunciation receive a weight of 3, and reaction/appropriateness and creativity/recombination receive a weight of 2.

Table 9
Evaluation of Oral Proficiency (I)

		1	2	3	4	5	
Function	Can't use language to communicate needs and ideas; has little functional ability; gropes for every word	_	_	_	_	_	Uses language to communicate needs and ideas; has good functional ability at his/her level of proficiency; language flows
Content/ Context	Has very limited vocabulary; uses vocabulary inappropriate to topic(s)	_	_	_	_	_	Has good command of vocabulary appropriate to topic(s)
Accuracy	Has poor word and sentence structure; has incomprehensible pronunciation	_	_	_	_	_	Has good word and sentence structure; has good pronunciation

Bruschke, 1989.

Table 10
Evaluation of Oral Proficiency (II)

		1	2	3	4	5
Function	Uses language to communicate needs and ideas; has functional ability at his/her level of proficiency; speaks at a normal pace	__	__	__	__	__
Content/ Context	Uses vocabulary appropriate to topic(s)	__	__	__	__	__
Accuracy	Uses correct word and sentence structure; pronunciation does not interfere with communication	__	__	__	__	__

Bruschke, 1989.

Table 11
Evaluation of Oral Proficiency (III) — Bruschke

I. *Vocabulary within Context*

0	1	2	3	4	5

minimal   extensive

II. *Functions/Use of Language*
(i.e., give information, enumerate/describe, ask questions, express likes/dislikes)

0	1	2	3	4	5

few   many

III. *Accuracy in Use of Basic Structures*
   (i.e., subject–verb, noun–adjective agreement, basic word order, negation)

   0   1   2   3   4   5

   | very poor, interferes with communication | few errors, does not interfere with communication |

IV. *Fluency*

   0   1   2   3

   | none | groping, slow | occasionally fluent | confident, language flows |

V. *Pronunciation/Intonation*

   0   1   2   3

   | no effort to use target lang. sounds | poor, greatly interferes with communication | occasionally interferes | does not interfere with communication |

VI. *Reaction/Appropriateness of Response*

   0   1   2

   | no reaction | sometimes appropriate | appropriate |

VII. *Creativity/Recombination of Learned Material*

   0   1   2

   | no attempt | some attempt | frequent attempts |

COMMENTS: _____
_____
_____
_____

Bruschke, 1989.

Pino (1989, p. 492) also presents two analytic scales in which the assignment of a score for the speaking test is greatly simplified (see Table 12 and Table 13). She also defines the five categories used in the evaluation. In Table 12, she presents a college or high school version that is appropriate for lower-level students, and in Table 13, a scale for more advanced students.

Table 12
Oral Language Rating Scale I

Categories	A+	A	B	C	D	F	Notes
Communication	40	37	34	31	28	25	
Accuracy	20	18	16	14	12	10	
Fluency	10	9	8	7	6	5	
Vocabulary	20	18	16	14	12	10	
Pronunciation	10	9	8	7	6	5	

Communication: Did you understand what was said to you? Are you talking about the right thing? Can you be understood despite errors? Have you conveyed your idea?

Accuracy: reasonable to inadequate grammatical correctness

Fluency: flow vs. hesitation

Vocabulary: adequate vs. inadequate

Pronunciation: good to bad

Pino, 1989, p. 492.

Table 13

Oral Language Rating Scale II

Categories	A+	A	B	C	D	F	Notes
Communication	25	23	21	19	17	15	
Accuracy	25	23	21	19	17	15	
Fluency	15	13	11	9	7	5	
Vocabulary	20	18	16	14	12	10	
Pronunciation	15	13	11	9	7	5	

Communication: purpose clearly conveyed for an average performance to purpose creatively and sensitively conveyed for an outstanding performance

Accuracy: grammatical correctness, especially _____ [teacher supplies grammatical features]

Fluency: amount of speech

Vocabulary: adequate for the purpose for an average score to advanced/new vocabulary for an outstanding score

Pronunciation: merely comprehensible to nativelike

Pino, 1989, p. 492.

It is again interesting to note the relative weight that Pino has given to categories on the two scales, especially the fact that *communication* is weighted the heaviest on Oral Scale I, while it is weighted equal to *accuracy* on Oral Scale II. Indeed, the effectiveness of the communicative effort is of utmost importance in oral communication. In speaking, the other participants can ask for repetition or clarification if there is misunderstanding or lack of comprehension, or if verification is needed; whereas with writing, the intended audience, a reader or readers, is not present and therefore cannot guide the writer by indicating problems with comprehension.

For nonnative teachers of another language, one of the most helpful criteria to bear in mind in evaluating speaking is the statement found in the ACTFL Proficiency Guidelines (1986, p. 2): "[T]he speaker can generally be understood even by interlocutors *not accustomed to* dealing with speakers at this level" [my italics]. In other words, one should ask, "Can I put myself in the place of a native speaker and understand what I have just heard?" With experience, we foreign language teachers tend to "understand" much more student language than the native speaker would understand, since we are accustomed to dealing with speakers at this level. In evaluating speaking performance, however, we cannot falsify student ability by rating it too high simply because we understand what the student is attempting to say. For inexperienced TAs especially, it is essential that they learn to hear their students objectively. Obviously, the same criterion can be applied to writing: "Writing is understandable to natives not used to the writing of nonnatives" (ACTFL, 1986, p. 5).

Table 14 offers another analytic scale for oral grading procedures, one developed by Hirsch and Thompson (1989, p. 24). This scale provides two different formulae for evaluating oral performance. Each formula gives different weighting to the categories. Note that Formula One does not evaluate content. Whatever categories and descriptions may be used, the relative differences in weight are based on the realistic expectations for student performance at a given level of study and can easily be varied.

Table 14
Oral Grading Procedures

GRAMMAR

A: Usage of required grammar concepts is almost perfect in given context.

B: Makes some grammar mistakes which generally would not affect meaning (i.e., agreements, partitive vs. definite article, wrong past participles, etc.).

C: Makes more serious mistakes which could give unintended meaning (i.e., conjugation, tense inconsistency, word order mistakes).

D: Meaning frequently obscured by grammar mistakes.

E: *"Épouvantable."*

VOCABULARY

A: Conversant with vocabulary required by given context.

B: Makes some vocabulary mistakes which generally would not affect meaning (i.e., wrong gender, wrong preposition [*finir à* + inf.]).

C: Makes more serious mistakes which could give unintended meaning (i.e., wrong gender, incorrect word choice, mangled words).

D: Meaning frequently obscured because of inadequate mastery of vocabulary.

E: "*Épouvantable.*"

FLUENCY

A: No more than a normal, "thoughtful" delay in formulation of thoughts into speech.

B: Hesitates longer than necessary to find the right word.

C: Narrative somewhat disjointed because of pauses.

D: Painful pauses make speech hard to follow.

E: "*Effrayant.*"

PRONUNCIATION

A: Demonstrates a knowledge of correct pronunciation and intonation; makes very few mistakes.

B: Some mispronunciation, but meaning is still clear.

C: Pronounced foreign accent which requires extra-sympathetic listening.

D: Meaning frequently obscured because of poor pronunciation.

E: "*Épouvantable.*"

CONTENT

A: Displays communicative ease within a given context.

B: Says more than the strict minimum.

C: Situation handled adequately though minimally.

D: Says less than adequate minimum.

E: Situation handled only partially or in totally unsatisfactory manner.

FORMULA ONE	*FORMULA TWO*
Grammar: ___ × 7 = ___	Grammar: ___ × 5 = ___
Vocabulary: ___ × 6 = ___	Vocabulary: ___ × 5 = ___
Pronunciation: ___ × 4 = ___	Pronunciation: ___ × 3 = ___
Fluency: ___ × 3 = ___	Fluency: ___ × 2 = ___
	Content: ___ × 5 = ___

$$A = 4.5 - 5.0$$
$$B = 4.0 - 4.4$$
$$C = 3.5 - 3.9$$
$$D = 3.0 - 3.4$$
$$E = 2.5 - 2.9$$

Hirsch & Thompson, 1989, p. 24.

Conclusion

To improve consistency when TAs evaluate their students' writing and speaking in ways that tend to call for subjective grading, this chapter has provided several guidelines and samples of scoring techniques. Whether holistic or analytic scoring and any of the scales presented are chosen, five points must be remembered:

1) All TAs who will score common tests should go through an intensive training period that will familiarize them with the techniques for scoring student work, allow for discussion of these techniques, provide sample texts for evaluation, and examine why selected samples were given certain scores, thereby ensuring consistency in the application of the scoring procedure. Such direction is vital for ensuring consistency among TAs, that is, for ensuring inter-rater reliability.

2) In multisection courses, it is extremely important to have clearly defined scoring criteria for all tests to ensure equal expectations and equivalent results on common tests that are scored by a number of different TAs.

3) Scoring scales should be created for each test administered. A common scoring scale for tests that cover an entire academic year is highly inappropriate.

4) Scoring criteria should include *all* types of items on the test, whether they are scored by discrete points or by holistic/analytic methods. These guidelines should be created *before* the test is administered.

5) For holistic scoring, descriptions for each level of performance should be general enough to include all varieties of anticipated student performance yet specific enough to give guidance in discriminating both quality and quantity of work between the ranges of levels of performance typical of the student population in the entire course. Categories and descriptions for levels of performance should be realistic, attainable, and commensurate with the students' level of study and degree of linguistic sophistication.

Consistency in grading provides the equitable evaluation of student performance across sections in multisection courses, especially in those courses taught by relatively inexperienced TAs. Such consistency can be improved — if not ensured — through rigorous training sessions in which TAs examine a variety of scoring scales and techniques, and practice scoring numerous samples of student performance in both speaking and writing. The scoring techniques suggested here will help reduce the gap between the totally impressionistic evaluation of student writing and speaking and the relatively objective evaluation of the various elements of effective language use.

Works Cited

"AATSP Program Guidelines for the Education and Training of Teachers of Spanish and Portuguese." *Hispania* 73 (1990): 785–94.

ACTFL Proficiency Guidelines. Yonkers, NY: ACTFL Materials Center, 1986.

"ACTFL Provisional Program Guidelines for Foreign Language Teacher Education." *Foreign Language Annals* 21 (1988): 71–82.

Bruschke, Dorothea. Personal communication and handout for "Teaching and Testing for Oral Proficiency." Wisconsin Education Association Council Meeting, Madison, WI, 1989.

Henning, Grant. *A Guide to Language Testing: Development, Evaluation, Research.* Cambridge, MA: Newbury House Publishers, 1987.

Hirsch, Bette G. & Chantal P. Thompson. *Ensuite: Cours intermédiaire de français.* Instructor's Manual. New York: Random House, 1989.

Johnson, Leonard W. *Grading the Advanced Placement Examination in French Language.* Princeton, NJ: College Entrance Examination Board, 1983.

Larson, Jerry W. & Randall L. Jones. "Proficiency Testing for the Other Language Modalities." *Teaching for Proficiency: The Organizing Principle.* Ed. Theodore V. Higgs. ACTFL Foreign Language Education Series. Lincolnwood, IL: National Textbook Company, 1984: 113-38.

Magnan, Sally Sieloff. "Teaching and Testing Proficiency in Writing: Skills to Transcend the Second-Language Classroom." In Omaggio, 1985: 109-36.

Medley, Frank W., Jr. "Designing the Proficiency-Based Curriculum." In Omaggio, 1985: 13-40.

Murphy, Joseph A. "The Graduate Teaching Assistant in an Age of Standards." *Challenges in the 1990s for College Foreign Language Programs.* Ed. Sally Sieloff Magnan. AAUSC Issues in Language Program Direction 1990. Boston: Heinle & Heinle Publishers, 1991: 129-49.

_____ & Jane Black Goepper (Ed.). *The Teaching of French: A Syllabus of Competence.* The Report of the Commission on Professional Standards, the American Association of Teachers of French. *AATF National Bulletin* 14 (October 1989). (Special issue.)

Omaggio, Alice C. *Teaching Language in Context: Proficiency-Oriented Instruction.* Boston: Heinle & Heinle Publishers, 1986.

_____ (Ed.). *Proficiency, Curriculum, Articulation: The Ties That Bind.* Middlebury, VT: Northeast Conference on the Teaching of Foreign Languages, 1985.

Perkins, Kyle. "On the Use of Composition Scoring Techniques, Objective Measures, and Objective Tests to Evaluate ESL Writing Ability." *TESOL Quarterly* 17 (1983): 651-71.

Pino, Barbara Gonzalez. "Prochievement Testing of Speaking." *Foreign Language Annals* 22 (1989): 487-96.

Reschke, Claus. "Global Assessment of Writing Proficiency." *Realizing the Potential of Foreign Language Instruction.* Ed. Gerard L. Ervin. Report of Central States Conference on the Teaching of Foreign Languages. Lincolnwood, IL: National Textbook Company, 1990: 100-11.

Richards, Jack C. "Error Analysis and Second-Language Strategies." *New Frontiers in Second Language Learning*. Ed. John Schumann & Nancy Stenson. Rowley, MA: Newbury House Publishers, 1974.: 32–53.

Virginia Department of Education Standards of Learning: French, Spanish, German, and Latin. Richmond, VA: Virginia Department of Education, 1988.

Contributors

Marva A. Barnett is Associate Professor of French at the University of Virginia. For a decade she has supervised French language programs and trained teaching assistants; she now directs the Teaching Resource Center, which promotes excellence in the teaching done by faculty and TAs throughout the university. Her research interests include the second-language reading process, with an emphasis on reader strategies, foreign language methodology, and teacher training. The author of the reading-strategies textbook *Lire avec plaisir,* she publishes in such journals as *Modern Language Journal, Foreign Language Annals,* and *The ADFL Bulletin.*

Robert Francis Cook is Professor of French in the Department of French Language and Literature at the University of Virginia, where he teaches the literature of the Middle Ages. He has published editions of Old French texts and studies on the epic genre, and is editor of the journal *Olifant.* He is a former assistant dean of the College of Arts and Sciences and former director of the Graduate Program in French.

Madeleine Cottenet-Hage is Associate Professor of French at the University of Maryland, College Park, specializing in francophone women writers and in film. Together with John Joseph, Pierre Verdaguer, and Celeste Kinginger, she is in charge of language instruction and TA training at Maryland. Her pedagogical publications include *Careers, Communication and Culture in Foreign Language Teaching* (with F. Grittner, S. Welty & T. Rose [National Textbook, 1976]), *Now It's Your Turn* (with R. Marret, L. Hefflin & C. Hamilton [Nathan, 1981]), and *Transition* (with R. Steele & P. Verdaguer [Prentice Hall, 1990]), as well as articles in professional journals.

Nadine O'Connor Di Vito is Senior Lecturer and Romance Language Coordinator at the University of Chicago. The application of research in sociolinguistics and sociocultural anthropology to foreign language teaching has consistently been the focus of her scholarly work. She teaches courses in foreign language teaching methodology, French language and linguistics, sociolinguistics, and cross-cultural communication.

Cynthia A. Fox is Assistant Professor in the Department of French Studies and the Department of Linguistics and Cognitive Science at the State University of New York at Albany. She coordinates the premajor French language sequence, supervises TAs, and teaches courses in French linguistics, teaching methodology, and sociolinguistics. Her current research focuses on linguistic and sociolinguistic aspects of North American varieties of French, as well as on applied linguistics.

Julia Herschensohn is Assistant Professor of Romance Linguistics at the University of Washington, where she is coordinator of French TAs and director of the first-year French language program. Teaching courses in French, linguistics, and language methodology, she is involved in the preparation of language teachers for the university and high school levels. Her primary research areas are theoretical linguistics, French syntax, and language pedagogy. Her most recent publications have appeared in *Modern Language Journal, French Review,* and *Lingvisticae Investigationes*.

Charles J. James is Associate Professor of German and Curriculum & Instruction at the University of Wisconsin-Madison, where he is coordinator of German TAs, director of the first-year German language program, and advisor for Secondary Education in German. He teaches courses in German language at all levels, as well as methods courses for both undergraduate and graduate students of German. He is a founding member of AAUSC and served as its first treasurer and first editor of its newsletter. He is also a member of ACTFL and MLA, as well as a life member of AATG. His research interests include language testing strategies and the educational systems in Germany. He has published articles and reviews in *Foreign Language Annals, Die Unterrichtspraxis, Modern Language Journal,* and *Polylingua*.

John E. Joseph is Associate Professor of French at the University of Maryland, College Park, where he specializes in language theory and its applications and directs the program in French linguistics. His teaching and research focus on the political and cognitive dimensions of language and how each impacts upon the other. His books include *Eloquence and Power* (Blackwell, 1987), *Ideologies of Language* (with T.J. Taylor [Routledge, 1990]), and *Linguistic Theory and Grammatical Description* (with F.G. Droste [Benjamins, 1991]); a book on autonomous and political approaches to French and Romance linguistics will be published in 1993.

Katherine M. Kulick is Assistant Professor of French at the College of William and Mary where she coordinates the elementary and intermediate French-language programs, and trains and supervises undergraduate teaching assistants in French and student teachers of French, German, Latin, and Spanish. She teaches courses in French language, phonetics, and foreign language teaching methodology. Her research interests include methodology, writing proficiency, adult learning, and francophone cultures. She is coauthor of the intermediate French textbooks *Interaction* and *Passerelles,* and of the introductory writing textbook, *Notez Bien!.* She is currently writing an advanced-level textbook on contemporary social issues in the francophone world.

Sally Sieloff Magnan is Professor of French at the University of Wisconsin-Madison, where she teaches courses in French language and teaching methodology and supervises teaching assistants. Her primary research interests are foreign language teaching methodology, error analysis, and proficiency testing. She is Editor of the 1990 Northeast Conference Reports entitled *Shifting the Instructional Focus to the Learner* and a coauthor of the introductory college French textbook *En Route.* She is a former President of AAUSC.

Keith Mason is Assistant Professor of Applied Linguistics in the Department of Spanish, Italian, and Portuguese at the University of Virginia, where he teaches courses in Spanish phonetics, phonology, methodology, dialectology, sociolinguistics, and bilingualism. He is the Spanish Placement Officer and Director of Basic Spanish Instruction. He has published articles in *Hispania* and *Polylingua.* His main research interests are phonetics, applied linguistics, methodology, and languages for specific purposes.

Benjamin Rifkin is Assistant Professor of Russian in the Department of Slavic Languages and Literatures at the University of Wisconsin–Madison, where he coordinates the introductory and intermediate Russian-language courses, supervises graduate student assistants, and teaches graduate courses in methodology and advanced Russian language. He has published articles and reviews in the areas of Russian-language teaching and contemporary Russian film in the *Slavic and East European Journal* and the *Slavic Review*.

Robert M. Terry is Professor of French at the University of Richmond, where he is chairman of the Department of Modern Foreign Languages and Literatures. He is also chairman of the board of directors of the Southern Conference on Language Teaching and the editor of *Dimension,* SCOLT's annual conference proceedings series. He is coauthor of three college-level French texts and the Teacher's Guide for *Systeme-D,* instructional designer for the videotapes accompanying *On y va!,* and the author of numerous articles. His primary research interests are proficiency-based testing, writing, and foreign language pedagogy.

Pierre M. Verdaguer is Associate Professor of French at the University of Maryland, College Park. He teaches courses in French culture and civilization, literature, and language, as well as courses in methodology for TAs. He recently developed an M.A. program with a concentration in French Civilization and an undergraduate major in Business French. His research interests are in the area of twentieth-century French culture and literature, and he has also coauthored a textbook, *Transition: Le plaisir des textes* (with M. Cottenet-Hage and R. Steele [Prentice Hall, 1990]), designed to develop reading strategies and critical skills.

Joel C. Walz is Professor of French in the Department of Romance Languages at the University of Georgia, where he supervises the graduate teaching assistants in French and teaches courses in methods, French phonetics, and applied French linguistics. He publishes articles in professional journals on the French language and language teaching with a special emphasis on pedagogical materials. He is coauthor of the elementary college French textbook *Rapports* (D.C. Heath).

Mary E. Wildner-Bassett is Assistant Professor of German and director of the Basic Languages program for the Department of German at the University of Arizona. She teaches courses in applied linguistics, second-language learning and teaching approaches, and language courses at various levels. Her research interests include language acquisition, cognitive styles, language learning strategies, pragmatics, and language analysis. She has recently authored a viewer's manual for the *Zielpunkt Deutsch* German language video program, and several articles and book chapters reporting her research findings.